Rough Collies

ROUGH COLLIES

AN OWNER'S COMPANION

Hazel Hunt

HOWELL
BOOK HOUSE
New York

First published in Great Britain in 1990 by The Crowood Press

Copyright © 1990 by Hazel Hunt

First American Edition, 1990

Howell Book House
Macmillan Publishing Company
866 Third Avenue, New York, NY 10022
Collier Macmillan Canada, Inc.

ISBN 0 87605 132 8

Macmillan books are available at special discounts for bulk purchases for sales promotions, premiums, fund-raising, or educational use. For details contact:

Special Sales Director
Macmillan Publishing Company
866 Third Avenue
New York, NY 10022

10 9 8 7 6 5 4 3 2 1

Printed in Great Britain

Contents

The Collie

I am the Shepherd of the sheep,
That I to serve was born,
Ewe, Hogg and Tup, I round them up,
The fleece, the hoof, the horn;
By dale and down and dipping-pan,
Crook, shears and wattle-shade,
I am the nearest brute to Man
That ever God has made.

I am the Shepherd of the Sheep,
Unto the hill I go,
When ways are blind and when the wind
Moans muffled with the snow;
When all familiar things are by
At freak of drift that's blown
By Grace of God through chaos I,
Still seek and find my own.

I am the Shepherd of the Sheep,
I am the Dog his Power,
I bid them be or march with me
At two good miles an hour,
I stem their scuffling panic wave,
I run, I crouch, I creep;
No Man who has a soul to save
Has wit to fold a sheep.

I am the Shepherd of the Sheep,
Their first and latest need,
Ewe, Tup and Hogg give heed to Dog
When Man may get small heed;
From the high places to the groves
Blue Grampian, Hampshire pine,
I am the Drover of the Droves,
The sheep are only mine.

I am the Shepherd of the Sheep,
You've met us on the way
To Fair and Town; my tongue drips down,
My coat with dust is grey,
I'm four-foot lame, I'm lame all round,
Yet here I run and there,
And bring my sheep in fresh and sound,
My honour and my care.

I am the Shepherd of the Sheep,
That I to serve was born,
I serve them true – Hogg, Tup and Ewe,
And hoof, and fleece and horn;
Since Lammas first to Lammas ran,
Day's light or lanter's glim,
The nearest brute am I to Man
That God has given to him.

Dogs of Every Day by Patrick R. Chalmers, 1933

Acknowledgements

I would like to thank all those whose conversations, articles and lectures have provided much of the information on Collies which I have absorbed over the years. In particular, Dr Peter Bedford FRCVS, Mr Neil King MRCVS, Bobby Roos, Linda Sparks, Kay White and Dr Malcolm Willis. Special thanks to Mrs Rosie Best MRCVS, for reviewing the chapter on ailments and diseases.

1

History of the Breed

The origins of the Collie are shrouded in mystery. From earliest times dogs have been used by man – first to help nomadic man in his hunting and later to guard the early settlements and to control his domesticated animals. From the descriptions of these ancient dogs, they would seem to bear little resemblance to the modern Collie but it seems highly likely that they evolved gradually. Dogs would have been selected purely for their ability to work, to respond rapidly to commands and to withstand hostile weather conditions. It is not hard to visualise a medium-sized, active dog with a weather-proof coat of conspicuous colouring and above average in intelligence gradually evolving as being the most suitable for this purpose.

Virtually all books written on the breed give credence to the theory that the Collie is descended from the dogs brought over with the Romans. I can find no evidence to support this. Such dogs as the Romans brought with them would not have been carried in crates – they would have followed the columns of marching men on their own four feet and they would have bred with any available bitches they met *en route* through Gaul and southern England. They certainly would not have remained celibate till they reached the north of England! Similarly, any bitches attached to the army that had the misfortune to find themselves in whelp, would have been left behind to fend for themselves when they produced their litter. You would expect to find a proportion of these whelps surviving on the Continent. Furthermore, if a few itinerant dogs made such an impression in England you would expect to find a much larger residual pool of superior animals remaining in their homeland. There is no evidence of that.

The Roman theory seems to have arisen from the desire of historians to give their breed a noble ancestry. They seemed unwilling to believe that a dog as beautiful and intelligent as the Collie could have originated in the British Isles. In fact, the Collies is one of our indigenous breeds – a 'True Brit' – hailing from the north of Britain.

The origin of the name Collie is as obscure as his history. Shakespeare refers several times to 'collied night' and 'collied brow' which would suggest that in Elizabethan times at least, the word meant dark or black. He also uses the word 'sable' to mean the same thing, which does not help us in our modern colour charts. It is usually accepted that the word derives from the Anglo-Saxon word, col, which meant black. Mrs Iris Combe puts forward the theory that the word is not derived from the Anglo-Saxon at all, but from the Gaelic, and means useful. Either explanation is plausible.

As a show dog, the Collie's history dates back to 1860, when, at Birmingham, a class was included for 'Sheepdogs'. This seems to indicate the ordinary drovers' dogs, usually Bobtails. Collies received no mention, although they were not specifically excluded. It would seem they must have made their presence felt, as, from then on, classes for herding dogs were divided into three categories – 'Rough coated', 'Smooth coated' and 'Short tailed'. By the time the Crystal Palace show was held in 1870, Roughs and Smooths had separate classes. Up to this time all the Collies shown were either black and tan, black and white or tricolour, but in 1871 a dog that was to change all that made his appearance in the ring. His name was Cockie, usually referred to as Old Cockie, and his colour caused a sensation. He was a very attractive sable and at this time sable was as rare in Rough Collies as it is in Border Collies today. He proved to be an extremely dominant sable and from then on this new colour became extremely fashionable. Queen Victoria who was much taken with the Collies working on her Balmoral estate in Scotland, had several Collies of different colours in her kennel and her patronage did much to popularise the breed. Two black and tan Collies from her kennel were exhibited to the public in the USA and proved a great attraction both for their beauty and their high-born connections.

In 1873, the great Trefoil was born. He was a tricolour well made, and with a great length of coat, although his picture shows him to have very little white. He was bred by Mr S.E. Shirley, one of the founders of the Kennel Club. Mrs Iris Combe has done considerable research into the antecedants of this dog and has discovered incontrovertible proof that the dog was born on one of Mr Shirley's Irish estates and did not originate in the Borders or North Country as had previously been accepted. Largely through his son, Ch. Charlemagne, every winning Collie today can trace his ancestry back to Trefoil. Mrs N.K. George of the Beulah Collies was always extremely proud that her Ch. Beulah's Golden Futureson could trace his tail-

Ch. Christopher, born 1887.

male line directly back through an almost unbroken line of champions for twenty-six generations back to Trefoil. When Ch. Charlemagne was bred to his litter sister, Flirt, they produced the dominant sable Ch. Eclipse who was considered to be the best of his sons. Charlemagne's grandson was the big winner Ch. Metchley Wonder, five times winner of the prestigious Collie Club Challenge Trophy, between 1887 and 1891. His most notable son was the handsome sable Ch. Christopher, sold to the USA for the record sum of £1,000, but not before he had sired, amongst his many winners, an unshown dog called Edgebaston Marvel, later sold to Mr Megson for £500, purely on his record as a sire.

Though not a great breeder himself, Mr Megson was always happy to pay a high price for a dog that he admired and, shrewd businessman that he was, he still made a handsome profit on the dogs he later sold to the USA. Edgebaston Marvel's most successful son in the ring was, undoubtedly, Ch. Southport Perfection who emulated his grandsire's achievement in winning the Collie Club Challenge Trophy five times. (It should be noted that, at that time, it was on offer three times a year and not, as at present, awarded annually to the winner of the British Collie Club's Championship show.) After Perfection's first win, Mr Megson bought him for £1,005 and the dog was then shown under his name. He also paid the record price of £1,300 for Ch. Ormskirk Emerald to his owner, Mr Stretch of the Ormskirk prefix.

Continuing our father-to-son, or tail-male line, we come to Perfection's grandson, Ch. Wellsbourne Conqueror, whose most notable son was Ch. Parbold Piccolo, sire of six champions, including the incomparable Ch. Anfield Model. At that time, high prices were being obtained from the USA where the rival financiers J. Pierpont Morgan and Sam Untermeyer competed with each other to obtain the best English dogs. Both had very strong kennels of mainly imported Collies and it is on record that, in 1887, J. Pierpont Morgan showed sixteen Collies at the Westminster show which is roughly equivalent to our Cruft's. Piccolo did not go to either of them, but to a Mr Behling at what was reputed to be the highest price ever paid for a Collie. Piccolo arrived safely at his new home where he appeared to be so happy and friendly that he was allowed the run of the place. Within a few hours he had disappeared, and, despite extensive searches and the offer of a substantial reward, he was never seen again. It was a great loss to the American fancy. English imports continued to beat American-bred dogs even though many in-whelp bitches were also being imported at that time.

It is noticeable in Collie history, right down to the present day, that every decade or so an outstanding dog is produced that raises the whole breed to a new level of perfection. Such a dog was Ch. Anfield Model that Piccolo had left behind in England. His photographs show him to be a dog of such beauty of head and expression that he could hold his own with today's Collies. His blood was much sought after on both sides of the Atlantic and considerable inbreeding was done to him in both countries. Beautiful dog as he was, Model did not have the best of temperaments and inbreeding only aggravated the problem in his progeny. Almost all the pedigrees of the time both here and in the USA show Model's name repeated several times.

It was around 1912 that the first Laund Ch. made its appearance. It was the first of some sixty champions produced by Mr W. W. Stansfield many of whom found their way across the Atlantic, mainly to the Bellhaven kennel of Mrs F.B. Ilch. This redoubtable lady produced 133 champions between 1920 and 1960. Ch. Laund Lero of Bellhaven was the first to win his group at Westminster in 1926 and Ch. Laund Loyalty of Bellhaven is still the only Collie to go Best in Show, at Westminster, in 1929. The great Am. Ch. Braegate Model was also

Ch. Laund Lukeo, born 1923.

imported from England and although contemporary critiques show him to have been a little big for English tastes he was undefeated in his brilliant career in the States while in Mrs Ilch's hands. Mr Stansfield made several trips to the USA taking some of his top English champions with him. Some of the most notable, who also gained American titles, where Ch. Laund Limitless, Ch. Laund Logic and Ch. Laund Lukeo.

In 1921, the great English sire Ch. Magnet was exported to the USA at the age of nine years. He still had time to sire two Am. Chs but his greatest influence was in England where he left behind such dominant sires as Ch. Laund Legislator and Ch. Poplar Perfection. His grandson, Ch. Eden Emerald, was one of the first of many great champions exported by Mr Fred Robson of Eden fame during his fifty years' activity in the breed. Emerald's great-grandson was the immortal Am. Ch. Honeybrook Big Parade from whom most of the winning Collies in the USA are descended, notably through his grandson, Am. Ch. Silver Ho Parader, sire of thirty-seven USA Champions. An extended pedigree of Parader reveals that he is descended from everything that was best in his English ancestry and

13

Ch. Magnet, born 1912.

Ch. Anfield Model occurs over twenty times. He can also trace his forbears back to the founder, Trefoil.

In England, Mr Robson was producing a string of champions such as Ch. Eden Extra, Ch. Eden Elegance and Ch. Eden Elenora. The 1920s and 30s were dominated by the powerful kennels of Laund, Seedley, Eden and later, the Backwoods kennel of Mr F. Ball. This latter kennel owed a great deal to the fortunate acquisition of Emerald's older brother Ch. Backwoods Fashion. Mated to Backwoods Famous, this lovely son of Ch. Poplar Perfection sired Backwoods Feature whose most notable claim to fame was as sire of Ch. Backwoods Fellow. Fellow was not a big dog, but had a beautiful head and expression, well carried ears and an immense sable coat. He was considered by many as the most perfect Collie yet seen.

I was never fortunate enough to see this dog who was so greatly admired by such fanciers as Mrs Nadine George and Miss Clare Maloney, but I was able to admire his son Beulah's Golden Shade. This huge coated parti-coloured dog carried more white than sable and his markings effectively prevented him from gaining his title. His son Ch. Beulah's Golden Future (who was the sire of my first Collie),

14

Ch. Backwoods Fellow, born 1930.

was a large dark-shaded sable who carried the white factor, which showed in his white blaze and big shawl collar. Like all this entailed line, he carried a stunning coat. He was the last champion to gain his title before war broke out in 1939.

Returning to that other son of the great Ch. Poplar Perfection, Ch. Eden Emerald, we find an extremely prepotent line following down through his grandson, Eden Extreme, to the merle Ch. Glenack Kingfisher who played a tremendous part in the production of all the merle Beulah champions, particularly through his tricolour grandson, Beulah's Night Victorious, and his litter brother, the merle Ch. Beulah's Silver Don Mario.

During the war, Mario and Ch. Beulah's Golden Sultan were sent to the USA to Mr and Mrs Christie. They were fortunate to arrive, as the ship on which they were booked to sail was torpedoed in mid-Atlantic. Due to a last minute hitch the Collies were transferred to

15

Eden Examine, 1 CC, born 1944, s. Lyncliffe Lancer, d. Seagull.

another ship and made the hazardous journey in safety. Sultan had a very successful career in the States and both dogs gained titles rapidly. Before he left England, Mario had sired one litter of great significance, for it contained the big war-time winner, the tricolour Lyncliffe Lancer, bred and shown by Mr and Mrs H. Cliffe.

Shows were restricted to Sanction Shows within twenty-five miles of the dog's home, during the war, and soon a sable and white appeared in the north that was to set everyone talking. It was a dog called Worsbro Model that had several Best in Shows to his credit and was receiving rave notices from the judges. He was sired by Lyncliffe Lancer and his fame was such that he was bought for an undisclosed sum by Mr Robson of the Eden kennel. His name was changed to Eden Examine and he became one of the three post-war sires who were to dominate British post-war breeding. The other two were Ch. Mywicks Meadow Lancer and Dazzler of Dunsinane.

Famous Post-War Sires

World War II saw the dispersal of many Collie kennels and most of the others were forced to reduce their numbers to one or two dogs. The exception was the Beulah kennel of Mrs N.K. George. Mrs George was able to maintain her kennel of some thirty Collies throughout the war years. She bred a litter of sable and whites by the last pre-war champion, Ch. Beulah's Golden Future, out of the lovely Ch. Beulah's Golden Feather. From this came the first post-war champion, Ch. Beulah's Golden Futureson, a dog that was considered to have the biggest coat yet seen. Another dog was sold to Miss P.M. Grey, at that time a hospital matron, and I was lucky enough to be able to purchase the only bitch in the litter, Beulah's Golden Fantasy.

Miss Grey, who had badly wanted a bitch, bought a later daughter of Futureson, Beulah's Golden Flora and in due course Flora was sent to Mr Robson's Eden Examine. There were only four puppies in the litter and Miss Grey kept the best bitch, Lass of Ladypark. The best dog was sold to my future husband Dr K.G. Collins and eventually became Ch. Lad of Ladypark. He won his first Challenge Certificate at eleven months and it was the first of many Challenge Certificates to be won by the Ladyparks.

Ch. Lad of Ladypark, born 1946, s. Eden Examine, d. Ch. Beulah's Golden Flora.

Ch. Ugony's Golden Gloria, born 1949, s. Ch. Lad of Ladypark, d.
Alphington Landgirl (left) and Ch. Ugony's Golden Son O' Lad of
Riffelsee, born 1948, s. Ch. Lad of Ladypark, d. Golden Rod of Wooden
(right).

Lad was a great character and sired six champions of whom the most renowned was Ch. Ugony's Golden Son O'Lad of Riffelsee, an exceptionally well-boned and coated golden sable. He had a good puppy career in our hands but his talent for poaching pheasants caused him to be hastily returned to his breeder, Miss D.M. Young, in order to save him from being shot by an irate gamekeeper. In her ownership he went on to win eleven Challenge Certificates. Son O'Lad was noted for his good movement and several times won the Non-Sporting Group at Championship Shows. He was the first post-war Collie to go reserve Best in Show at a Championship Show. He had a great influence on the Ugony Collies which have produced some eight or nine champions of whom the most illustrious must be the lovely Ch. Collydean That's My Sheila at Ugony, winner of eight Challenge Certificates.

Miss Grey was elated with the success of her first litter and dis-proved for ever the old wives tale that repeat matings are never a success by dispatching Flora to Eden Examine again the very next year. This time it produced her great favourite Int. Ch. Lochinvar of

Int. Ch. Lochinvar of Ladypark, born 1947, s. Eden Examine, d. Ch. Beulah's Golden Flora.

Ladypark. This dog is a prime example of how one dog can change the whole future of the breed.

Lochinvar was a big, heavily coated, sweet natured and sweet expressioned golden sable that bred pure for sable. He never sired a tricolour even to tricolour bitches and his services were in great demand. Most of the top bitches in the country were sent to him but Lochinvar had the happy knack of stamping all his offspring with his own unmistakable type and sweet temperament, irrespective of the quality of the dam. No dog ever did more for a breed than Lochinvar did for the Rough Collie.

In his first litter he sired three champions and among his more famous sons were Ch. Laird's Galway Sun, Ch. Loyal of Ladypark, Ch. Leonertes of Ladypark, Ch. Eden Rip of Ladywell, Ch. Lena's Golden Son, Ch. Walbrooke Stormy Petrel, Ch. Westcarr's Whistler and Pattingham Kismet, winner of two Challenge Certificates. Add to that some very lovely bitch champions and a large number of overseas champions and international champions and it is doubtful if his record will ever be surpassed.

19

Among his sons to gain his title abroad was Int. Ch. Libretto of Ladypark who was exported to Italy to the Cambiano kennels of Mrs Garabelli senior. Before he left, he sired Ch. Liberty, Ch. Legend, the gorgeous Ch. Limpid of Ladypark and Ch. Pattingham Lullaby. Had he remained, he might have equalled his sire's record. Liberty sired no less than eight champions and Legend a further five. Pattingham Kismet, who himself gained two Challenge Certificates, proved a most successful sire for Mrs Margaret Franklyn and his progeny included Ch. Debonair of Glenmist (sire of the two litter brothers, Ch. Golden Legacy of Glenmist and Ch. Pattingham Gay Legend of Glenmist), and Ch. Pattingham Pacemaker. This last dog, a big free-moving sable of great ring presence, achieved immortality when, in 1964, he won the Non-Sporting Group at Cruft's. This group has since been split into the Working and Utility groups.

Of the eight champions sired by the very showy Liberty, only one was a dog and this was Mrs Newbury's Ch. Alphington Sociable who had a great influence on her strain. Ch. Legend proved very useful for the Ladypark strain because he brought a complete new set of genes with him as his grandam, the lovely Ch. Lena, although a sable, was the daughter of the blue merle Lilac of Ladypark. Lilac was a dark-eyed merle and both Lena and Legend were noted for the beauty of their dark eyes. Among Legend's sons were Ch. Statesman of Southwardedge, Mr Rodford's Ch. Statesman of Skellvale, sire of Ch. Sovereign of Skellvale, and the last of the Ladypark champions Ch. Legendary Prince of Ladypark, owned by Mrs Terry Taylor.

Ch. Lad of Ladypark had a great deal of influence in the West Country and apart from Ch. Son O'Lad, sired Ch. Riffelsee Resplendence who, because of his great friendliness, was given the run of the ship on which he was exported to Australia (who at that time did not allow imports by air), spending many happy hours sitting on the ship's hatch with the crew. Sadly, when the ship docked at Singapore the hatches were removed and this lovely dog leapt on to the open hatch and fell to his instant death in the ship's hold.

Resplendence sired only one litter before he left England and Lad's greatest influence has come down through his tricolour son Riffelsee Royalist, more by accident than design. His history is a series of coincidences. Royalist's dam was the tricolour Beulah's Night Flare who had already blotted her copy-book when I loaned her to Miss Grey on breeding terms for her first litter.

For her second litter, she was mated to Lad and produced seven puppies which she was unable to nurse. A foster mother was found

Riffelsee Royalist, born 1948, s. Ch. Lad of Ladypark, d. Beulah's Night Flare.

for the litter but it was decided to try and rear two badly marked tricolour dogs on the bottle. One died but the smaller of the two battled on and though he was only about half the size of the rest of the litter by the time they were weaned, he seemed lively enough. He was extremely ugly with the typical 'bats' ears' of the runt of the litter and no one would buy him even as a pet. He was six months old before we noticed that our ugly duckling was turning into a swan and another two months before he made a successful show debut and Mr Robson offered to buy him before he went into the ring. He was a small, rather feminine looking dog with an immense coat who many thought should have made a champion. Due, probably to his lack of colostrum when he was a puppy, it was found impossible to bring him into good condition and he was retired from the show ring after a successful puppy career.

He bore a great resemblance to his famous grandsire, Beulah's Night Victorious and like him was to prove a great sire. Though very little used, he sired in his first litter Ch. Westcarr's Blue Minoru and his little sister Westcarrs Blue Minerva, winner of two Challenge

21

Certificates, and in his second litter to Ch. Sapphire of Glenmist the two litter sisters Ch. Lovely Lady of Glenmist and Ch. Pattingham Gay Lady of Glenmist the dam of the immortal Ch. Pattingham Pacemaker. Pacemaker seems to have left only one son of much influence in the breed and that is Glamour Boy of Glenmist who sired Mrs Aileen Speding's Ch. Antoc The Boy Friend who, in turn, sired the elegant sable Ch. Antoc Haymaker. Mrs Speding's first champion Ch. Antoc Tawny Tattoo also traces back to Eden Examine as he was by Ch. Westcarr's Whistler, a sable son of the great Lochinvar.

Eden Examine left another line of note through his son Rimington Kittieholm Pilot. Pilot was a well-boned, sound, shaded sable who lacked a little in quality of skull but who proved an excellent sire as did so many of Examine's sons. He sired three champions in all but probably his greatest contribution was through his tail-male grandson Ch. Mywicks Meadow Lancer, a dog who was to set new standards for the breed. Yet another son of Examine's that was to have great influence was Abbott of Arranbeck who sired Dunsinane Alaric of Arranbeck who, in turn, sired the first of the Dunsinane great sires Ch. Defender of Dunsinane for Mrs Audrey Chatfield.

The third champion son of Eden Examine was Mr Tomlinson's Ch. Selstoma Safeguard who sired Ch. Forth of Naragansette for Mr McLaren of Scotland who is still producing champions today. One other shaded sable champion sired by Examine was the good-looking Ch. Mywick's Model Examiner who left no sons of note behind. Rather more influential was Mr Tomlinson's Longmeadow Lancer, winner of one Challenge Certificate, who sired for him Ch. Selstoma Sequence. The only champion daughter of Examine's was Mr Mywick's pretty Ch. Mywick's Fashioness.

Of all the prepotent sons of Eden Examine, Lochinvar is rightly the most famous and he was the only golden sable – all the others were shaded – but all had a tremendous influence for good on the immediate post-war breeding. There is scarcely a Collie in the country today who cannot trace his ancestry back to Examine, who although he gained one Challenge Certificate in his old age, was undoubtedly robbed of his title by the lack of wartime Championship Shows. Before he died, Examine had one more change in ownership and ended his days in the kennel of Mr Mycroft for whom he sired some very valuable litters. His influence ran right through the Mywick strain, culminating in the production of his great-grandson Ch. Mywick's Meadow Lancer, born in 1955.

Meadow Lancer was a shaded sable who, although he lacked something in coat and conformation, was possessed of a beauty of head and expression that was a revelation to contemporary breeders, who flocked to use him. Considerable line breeding was done to this dog in an attempt to fix this beautiful head in the breed. He was the second of the three post-war sires that were to lift the breed to new heights. In all, he sired thirteen champions – five dogs and eight bitches. He was the sire of the most successful tricolour bitch ever bred, the lovely Ch. Satine of Simbastar winner of fifteen Challenge Certificates.

Amongst the male champions he sired was the sable Ch. Duntiblae Dog Watch who successfully carried on the line for Mrs D. Cochrane with his son, Ch. Duntiblae Dog Star, and grandson, Ch. Duntiblae Dingo, who in turn sired Ch. Collydean Fair Dinkum at Ugony for Miss D.M. Young. Meadow Lancer also sired the tricolour Ch. Rhodelands Boy the sire of the sensational merle Ch. Carramar Boy Blue whose name is writ large in blue merle history.

Mr and Mrs Alan Jeffries sent their Jesfire Fashion to Meadow Lancer and were rewarded with the two sable brothers Ch. Jesfire Happy By Name and Ch. Jesfire Lucky by Name. Happy was exported but Lucky remained in England and sired five champions. They included the magnificent tricolour owned by Mr L. Casely, Ch. Thistleblue Blueland Boy, who started a highly successful dynasty for Mr and Mrs Hickson with three generations of champions, Ch. Bririch Black Keino, Ch. Blue Rock of Bririch and Ch. Bririch Blue Unit. All these lines have been influential but it was through his grandson, Ch. Defender of Dunsinane, and his son, Ch. Dorgano Demander of Dunsinane, that Meadow Lancer was to have his greatest influence on posterity.

It came, unobtrusively enough, in the shape of a small sable and white dog bred by Mrs Audrey Chatfield and registered by her as Dazzler of Dunsinane. There was nothing remarkable about this dog, indeed Audrey herself has described him as insignificant, but he had a touch of class about him and he had no major fault. He hated the show ring and after a short but reasonably successful puppy career he was retired to stud. All truly great sires are capable of stamping their type on their progeny regardless of the type of the bitch that is sent to them and Dazzler was to prove himself one of the greatest of all post-war sires.

Just as in Lochinvar's first litter, which produced three champions, so in Dazzler's first litter the type was there for all to see. The classic heads, the sweet expressions, the conformation, the short hocks and the wealth of well-fitting coat that were all to become his trade-mark. He was perhaps fortunate in the first bitch sent to him (who was to become a champion herself later), the tricolour Witchcraft of Rokeby. She has earned her own accolade in the chapter of great brood bitches but in this first litter she produced Ch. Royal Ace of Rokeby and his sister Ch. Romney of Rokeby for their breeder Mrs Betty Eglin. In all, Dazzler sired ten English champions beside a number of Continental ones, but none made more impact on the breed than did his son Royal Ace.

No fewer than twelve English champions can claim Royal Ace as their sire. Of the two litter brothers bred by Mrs Vera Hickson, Ch. Bririch Gold Emblem was exported to the USA but Ch. Bririch Gold Edition remained in England and sired five champions including the dogs Ch. Fernmoss Editorial of Bririch and Ch. Kidlaine Konrad. Konrad left only one son of note but he was the immortal Ch. Aberthorne Arrester. This sable and white dog out of Ch. Kreba Contemplation and bred by Jimmy Tait and Joyce Skilbeck has sired nine English champions to date and an even larger number of continental champions. The 'Arrester' type with their sweet expressions, dark

Ch. Aberthorne Arrester (centre) with his daughter, Ch. Brettonpark Country Fair (left), and his son, Ch. Mybern's Minstrel (right).

Ch. Aberthorne Arrester, s. Ch. Kidlane Konrad, d. Ch. Kreba Contemplation.

Ch. Mybern's Minstrel, born 1977, s. Ch. Aberthorne Arrester, d.
Mybern's Mistibelle, brs M. and B. Harris, ow. D. Crapper.

eyes, arched necks and immensely thick straight coats are still very distinctive in the ring.

His sons, Ch. Dunsinane Detective, Ch. Heighinglea Black Knight of Rixown, Ch. Mybern's Minstrel, Ch. Tameila Casey Jones and Ch. Tashedon Tommy Tucker, all look set to distinguish themselves in the siring stakes. Minstrel has a head start by siring Ch. Mybern's Mandane and Ch. Brilyn Super Tramp. Mandane, noted for his beautiful head properties has already sired eleven champions and Super Tramp, six, including Ch. Rockbar Gentle Gypsy Cruft's Best of Breed, 1987, Mandane's son, Ch. Jankeith Gideon of Mybern, who is a tricolour and has, to date, produced two champion sons, the merle Ch. Bririch Blue Ripple and the tricolour Ch. Mybern's Merideon.

One of Mandane's sons made history by gaining his title in three weeks. This was the Jeffries sable, Ch. Lasheen Stolen Property from Jesfire, a truly spectacular animal. Another of Mandane's sons that is emerging as one of the country's top sires is Mr and Mrs Clarke's Ch. Lynway Sandknocker. He has sired many winners including Mrs Hope Jones' Ch. Matai Don Quixote and Ch. Emryks Owd Peculiar who, in turn, has sired a champion son in Ch. Emryks Runnaway for his breeders Brian and Pauline Skyrmes.

Ch. Brilyn Supertramp, born 1979, s. Ch. Mybern's Minstrel, d. Brilyn Duchesse Lace, br. and ow. B. Hawkins.

Ch. Wardette Cuddly Dudly,
s. Ch. Brilyn Supertramp,
d. Sangreat Sweet Cherub of
Aberhill, brs and ows J. and P.
Stickler.

Ch. Lynway Sandknocker,
born, 1982, s. Ch. Mybern's
Mandane, d. Arranbrook
Cleopatra of Lynway.

*Ch. Matai Don Quixote, born 1985, s. Ch. Lynway Sandknocker, d.
Ch. Matai Flaming Jenny.*

Ch. Tameila Casey Jones has already sired Ch. Storwill Joe Soap of
Tameila and Tommy Tucker, himself a Cruft's Best of Breed winner,
has succeeded in siring another two – Tashedon Jenny Wren who won
Best of Breed of Cruft's in 1988 for her breeders, Mr and Mrs Staniland, and Ch. Coldamar Wor Geordie who won the Dog Challenge
Certificate in 1989 for Mr and Mrs Williamson. Before he left these
shores, Tommy Tucker's tricolour son, Spanish Champion Tashedon
Hot Chocolate, sired only a handful of litters yet amongst them have
been three champions and a Challenge Certificate winner.

One of them, Roy Williams' Ch. Byllsacre Just Kate, made history
when she won the Working Group at the Border Counties Championship Show in 1988. Her litter brother, Ch. Byllsacre Just So, made a
good double for their breeder Rene Cozens when he won his title. The
first of Hot Chocolate's daughters to make a name for herself was the
pretty sable, Ch. Saheltra's Talk of the Town of Felray, and the most
recent, the Challenge Certificate winning tricolour, Mr Greenhalgh's
Edgemont Katarina. It would seem that as with Libretto of Ladypark,
Chancellorville Aquitane and Lynnaire Man in Black, a potentially
great sire has been lost by British breeders before his full worth could
become established.

Ch. Tameila Casey Jones, born 1979, s. Ch. Aberthorne Arrester, d. Ch. Dark Delight of Tameila, br. and ow. A. Hodgson.

Ch. Emryks Owd Peculiar (right) and his son Ch. Emryks Runnaway (left). (Photograph by D. Pearce.)

*Ch. Coldamar Wor Geordie,
born 1984, s. Ch. Tashadon
Tommy Tucker, d. Coldamar
Dark Secret, Cruft's Ch. 1989.*

*Sp. Ch. Tashadon Hot Chocolate, s. Ch. Tashadon Tommy Tucker, d.
Glory at Tashadon, br. J. Staniland, ows Momediano.*

31

All these dogs can trace their antecedants back in eight or nine generations of tail-male champions to Dazzler of Dunsinane, using, of
course, the top line of the pedigree.

On the Continent, Royal Ace proved a most potent sire and eight of
his progeny carrying the Rokeby prefix became Int. Chs. The Laund
kennel also sent out three that became champions by him and the
Sandiacre strain, one. All these dogs have had a strong influence on
the European Collie scene.

Dazzler's other son, Ch. Ramsey of Rokeby, was noted for the sweet
expressions he passed on to his offspring and another line of great
sires has come down from him through Ch. Brettonpark Whatziz-
name (himself sire of five champions), through his son Sangreat
Sorocco of Arranbrook to that other great sire of the eighties, Ch.
Arranbrook Mr Chips of Aberhill. Once again we have a sire capable
of transmitting his outstanding qualities, including his glorious temperament, to his progeny, irrespective of the type of breeding of the
bitches sent to him. To date, Mr Chips has sired eleven champions

Ch. Karava Kornishman, born 1980, s. Ch. Geoffdon Lawmaker, d.
Karava Kastille.

*Ch. Jasand Young Winston,
born 1983, s. Ch. Karava
Kornishman, d. Jasand
Tuppencee Coloured.*

*Ch. Jasand Master Ziggy,
born 1982, s. Ch. Arranbrook
Mr Chips of Aberhill, d.
Aberhill Prima Donna of
Jasand.*

and several lines from him are emerging, the most successful probably being through Mr Geoff Mildon's Ch. Geoffdon Lawmaker who has so far sired three champions. From his tricolour son , Mr and Mrs Anderton's Ch. Karava Kornishman, has come Mrs Jasmine Round's shaded sable, Ch. Jasand Young Winston, the tricolour Ch. Keegan of Karava, the sable bitch, Ch. Kidlaine Kwaeola of Karava and the merle Ch. Karava Blue Kreation. Another highly successful son of Mr Chips, who has already sired two champions to date, is the sable Ch. Pelido Double Fantasy. Mr Chips is also the sire of Ch. Jasand Master Ziggy.

My favourite son of Ramsey's was the striking sable Ch. Rauno of Rokeby. Others were Ch. Lynway Sundance and Ch. Claredawn Clansman. Another of his sons was the beautifully bred sable Ch. Geoffdon's Westlynn Wayside Boy, owned by Geoff Mildon. This dog sired six champions and his son, Ch. Sonza Star Wars, is the sire of Mrs Read's Ch. Volterra King of the Stars, so another champion line seems to be developing there. Ramsey did not sire many tricolours but one of this colour, Mr and Mrs Blake's Ch. Corydon Quinault, has had great influence on the breed, both here and in Australia, mainly through his two sons, the litter brothers bred by Mr and Mrs Derek

Ch. Geoffdon Westlynn Wayside Boy and his granddaughter, Ch. Kaywell Babooshka of Geoffdon.

34

Ch. Chrisarian Capricious, born 1979, s. Ch. Little Caesar at Corydon, d. Ch. Chrisarian Chantelle at Corydon brs and ows C. Black and M. Penwarne.

Ch. Corydon Handsome Hotspur with the British Collie Club Trophy, born 1980, s. Ch. Little Ceasar at Corydon, d. Corydon Pollyhanna.

Field, the sable Ch. Little Caesar at Corydon and the tricolour Ch. Dameral Aristedes. Unfortunately for English breeders, Little Caesar was exported to Australia before his full potential as a sire was realised, but before he left he sired Ch. Jeffield Esquire, a shaded sable of great merit, Ch. Chrisarian Capricious and the noted sire, Ch. Corydon Handsome Hotspur. Ch. Dameral Aristedes remained in England and sired, amongst many winners, the elegant blue merle Ch. Saheltra's Sally Sunshine of Clickham (who Derek Smith has since sent out to the kennel of Mr Bellini of Italy), and Ch. Lowerpark Star Spangled for Mrs Lynn Westby. Another son of Quinault's that enhanced the English show scene before he too left for Australia was Ch. Corydon Handsome Hero. This sable dog was noted for his soundness and, perhaps as a result, was one of the handful of post-war Collies to distinguish themselves in the Working Group.

The Sandiacre kennel of Mr and Mrs Jack Wigglesworth owes, as they would be the first to admit, a great deal to another son of Dazzler's, Sandiacre Softly-Softly, winner of one Challenge Certificate. His mother was the lovely Ch. Sandiacre String of Pearls and he himself was the sire of beautiful bitches, siring five champions in all. Many of his progeny were exported to Scandinavia and other parts of Europe where they met with striking success. Ch. Dunsinane Robin Hood of Rokeby was another son of Dazzler's that was was entitled to prefix his name with the magic 'Ch.'. Less successful in the ring, perhaps, but an outstandingly successful sire, was Brettonpark Highlander of Dunsinane. He sired eight champions. The first was Ch. Drum Major of Dunsinane whose greatest contribution to the breed was his son, the beautiful Ch. Melzars Marvin of Dunsinane whose death, at four years of age, was a blow to his owner, Mrs Audrey Chatfield, and to the fancy as a whole. Highlander was also the sire of the two tricolours, Ch. Jesfire Clean Sweep, who won Best of Breed for his owners Mr and Mrs Alan Jeffries at Cruft's and has left us with Mrs Evan's blue merle dog, Ch. Carrastina Silver Shadow, and Mr and Mrs Burtenshaw's Pelido Black Prince. Black Prince has sired a champion in all three colours, the most noted being the blue merle dog, Ch. Cathanbrae Polar Moon at Pelido, as well as the sable dog, Ch. Pelido Sparticus, and the tricolour bitch, Ch. Pelido Black Belle.

From the above history, the significance of Dazzler as a sire can readily be deduced. Even more remarkable is the astonishing success of his sons and grandsons as reproducers of the same type. It has been calculated that 85 per cent of all present-day winners are descended from him and there are many top winners that can trace every line of their pedigree back to Dazzler. It is not surprising that the 1970s have earned the title 'The Dazzler Decade' in Collie circles.

Famous Brood Bitches

In every breed history, great credit is awarded to the dominant sires of the breed. I feel that not enough emphasis has been placed on the debt the breed owes to the great brood bitches of the past. If you study Collie history, you cannot help but be struck by the number of successful strains that have been founded on just one bitch. Some have produced a champion in every litter they bred, it seeming almost immaterial to which sire they were put. It has been stated that champion bitches seldom make good brood bitches and that their less illustrious relations are the better producers so often that we accept this as a fact. I believe this to be a fallacy. When you consider that approximately three thousand Collie bitch puppies are registered every year and that, out of this number, scarcely more than eight will gain their title, then the odds against these eight being the best brood bitches are high. Yet very often they are. Sometimes, we get whole strains of champion bitches that continue to breed their like for several generations, and it is these strains that have proved the backbone of many illustrious kennels. A study of the pedigrees of those bitches who have produced two champions or more, reveals some interesting facts about the part they have played in the establishment of some famous lines.

Mr Fred Robson was an extremely successful breeder and many of his Eden champions were exported to the USA. He came on the show scene round about 1913 and remained active in the breed until his death in 1966. He was fortunate in securing as one of his foundation bitches a daughter of Ch. Laund Limit out of that great brood bitch Denny Lively Bird, which he named Eden Emily. Emily obviously inherited her mother's talents as a reproducer and was the dam of Ch. Eden Elenora (by Ch. Eden Extra). When mated to the great sire, Ch. Poplar Perfection, Elenora gave Mr Robson Ch. Eden Etiquette, Ch. Eden Enrapture, Ch. Backwoods Fashion and the great sire, Ch. Eden Emerald, who played such a prominent role in American Collie history.

After the last war, the Eden strain was one of the first to re-establish itself, largely with the help of a bitch called Eden Effigy who produced three champion daughters – the lovely Ch. Eden Endearing and her litter sister Ch. Eden Estrella by Eden Excellent, and Ch. Eden Elation by Chapelburn Ronald.

Mr Robson and his kennel man, Harry Ribbins, were a familiar sight at the shows. Mr Robson was always on the look-out for a good Collie and it was his habit to inspect the benches catalogue in hand during the show. If a Collie took his fancy, he would, with the utmost courtesy, ask if he could see him move, and get Harry Ribbins to run the dog up and down. They would then confer and if they liked what they saw, Mr Robson would offer £100 for the animal. This was a very fair price in those days, when the average weekly wage was around £5. If the breeder did not succumb to temptation, it was still a matter of self-congratulation that the great Mr Robson had made an offer for your Collie. I never knew him to raise his bid.

Mrs N.K. George of the Beulah Collies always said that she owed a great deal of her success to one of her early tricolour bitches, Beulah's Night Shade, dam of Ch. Backwoods Fanfare, and one of the earliest of the Ladyparks, a bitch called Lyric of Ladypark who became the grandam of Ch. Lena of Ladypark. Mrs George may well have been right but history records that it was another of her tricolour bitches that was to have the greater influence. This was Beulah's Night Black and Beautiful who was one of her favourite house dogs. She was a sister of that prolific war-time winner, the tricolour Lyncliffe Lancer and was bred by Mr and Mrs H. Cliffe. She was the first tricolour I ever saw and I thought she was perfection itself. Like her brother, she was robbed of her title by the war. Mated to the tricolour, Beulah's Night Victorious, she produced, inevitably, an all-tricolour litter which contained Ch. Beulah's Night Glorious and the two sisters, Beulah's Night Gorgeous and Miss Maloney's Beulah's Night Glamorous who both won Challenge Certificates. Mated to Ch. Beulah's Golden Futureson, Night Glamorous produced Ch. Westcarrs Whitethroat, and bred Ch. Westcarrs Whistler when sent to Lochinvar. Both were sable-and-whites.

Night Black and Beautiful had another daughter that was to play a very significant role in the future of the breed. Her name was Beulah's Golden Kiska and she was the dam of the spectacular sable, Ch. Beulah's Golden Fusonkin, Ch. Beulah's Golden Flora and the tricolour, Shiel's Beulah's Night Flower, who was the dam of Ch. Beulah's Night So Neat. Flora is immortalised as the dam of Chs Lad and Lochinvar of Ladypark. She was not renowned for her head properties, but she was a beautifully constructed and free-moving bitch who completed her title after she had finished her maternal duties.

Another of Mrs George's excellent brood bitches was Beulah's August Princess. Mated to Ch. Beulah's Golden Mightyatom, she bred Ch. Beulah's Golden Mightysol and when mated to Ch. Beulah's Golden Fusonkin, she bred Ch. Beulah's Golden Sunfu Son.

Every now and again you get a bitch of unremarkable breeding who seems to release from within her a stream of such quality that it carries on through her sons and daughters to her grandchildren and beyond. She becomes the founder of a new dynasty. Such a bitch was Laird's Rose. Others include Lilac of Ladypark and Ch. Witchcraft of Rokeby.

According to Miss Grey, at the time, Laird's Rose was a somewhat undistinguished looking bitch and she was astonished at the quality of the litter she produced to Lochinvar. It was his first litter. From it came three champions – Ch. Laird's Galway Sun and two daughters, Ch. Rose of Ladypark and Ch. Maid of Ladypark. Rose was sold to Dr Collins and myself at the age of ten weeks and completed her title just out of puppyhood. She was mated three times to our Ch. Lad of Ladypark and bred a champion in each litter. The dog Ch. Riffelsee Resplendence won his title in the spring of 1954 in just five shows, Int. Ch. Riffelsee Regality of Dunsinane, was the first Dunsinane champion and later produced Ch. Darling of Dunsinane, and probably the most remarkable of them all was Ch. Riffelsee Reward of Glenmist CD.

Reward was purchased from us, at the age of eight weeks by Frank Mitchell and was the foundation of his most successful Glenmist kennel. She must hold the record of the best all-round bitch that the breed has ever produced. Not only did she annex her obedience CD as well as three Challenge Certificates but, in between, she bred three litters containing four champion daughters – Ch. Sapphire, Ch. Sceptre, Ch. Spellbinder and Ch. Starlet of Glenmist. Sapphire carried on the family tradition by also producing four champions – two dogs by Ch. Debonair of Glenmist, Ch. Glenmist Golden Legacy and Ch. Pattingham Gay Legend of Glenmist, and two daughters by the tricolour Riffelsee Royalist, Ch. Lovely Lady of Glenmist and Ch. Pattingham Gay Lady of Glenmist.

It was said of Frank Mitchell, at the time, that he produced a succession of beautiful bitches, each one lovelier than the last. Lovely Lady was the dam of Ch. Gay Cascade of Glenmist and Gay Lady was the dam of the history making Ch. Pattingham Pacemaker who won the Non-Sporting Group at Cruft's. Ch. Starlet of Glenmist also produced two champions – Ch. Debonair of Glenmist and the important sire, Ch. Larkena Vanara Golden Victor, bred by Mr and Mrs J. Parrot.

Ch. Riffelsee Reward of Glenmist CD, born 1953, s. Ch. Lad of Ladypark, d. Ch. Rose of Ladypark.

Ch. Rose of Ladypark had a fourth litter by Riffelsee Royalist and a sable bitch called Riffelsee Rosemary was purchased from us by Mr and Mrs Alan Jeffries. She never distinguished herself in the show ring but her tail-female line (the bottom line in the pedigree), led to her granddaughter, Sandiacre Jesfire Gay Tweed. Tweed was the dam of the bitch Ch. Jesfire Gay Return who produced the sensational sable dog, Ch. Jesfire High Regard, and she was also the dam of Seawitch of Sandiacre who takes her place in the history books by virtue of being the dam of the lovely Ch. Sandiacre String of Pearls. She very quickly gained her title and set about proving that she was a worthy descendant of Laird's Rose by producing, in her first litter to Dazzler, the notable sire Sandiacre Softly-Softly winner of one Challenge Certificate. In her remaining two litters to Ch. Rauno of Rokeby and Brettonpark Highlander of Dunsinane, she bred Ch. Sandiacre Sweet Lorraine and Ch. Sandiacre Seed Pearl. Sweet Lorraine carried on the family tradition by also producing three champions, all to diff-

*Ch. Sandiacre String of Pearls, born 1968, s. Ch. Royal Ace of Rokeby,
d. Colrenes Seawitch of Sandiacre.*

*Ch. Sandiacre Sweet Lorraine, born 1973, s. Ch. Rauno of Rokeby, d.
Ch. Sandiacre String of Pearls.*

41

erent dogs – Ch. Sandiacre Sweet Valentine, Ch. Sandiacre Stripper and the dog, Ch. Sandiacre Silence is Golden. Ch. Seed Pearl is the dam of Ch. Sandiacre Sweet Georgia Brown.

Returning to the Ladypark strain we find that the influence of their great sires was so dominant that they tended to overshadow the excellence of their brood bitches. One of the best of these was Lindy Lou of Ladypark, a very striking bitch with a big white collar, a white patch on her nose and a particularly strong, round foreface. There is no doubt in my mind that she would have made a champion if she had been shown. However, Miss Grey was extremely proud of the confident temperament of all her Collies and the lovely Lindy Lou was shy of strangers so she was never exhibited. She made up for it by producing three great champions – the showy Ch. Liberty of Ladypark followed by the aptly named Ch. Lovely of Ladypark and finally, the exquisite Ch. Limpid of Ladypark.

One little bitch that had a great influence, both on the Ladyparks and the breed as a whole, was the merle Lilac of Ladypark who had an interesting history. I had taken my tricolour bitch Beulah's Night Flare to Maroel Blue Mandarin, the dark-eyed merle son of the

Ch. Limpid of Ladypark, born 1953, s. Int. Ch. Libretto of Ladypark, d. Lindy Lou of Ladypark.

Lilac of Ladypark, born 1946, s. Maroel Blue Mandarin, d. Beulah's Night Flare.

tricolour Ch. Eden Diadem who proved such a successful sire in the USA. Mandarin was owned by a Mr Lloyd of Risca and I was surprised to find the dog sitting outside his front door on the pavement, waiting for the children to arrive home from school. He seemed far more interested in the children than in Flare but I left her there and in due course I sent her to Miss Grey on breeding terms. She whelped two puppies – one tricolour and one merle bitch. I was very anxious to preserve the Diadem breeding and it was agreed that I would take the tricolour and Miss Grey would keep the merle. A fortnight later, Flare was sent home, by train, in disgrace. She had killed the tricolour puppy and savaged the merle to such an extent that she could never be shown; only Miss Grey's devoted nursing saved her life. Later, a bone was found in the straw and it was a lesson to both of us never to feed or allow food near the nest.

Lilac was hand reared and proved of great importance in both sable and blue merle post-war breeding. Her first litter was to the sable, Lucky of Ladypark, one of Miss Grey's first Collies. It produced the beautiful sable Ch. Lena of Ladypark who was much admired for the darkness of her eyes. She was yet another champion to breed three champions – Ch. Lilt of Ladypark, Ch. Eden Rip of Ladywell and

Ch. Lena's Golden Son – all by Lochinvar. Lilac's part in blue merle history can be found in the section on blue merles. She was the source of all that was good in post-war merle breeding. Today the sable/merle cross is much advocated by USA breeders who have achieved some marvellous results with it. British breeders are very prejudiced against it. I can only say that, in Miss Grey's hands, it was magic.

Mr Tom Purvis, that sadly missed Geordie personality, owed a great deal to one of his early foundation bitches, Ch. Danvis Deborah, who produced three bitch champions for him. Two were by Lochinvar, namely Ch. Lottery of Ladypark and Ch. Danvis Dyllorna, and the third, Ch. Danvis Daytime, was by Ch. Cezar of Corbieux. Deborah was also the dam of two Challenge Certificate winners, Diadem and Devotion, both by Lochinvar. Tom had another good line running down from the bitch Danvis Daphne who not only produced the dog, Ch. Danvis Driver, but also the bitch, Ch. Danvis Deanna, who left one champion daughter, Ch. Danvis Derna. Derna proved an excellent brood and presented Tom with the dogs Ch. Danvis Duffer and Ch. Danvis Dooley as well as the winning bitch Danvis Dorabelle.

Mention has already been made of Mrs Margaret Franklyn's Pattingham Collies which are behind many of today's winners, but she would be the first to acknowledge that she owes a great deal to one of her foundation bitches, Danethorpe Laugh of Ladypark, who bred for her the two champions Ch. Pattingham Lullaby and Ch. Pattingham Prelude.

Even so, it was their sister, Polka, purchased from Mrs Franklyn at eight weeks, that was to have the greatest success as a brood bitch for her new owner Mrs Florence Chapman. Mated three times to three different dogs, Polka bred four Deloraine champions – the bitches Decorative, Distinctive and Dinah-Mite and the dog Ch. Deloraine Don Juan.

Another brood bitch that was to have a tremendous influence on post-war breeding was Leecroft Ladyfair for, in one litter to Ch. Mywicks Meadow Lancer, she produced three champions, Ch. Deborah of Dunsinane, Ch. Danvis Sheba of Simbastar and the incomparable tricolour Ch. Mywick's Satine of Simbastar winner of fifteen Challenge Certificates who was the dam of Ch. Colrenes Mywick's Merlow Moonbeam.

In 1965, a tricolour bitch was born that was destined to become the greatest brood bitch of all time. Like Laird's Rose she came from an undistinguished background, but such was her prepotence, she was to found a dynasty that has produced, and is still producing, champions in virtually every European country in which Collies are known. Her name was Ch. Witchcraft of Rokeby and she was bred by Mrs Betty Eglin. She was the dam of five top-class English champions – Ch. Royal Ace of Rokeby, Ch. Rauno of Rokeby, Ch. Dunsinane Robin Hood of Rokeby and the two bitches, Ch. Romney of Rokeby and Ch. Derburgh Rosemarie of Rokeby. She was also the dam of a further ten international champions – Int. Ch. Riff (Czechoslovakia); Int. Ch. Craftsman (France); Int. Chs Knight Matchmaker, Reporter and Response (Germany); Int. Chs Rival and Razina (Italy); Int. Ch. Ronan (Norway); Int. Ch. Witch Hazel (Spain) and Int. Ch. Rangefinder (Sweden), all of Rokeby. For one bitch to produce fifteen champions is amazing and when you consider that almost all of them carried on this champion-producing line, the number of her champion grandchildren and great-grandchildren is quite staggering.

Romney was the dam of the lovely Ch. Dunsinane Rosalinda of Rokeby, also that great sire, Ch. Ramsey of Rokeby, and the important brood bitch Corydon Regality of Rokeby. Derburgh Rosemarie was the dam of several international champions. Mr and Mrs Blake's Corydon Regality of Rokeby was a daughter of Ch. Witchcraft's two very successful children, Ch. Royal Ace and Ch. Romney of Rokeby. This bitch produced the tricolour bitch, Ch. Corydon Qui Vive in her first litter and in her second, the sable dog, Corydon King Hector. Mated together, these two produced the lovely Ch. Corydon Hyppolita. Qui Vive was also the dam of the tricolour dog Ch. Corydon Quinault.

Hyppolita carried on the family tradition by also producing two champions – the dog Ch. Corydon Polymeros of Bririch and Ch. Corydon Polly Hera. Hyppolita's other daughter, Pollyhanna, was the dam of those two outstanding males, Ch. Corydon Handsome Hero and Ch. Corydon Handsome Hotspur. The successful formula of half-brother and sister mating was repeated when Regality's two offspring, King Hector and Clear Majority of Corydon, were mated together and produced that great little show girl, Ch. Everlovin Emily of Corydon, bred by Mrs Elizabeth Webb. Emily wrote her name in indelible ink on the role of honour when in one litter, by Ch. Corydon Quinault, she bred three dogs of great excellence for her owners Mr and Mrs Derek Field. They were the sable dog, Ch. Little Caesar at Corydon, the tricolour dog, Ch. Dameral Aristedes and their sable brother Dameral Tawny Tobias, winner of two Challenge Certificates.

Ch. Witchcraft of Rokeby had one granddaughter that had obviously inherited her grandmother's genius for producing only the best and that was the elegant Ch. Rosalie of Rokeby. She was the dam of four English champions and several international champions. In England, her only champion son was the notable winner Ch. Dunsinane Radar of Rokeby, but she produced three very good bitches in Ch. Ravissant of Rokeby, Ch. Jimalyn's Rejoice of Rokeby and Ch. Sandiacre Request of Rokeby, the latter being the dam of Ch. Sandiacre Smartie Pants.

Another bitch who joined the select band who bred three champions was the sable bitch Bririch Golden Belita by Dazzler of Dunsinane. Mated to her half-brother, Ch. Royal Ace of Rokeby, also by Dazzler, she gave Eric and Vera Hickson three champions in just one litter. Ch. Bririch Gold Edition remained in this country where his contribution to Collie breeding can hardly be overestimated but his brother, Ch. Bririch Gold Emblem, was exported to the USA where he proved a most successful sire, his blood combining well with their breeding. The third member of the trio was the tricolour bitch, Ch. Bririch Night Enchantment.

The Arranbrook strain of John and Sue Basing owes a great deal to their purchase of Brettonpark Burnished Gold of Arranbrook, for in one litter to their own Sangreat Sorocco of Arranbrook she produced the lovely Ch. Arranbrook Polly Peachum, that great show dog and sire Ch. Arranbrook Mr Chips of Aberhill and his brother, Ch. Arranbrook Summer Wind of Camanna.

Yet another Ch. bitch who disproved the theory that champions do not make the best brood bitches was Ch. Kreba Contemplation. Put to Ch. Kidlaine Konrad, she produced, in one litter, the immortal Ch. Aberthorne Arrester and his tricolour sister, Ch. Aberthorne Aphrodisia, for Joyce Skilbeck and Jimmy Tait.

Another bitch to emulate this feat was Mrs Rene Cozen's great little show lady, Ch. Querida Mia who, put to Byllsacre All in Gold JW, gave birth to two champions – the sisters, Ch. Byllsacre Mia'ly Golden and Ch. Byllsacre Mia'ly a Dream. Another Byllsacre bitch that has earned her own niche is Byllsacre Hi-Society. When put to the tricolour Spanish Ch. Tashedon Hot Chocolate, she produced the Group Winner Ch. Byllsacre Just Kate and her brother Ch. Byllsacre Just So.

Ann and Norma Lister's sable Abbestone Ruby Red Dress joined the very select band of bitches that have achieved the distinction of breeding three champions in one litter – Ch. Abbestone Ruby Tuesday, Ch. Abbestone Ruby's Love at Mybern and Ch. Abbestone Red Adair by Ch. Mybern's Mandane.

46

Ch. Byllsacre Querida Mia, born 1979, s. Ch. Rokeby the Radical, d. Byllsacre Limelight. (Photograph by J. Kelly.)

Ch. Byllsacre Just Kate (winner of the Working Group, Border Counties, 1988), born 1985, s. Sp. Ch. Tashedon Hot Chocolate, d. Byllsacre Hi Society. (Photograph by D. Freeman.)

Ch. Brilyn Dawn Delight, born 1980, s. Ch. Brilyn Supertramp, d. Brilyn Band of Gold, ow. and br. B. Hawkins.

Readers must draw their own conclusions from this section but one thing is indisputable – the more you study the great winner-producing lines before making your initial purchase, the greater will be your chances of founding your own successful dynasty.

Blue Merle History

In the opinion of many, myself included, the blue merle is the most beautiful of the three colours of Collie. It is also the most difficult to breed and herein lies its fascination. The blue should be a soft, silvery blue spotted or marbled with black which should not run together or extend to large black patches. Merles normally carry very large white collars and white blazes are more acceptable than those in the other two colours. Bright tan markings on the face and legs add yet another shade to this most colourful of dogs.

It is largely thanks to the efforts of Mr W. Arkwright that the blue merle survived at all as a show specimen. Prior to his interest in the early 1870s, most merles were drowned at birth. There was no demand for them at all but Mr Arkwright changed all that. He made a considerable study of blue merle breeding and came to the conclusion that the merle/black and tan cross produced the best coloured merles, closely followed by the merle/tricolour cross. Sables bred to merles, he maintained, resulted in muddy coloured merles and blue-eyed sables. This view has been handed down from generation to generation in England and is generally regarded as indisputable. In the USA the sable/merle cross is common and the wider gene pool that becomes available to breeders through its use is considered to be of the utmost benefit to the breed.

Mr Arkwright was a great admirer of the merle dog, Scott, whom he considered to have the perfect colour and markings for a merle, namely, 'silvery blue, beautifully clouded with black, white collar, chest, feet and tag, face and forelegs bordered by bright red, with one china eye'. He mated a granddaughter back to Scott and produced the sensational dog, Blue Sky, and his sister Blue Thistle. From her came the first merle champion, the lovely Ch. Blue Ruin. She was described as being of a beautiful blue colour, of such a lovely shape that out of coat she could easily have won her title as a champion Smooth. In 1888, she created a sensation by winning the Collie Club Trophy for Best of Breed at the Kennel Club Show, the first of her colour to win such a prestigious award. From that moment on the status of the blue merle as a show dog was assured.

Two years later, at the age of six, she was sold to America, but not before she had left some useful progeny in this country. In the USA she proved the springboard for successful merle breeding and the colour proved immediately and immensely popular. During the reign of Edward VII, more merles were sent to the USA than any other colour, many of them in-whelp bitches. Many merles were exported to Europe. Some travelled as far as Russia. Yet still the classes in England continued to be well filled. This was partly due to the fact that at this time merles had special classes of their own (as they still do on the Continent), and to the formation, in 1907, of the Rough Blue Merle Collie Club.

At the turn of the century, Mr W.E. Mason began to take an interest in the colour and his Southport kennels housed many high-class merles, several of them sired by his famous dog, Ch. Southport Sample. A large number of Mr Mason's merles found their way across the Atlantic where the demand seemed insatiable. Meanwhile, more and more English breeders were taking up the colour. Mr C. White had many beautiful merles in his collection of Collies and his Ch. Blue

Princess Alexandra was considered to have the ideal colouring and markings. He was also the breeder of USA Ch. Leabrook Enchantress who was the first of her colour to become a champion in that country.

Among the British breeders specialising in merles was Mr H.E. Packwood who produced such notable dogs as Billesley Blue Coat, Blue Bonnet and Blue Blossom who all made considerable inroads on the prize list. Even Mr Ainscough of the famous Parbold Collies was to add merles to his kennels and he bought a bitch he called Parbold Blue Luna from Mrs Hume-Robertson. Luna was litter sister to the first English merle dog champion, Ch. Porchester Blue Sol. Blue Sol was a beautiful coloured and marked dog that also had a head that was good enough for him to defeat many of the best sables in the country which he duly did when he won the Challenge Certificate at the Ladies' Kennel Association in 1911.

After World War I, the popularity of the blue merle declined. Only a few, like the Rev. T. Salter with his Mountshannon Collies (in particular his Ch. Mountshannon Blue Splendour), and Miss Daisy Miller with her Knight O' Blue Mist and Gypsyville Blue Minx, kept the merle flag flying. In 1927, Ch. Glenack Kingfisher, bred by Mr and Mrs Pyle, was born. He played a big part in the pedigrees of the early Westcarr kennels of Miss Clare Maloney and the Beulah kennels of Mrs N.K. George. His daughter, Beulah's Silver Tern, was the dam of the litter sisters (by Ch. Backwoods Flutter), Ch. Beulah's Silver Marina and Ch. Beulah's Silver Merienda. Merienda was the dam of the spectacular merle USA Ch. Silver Don Mario, who was sent to the USA to conserve English blood lines during World War II. Before he left, he sired one litter to Mr and Mrs H. Cliffes' beautiful tricolour bitch, Leyland Lima, winner of two Challenge Certificates, which contained Beulah's Night Black and Beautiful and that great tricolour wartime winner, Lyncliffe Lancer, who sired the immortal shaded sable, Eden Examine.

Mrs Nadine George retained in her kennel the unshown tricolour brother of Don Mario's called Beulah's Night Victorious, so named because he was born on the night of the battle of the River Plate. He was a big dog, as near a black and tan as it was possible to be. He had scarcely any white on him but he had immense influence on post-war breeding, mostly through the use made of him by Miss Maloney and Miss Osborne. The first Collie that I owned, called Beulah's Golden Fantasy, was mated to him and produced Ch. Beulah's Night Fame, Night Flame and my Night Flare. In her first litter, Night Flare bred that great brood bitch, the merle Lilac of Ladypark, and in her second, the tricolour Riffelsee Royalist. He sired just three merle litters and yet every merle in the country can trace their pedigree back to him. Like his grandfather, Beulah's Night Victorious, Royalist had very little white on him yet when Miss Maloney mated a very heavily marked merle, Lobelia of Ladypark, to him, she produced one of the most beautiful merles yet seen – Ch. Westcarrs Blue Minoru.

Lobelia was another daughter of Lilac of Ladypark, so it was an interesting experiment in line breeding for which Miss Maloney received much commendation. Now that she is no longer with us, I can reveal it was purely a chance mating. Lobelia had been sent to our shaded sable Ch. Lad of Ladypark but would have none of him. She was an extremely cantankerous bitch and was put in with the young Royalist who was considered too young to be used, a supposition with which he wholeheartedly agreed. Such is the perversity of the female kind, that his complete indifference to her charms trans-formed her behaviour. From a snapping, snarling harridan she became a sweet, gentle alluring creature and eventually succeeded in getting a somewhat reluctant Royalist to mate her. Thus was the course of Collie history changed, for the resultant litter contained the immortal Ch. Westcarr's Blue Minoru and his sister Westcarr's Blue Minerva, winner of two Challenge Certificates.

Minoru was a magnificent, large, well-boned, free-moving beauti-fully coloured and coated dog, with an excellent head and conforma-tion. He was the first blue merle since Ch. Blue Ruin to win the coveted British Collie Club 60gn Trophy and he won many new admirers for his colour. He was the sire of Ch. Crosstalk Silver Bridholme Rambler, Ch. Silvasceptre from Shiel and Ch. Crosstalk Silver Belle. Rambler, in turn, sired Ch. Fourjoys Blue Danny and Ch. Fourjoys Blue Minstrel of Whitelea for Mr W. Richmond. Lilac of Ladypark was the dam of the first post-war blue merle champion in Miss Osborne's dark-eyed Ch. Silva-Seabear from Shiel (Lobelia's litter sister). Silva-Seabear was the first of many lovely dark-eyed merles produced over the years by the Shiel kennel.

Mrs George always held a strong hand in merles and, in 1951, bred an incredible litter by Beulah's Silver Don Glorio out of Beulah's Night Vivid which contained three champions and one Challenge Certifi-cate winner, all of a most beautiful silver blue colour. Two of them were bitches – Ch. Beulah's Silver Medialuna and Ch. Beulah's Silver Mantilla – and two were dogs – Ch. Beulah's Silver Don Marjo and Beulah's Silver Don Mero. Don Marjo was the sire of yet another Beulah merle champion in Ch. Beulah's Silver Maravella.

It was a grandson of Minoru's, Ch. Carramar Boy Blue, bred by Mrs Joyce Sargeant that electrified the Collie world when he appeared on the show scene in 1962. This lovely blue merle dog lit up the ring with his luminous colour as he glided elegantly round it. He won ten Challenge Certificates altogether and almost every major award available. He was the sire of an even heavier coated merle in Ch. Carramar Blue Tweed and the beautifully coloured Ch. Cheryldene Moonskater of Dunsinane. Blue Tweed sired Ch. Clickam Night Superior for Mr Derek Smith. Boy Blue was his grandsire on both sides so it is not surprising that Superior, who was the sire of Ch. Clickam Ciraveen Black Cavan, is to be found behind many of today's winners. Boy Blue also sired some beautiful bitches including the tricolours Ch. Shearcliffe Black Belle of Dunsinane bred by Mr J. Broderick and Ch. Carramar Pollyanna, bred in the home kennel by Joyce Sargeant.

One of the last champions to carry the Ladypark prefix was Mrs T. Taylor's Ch. Cathanbrae Ladypark Lavender Blue. She was the dam of two great blues, Ch. Cathanbrae Smokey Joe by that marvellous sire

Ch. Carramar Boy Blue, born, 1960, s. Ch. Rhodelands Boy, d. Westcarr's Blue Myrobella.

Ch. Antoc Midnight Cowboy, and the descriptively named Ch. Cathanbrae Willow Pattern sired by Knight Marksman of Rokeby. Willow Pattern's grandson was the notable winner and sire Ch. Cathanbrae Polar Moon at Pelido.

It is impossible to complete a history of blue merles without mention of the famous brothers Ch. Danvis Ladyvale Blue Mist and Ch. Danvis Ladyvale Blue Macade. They were bred by Mr P. Davison, sired by a tricolour Danvis Jesfire Johnny Walker out of Sea Dreamer a merle who combined Carramar and Clickam breeding. Blue Mist was the first to make his appearance, winning twelve Challenge Certificates in all including Cruft's and British Collie Club, twice taking home the famous trophy on which all the great winners of the past have their names inscribed. He sired the merle Ch. Rubec Mist 'n' Blue of Aberhill before leaving to carve out a new career for himself as a very successful sire and show dog in Australia. His blood was then lost to England but not to the Continent, as Mrs M.T. Garabelli imported into Italy a son of his, Ch. Dornbrae Misty Blue, who has proved a most useful out cross for her.

Back in England, the resourceful Tom Purvis, who owned and had handled Blue Mist to all his triumphs, went in search of his litter brother. He remembered him well as being of equal high quality but he had been sold as a pet. Tom told me that he found Macade wandering round a housing estate and had little difficulty in persuading his owners to part with him. Blue Macade had an even more sensational show career than his brother. With one Challenge Certificate to his credit, he went to Cruft's in 1979 and won Best of Breed. For those of us watching that day, he made an unforgettable appearance in the big ring with a wonderful luminous blue colour that lit up the ring in the way only a good merle can. It was a thrill for all of us when he went Reserve in the group. The following year, he repeated his Best of Breed win, taking his ninth Challenge Certificate, at Cruft's. He too had his name inscribed on the British Collie Club trophy for winning Best of Breed in 1979 making three wins in a row for the late Mr Tom Purvis. After his owner's death, Macade was sent to join his brother in Australia.

Over the years, great success in blue merle breeding has been achieved by Mr and Mrs Eric Hickson of the Bririch strain. A son of their great tricolour, Ch. Bririch Black Keino, the blue merle, Ch. Blue Rock of Bririch, sired three champion merles – Ch. Bririch Blue Unit and two beautiful daughters, Ch. Mossylea Moody Blue and Ch. Ingledene Blue Rain. One of the prettiest blue merle bitches that I can recollect was the home-bred Ch. Bririch Blue Yvette and she, in turn, has produced a champion son in Ch. Bririch Blue Ripple.

A whole new set of genes were brought into this country with the arrival of the merle bitch, the aptly named Ink Spotted Blu di Cambiano. Mated to Beaublade Black Faustus at Sangreat, she produced, in her first litter, the beautifully coloured and coated Ch. Sangreat Snow Sapphire of Rubec for Maud and Alan Mather. Encouraged by this first venture into the English ring, Mrs M.T. Garabelli sent over another Italian ambassador. This time it was Ink Spotted's brother It. Ch. Incredibly Blu di Cambiano. They were both by her famous sire Int. Ch. Lupupick Blu di Cambiano out of the English bitch Int. Ch. Grimhaven Blue Opal. I had been greatly impressed with this dog the previous year when I made him Best in Show at the Italian Collie Club. I was delighted to be asked to handle him when he emerged from quarantine and he quickly gained his British title. He was a spectacular looking dog but it was his gentle yet fearless nature that won all hearts. Coupled with the fact that he obtained eye and hip clearance certificates, his importation has proved a resounding success.

Eng., It., and Int. Ch. Incredibly Blu di Cambiano, born 1980, s. Int. Ch. Lupupick di Cambiano, d. Int. Ch. Grimhaven Blue Opal. (Photograph by D. Pearce.)

Before he left for an equally short stay in Sweden, he had gained the Pedigree Chum/Our Dogs Trophy for the top sire in the breed, the first time it has been won by a merle. At the time of writing he has sired nine champions in five different countries, a record unequalled in the breed. He has left one champion son in this country in Ch. Rubec Blue Peter and a Challenge Certificate winner in Lynway Spotted Dick. The Mathers have done a very neat bit of line breeding in mating their Ch. Snow Sapphire to her cousin Ch. Blue Peter to produce the young blue merle, Ch. Rubec Snow Symphony, for the Magills. So far, she has won five Challenge Certificates in four months.

Recently a new star has arisen in the blue merle firmament. This is Angela Hodgson's Ch. Tameila Gordon Bennet. He is a son of Ch. Upperton Blue Brand out of a daughter of Int. Ch. Incredibly Blu, and, at the time of writing, has notched up a total of nine Challenge Certificates, including Cruft's 1988 and the Challenge Certificate and Best of Breed trophy at the British Collie Club show 1989.

I have seen many blue merle champions in this and other countries. Some go back to the pre-war years. Of them all, four stand out in my memory. All of them were outstandingly beautiful, with excellent heads, glorious colouring, conformation and movement. Each of them raised the standard of merles in this country to new heights.

Ch. Rubec Blue Peter, born 1985, s. Int. Ch. Incredibly Blu di Cambiano, d. Rubec Snow Dove.

Ch. Tameila Gordon Bennet (Cruft's CC 1988), born 1986, s. Ch. Upperton Blue Brand, d. Tameila Blue Charm.

Ch. Rubec Snow Symphony JW, 1 CC, born 1987, s. Ch. Rubec Blue Peter, d. Ch. Sangreat Snow Sapphire of Rubec. Top winning Collie 1989.

They were Ch. Westcarr's Blue Minoru, Ch. Carramar Boy Blue, Ch. Danvis Ladyvale Blue Mist and Int. Ch. Incredibly Blu di Cambiano. Further information on the breeding of merles can be found in the section on colour inheritance.

The History of the Collie
World-Wide

From the time that Queen Victoria sent a pair of Collies to be exhibited in the USA to the present day, Rough Collies have continued to leave these shores in ever increasing numbers. Now there is scarcely a country that does not have its own flourishing Collie Society.

The days when fabulous prices could be obtained from the USA are long since gone, but there is still a steady stream of high-quality Collies leaving these shores each year. Nowadays, overseas breeders have much more information at their command. Colour photographs and videos are freely available and travelling is so much easier that many potential purchasers prefer to travel to Britain and select their own stock. On their return to their own countries, they have skilfully blended the breeding of their new stock with the old, often with spectacularly successful results as I hope to be able to show.

The history of the breed in most countries is so intertwined with Britain's that it is difficult to disentangle the threads. All of these Collies can trace their family tree back to the founder, Trefoil. I wonder if the writer of the following extract had any inkling of the world-wide impact this dog was to have when he wrote of Trefoil's first appearance at a show in Northampton in 1874: 'Sheepdogs were well represented, but a young dog named Trefoil came and astonished all. He is what we have been looking for, but never seen before in a Colley class: a really magnificent stamp. Here you had all you could desire – head long, slightly conical, and with a foxy intelligent appearance; long jaw; eye quick and expression soft; with a neck and bosom very full of coat; body well ribbed up and coat harsh to the touch; on good legs and feet; with a short stern carried almost straight out and not over the hindquarters. Not quite twelve months old, this new-comer "made his mark" and will keep to it.'

'Keep to it' he certainly did and now his descendants have spread to all parts of the world. In England, our Collies are tied in so closely with European Collies that the type is indistinguishable one from another. In America, something very different has happened. From the expensive blood lines which they obtained from Britain, they have bred a type of Collie that is two inches (5 cm) bigger and ten pounds (4.5 kg) heavier.

Until the last war, British dogs continued to be imported into the USA and were very successful. Since then, the type has diverged. American breeders have concentrated on producing large, upstanding, showy Collies with great emphasis on strong, well-rounded forefaces and well-blunted muzzles. So much so that it is conceivable that their Collie will one day be recognised as a separate breed as has happened with the American Cocker Spaniel. I feel this would be a great pity. The American Breed Standard is merely a fuller, more explicit version of our own. We, in Britain, have turned to producing a smaller dog with a shorter head and less strength in the foreface. If both countries could revert to the classic head that was once so much admired on both sides of the Atlantic, we would produce a Collie without exaggerations that would win in either country.

Mrs Bobby Roos who was familiar with our war-time Collies and whose Wickmere Collies are world-famous has kindly written the following short history of American Collies.

Three thousand miles from the parent source of the breed the Collie found strong roots on the eastern shores of the USA. The earliest stud book, printed in 1878, contained no Collie registrations. The second volume, printed in 1885, listed twenty-two Collies, nineteen of which were bred by Americans. By the middle 1880s the breed was distributed further west and south.

The Collie Club of America, founded in 1886, adopted the Standard which appeared in the American Kennel Club Gazette, July 1900, under the heading, 'The True Type Collie'. It is not the same Standard in use today but any alterations are studied carefully to avoid hasty, whimsical changes.

In 1900, about 675 Collies were registered (in 1890 there were about 265). Since the turn of the century, the numbers have increased rapidly. In 1988 there were 18,931 Collies registered with 6,173 litters. From the twenty-two all-breed shows in 1900, there were 1,056 in 1987. The possibility of acquiring championships was made more available with 1,051 specialty shows.

American breeder/fanciers have embraced and promoted not only the variety in coat but endorsed the white Collie (sable, tricolour or blue markings) and the past decade has witnessed more sable/merles exhibited. From December 1949 to, and including, November 1950, forty-five roughs and one smooth became champions. In 1987 there

USA Ch. Kingsmark Out of the Blue at Rainshade, s. USA Ch. Kingsmark El Capitan, d. Kingsmark Merri Roane, ow. Dr Sharon Vanderlip.

Rainshade Carte Blanche at 8 weeks of age, ow. Dr Sharon Vanderlip.

USA Ch. Milas Kimet Glittering Gem, ow. Kim Spencer Morgan.

were 173 roughs completing titles and 125 smooths added the coveted prefix 'champion'.

Ch. Black Hawk of Kasan, a tricolour smooth, won Best of Breed over the Best of Variety rough at the National Specialty in 1970. Hawk's siring record proved his quality. Then a blue smooth appeared – Ch. Lisara's Morning After – and she compiled a show record which includes nine Best in Show, all breeds, sixteen specialty wins and Best of Opposite Sex to Best of Breed at the 1984 and 1985 Collie Club of America National Specialty. She is the dam of three smooth and three rough champions.

It had been a male dominated breed for many years and a blue rough bitch, Ch. Starr's Blue Jeans, made feminine Collie history by winning Best of Breed at two National Specialties of the Collie Club of America in 1982 and 1986.

It is apparent in the photograph of Blue Jeans that American breeder/exhibitors are unconcerned about large, black patches on blue merles. Sable/merle is still a controversial issue with some of the American fan-

USA Ch. Starrs Blue Jeans (BOB CC of America, 1982, BOB CC of
America Centennial Show, 1986) s. Ch. Karavel Sudden Windfall,
d. Hi Vu Silver Mystery, brs and ows L. and P. Durazzano.

ciers. When Ch. Wayside After The Gold Rush was Winners Bitch and
Best of Winners at the 1981 Collie Club of America show she was
deluged by foreign and American spectators during the photo session.
Phenotypically a sable with dark eyes, an observer is unaware that
some of the 'sables' are genetically sable/merles. A male sable/merle,
Ch. Candray Constellation, won the breed at the 1988 Collie Club of
America National Specialty.

The Collie migration from the east coast preceded the dispersal of the
large kennels of the breeders who had developed recognisable lines
and had closely bred males which were dominant for virtues which
breeders were seeking.

With the expansion of the show and breeding activities across the
North American continent, many Collies will never compete against
each other or be seen by fanciers, unless owners exhibit at the National
Specialty. However, breeding and showing has become more mobile
and owners can travel the 3,000 miles (4,800 km) from one coast to
another, by air, to breed or even attend a show. It is now commonplace

USA Ch. Wayside After the Gold Rush, Winners Bitch, Best of Winners, CC of America, 1981.

for exhibitors to drive 1,500 miles (2,400 km), or more, to show on circuits or at one or two shows where the possibility of winning is more likely.

American champions represent a kaleidoscope of colours in both the rough and smooth variety.

Australia is another country where vast distances have to be travelled by exhibitors to attend their beautifully run open-air shows. For over one hundred years Collies have steadily been gaining in popularity and British imports, notably from the Eden and Laund kennels, have all played their part. Until recently, all dogs had to make the long journey by sea, but in recent years dogs have been allowed on the airways which has greatly facilitated imports. Aust. Ch. Eden Exemption was imported by Mrs Zora Mitchell in 1946. He was a litter brother of Ch. Eden Elation and he proved a very influential sire. Among his descendants is Australia's top winning Collie Aust. Ch. Braeden Show Dancer, winner of fifty-eight groups, twenty-six Best in Shows and ten Royal Show Challenges.

Australia has also imported Collies from the USA and seems to have established a type somewhere between the two. I have not been able to visit Australia but such English judges who have been there have been impressed, particularly by their conformation and movement. A dog that improved heads – especially skull and muzzle planes – was Aust. Ch. Shaun of Sandiacre. He was taken out as a puppy by Mrs Elsa Moxham when she moved from England to Australia.

Shaun's best win was probably in 1978 when he took Best in Show at the Collie Club of Victoria Championship Show under Mrs Aileen Speding, but it is as a sire that his record is unsurpassed. By the time he died at the age of fourteen he had sired the incredible number of fifty-nine champions.

In 1980, Mr and Mrs Marcovich imported into their Dornbrae kennels two spectacular blue merles from Mr Tom Purvis. First, British and Aust. Ch. Danvis Ladyvale Blue Mist and later, his litter brother, Ch. Danvis Ladyvale Blue Macade. During their show careers in England these two dogs won twenty-one Challenge Certificates between them, including three at Cruft's, and won the British Collie Club Challenge Trophy in 1977, 1978 and 1979. Macade, who was the better showman of the two, won the Working Group at Man-

Aust. Ch. Braeden Show Dancer, Australia's top winning Collie, born 1978, br. Mrs Zora Mitchell.

63

Aust. Ch. Cnocmoy Mr Aristocrat, born 1983, brs Mr and Mrs B. Heath. He gained the title at 12 months of age and has numerous Best in Group and Best in Show awards to his credit.

chester Championship Show going on to be Reserve Best in Show and was also Reserve in the Group at Cruft's, so their acquisition was a major boost for Australian Collie blood lines.

In recent years, the greatest British influence has undoubtedly come from the importation of a succession of Corydon champions, sent over by Mrs and Mrs Blake. The tricolour Ch. Corydon Quinault arrived in 1976. He carried the finest possible breeding being by Ch. Ramsey of Rokeby out of Ch. Corydon Qui Vive and sired twenty-two champions in his adopted country, doing much to improve the heads, eyes and expression of the Australian dogs. He was followed by the big winning Ch. Corydon Handsome Hero, who was noted for his soundness, and Ch. Corydon Little Caesar at Corydon. Both of them quickly gained their Australian titles and sired many champions. A later import, Ch. Corydon Glory Alleluia became an Australian champion in five shows, notching up a major Best in Show, all breeds, on the way. Recently, Ch. Corydon Tuck's Tiger and Ch. Corydon Gold Star have joined them, down under, where they look like continuing their highly successful show careers.

Collies have also reached a very high standard in Holland, as anyone who has judged over there recently will confirm. Things have not been easy for Dutch breeders, particularly during the last war when they were an occupied country. Mrs Tonny Heig explains some of the difficulties:

The first Collie registered at the Dutch Kennel Club with full details was a tricolour bitch of Seedly breeding, in 1913. The second was a sable dog by Parbold Picardo ex Eden Excellence. During the 1920s, Laund imports dominated the scene and Laund Lockhart gained three championship titles. It was not until the 1950s that Collies began to make progress and such well-known prefixes as Biancas Home, Cleveland Hills, Conny House, Meerval, Lansing and Noble Heart came to the fore. These still dominate the Collie scene in Holland.

Until that time, Dutch breeders had favoured the broader-skulled type of Collie, but around that time Mr and Mrs Joe Kat settled in Holland from England, bringing with them some very fine Ladypark stock. They produced the first Dutch champion in Maramin Golden Adonis. So beautiful was this dog that Dutch breeders were completely won over to the 'English' type and began to discard the heavier-boned broader-headed Dutch type. They began to visit Cruft's and took back with them some excellent English blood lines, notably Dunsinane, Rokeby and Bririch. Blue merle breeding was greatly influenced by the importation of Bririch Silver Dew and Bririch Silver Spray and also the tricolour Bluemecos Fire Spray who won many championships.

During the 1970s, Don Sirocco of Dunsinane had great influence as a sire, particularly through his son, Lansing Super Stranger, who not only became a Dutch champion but won his international title at eight years of age. He is still a beautiful dog at fifteen years. His son, Nesting Topper of the Noble Heart, who closely resembles his sire has emulated his success as a sire of winners. Int. Ch. Response of Rokeby had immense influence in Holland and one of his sons, Light Shadow of the Cleveland Hills, became the leading sire in Holland. Of his many champion children, Ch. Ualpha of the Cleveland Hills is probably the most notable. At the time of writing, the three most successful sires in each of the colours are the den Otters sable, Ch. Aberthorne Altered Image, Tonny Heig's tricolour Knight Black Joe of the Noble Heart and Brenda Teel's blue merle, Pelido Blue Rolls Royce. For some years, the country's top winner and sire was Ch. Antoc Starboy who left many notable winners and his mantle now seems to have fallen on Ch. Aberthorne Altered Image.

Dutch breeders are not only concerned with producing beautiful Collies, they aim to make them genetically healthy as well. When a Collie reaches three years of age, the Dutch Collie Club sends out a

Int. Dutch and Belgian Ch. Aberthorne Altered Image, born 1987, s. Ch. Aberthorne Arrester, D. Conkesbury Tried, brs J. Steilbech and J. Tait, ow. Den Otter.

Knight Black Joe of the Noble Heart, s. Little Joe of Tameila, d. Needed 'n' Wanted of the Noble Heart, br. Tommy Heig.

Pelido Blue Rolls Royce, s. Ch. Alenzones Blue Stratos at Pelido, d.
Pelido Chequita Rosa, brs Mr and Mrs Burtenshaw, ow. Brenda Teel.

questionnaire to the owner asking for details of the dog's health and
social behaviour, also the results of eye and hip tests. The answers are
computerised and sent to a panel of scientists working for the club,
who advise on what should be done to avoid the spread of any fault or
disease that shows up on the computer. These results are published
twice a year in the club magazine. The Dutch Collie Club holds regular
eye testing sessions and offers a 20 per cent reduction on all Collies that
have also been hip tested. The club also sends out lists of puppies available to potential buyers, with details that include both parents' wins
and their hip and eye status. To get on the list, at least one parent must
be free from CEA. If any breeder breeds from badly affected puppies
then his name will not be included on the list. In this way, the Dutch
Collie Club is actively engaged in raising the standard of the breed both
genetically and in appearance.

Collies in Germany have had a mixed reception but are now firmly
established as one of their most popular breeds and have reached a
very high standard in quality. Eva Maria Kramer has kindly sent me
a history of the Rough Collie in Germany, which is reproduced here.

67

Dutch Ch. World Junior Ch. Cramer, the Commander at Lynway, s.
Mossylea Shades of Glory, d. Cramar Golden Aurora, ows Mr and Mrs
Boerema.

Due to the close relationship between British and German royalty, in
Victorian times, everything British was highly fashionable in Germany.
Soon after becoming popular in England, dog show activities started in
Germany. Happy days without quarantine saw many British exhibitors
showing famous champions in Germany. The Collie became popular in
the better-off circles of Germany, long before the German Shepherd
was even recognised as a show and sport breed. Collies excelled as so-
called 'war dogs', when they were trained to do many dangerous
chores as messenger dogs, carrying cable to the front, finding
wounded soldiers etc. In 1889 the first stud book was published which
included show records, and at Frankfurt in 1888, the famous English
Ch. Eclipse, bred by Mr Bissell and owned by George R. Krehl of
London, shared first prize with Achmet, owned by Max Feer. Two
prizes were won by bitches from a Mrs Fielding-Kane from London.
Max Feer was the leading Collie breeder at the time, and he was
breeding from the finest English blood lines, for example, Ali Baba, son
of Ch. Metchley Wonder. In 1889 the predecessor of the Club für

Britische Hütehunde e.V. was founded, and the Collie's popularity lasted well until the beginning of World War I. Meanwhile, the German Shepherd Dog had come into its own. Nationalism and skilful promotion of his admirers quickly made him top dog in Germany, and he took over the Collie's task at war and police service.

World War I saw the cessation of all dog activities. A handful of dedicated breeders saved a few dogs over the difficult times until, in 1931, a Collie association was refounded. Soon followed imports from famous English kennels such as Laund, Eden, Ashtead and Southport. By the beginning of World War II, the Collie was a well-respected breed again – not the most fashionable one, but with a sound background, producing good dogs that did very well in the now popular dog training circles. Collies competed successfully as Schutzund against German Shepherds, Boxers etc. Many of the good breeding stock of the time had Sch. H I, II or III. Again the war ended it all – until, in 1948, Mr Paul Tischler of Hamburg called the remaining Collie friends together to refound the Club which was now named Club der Britischen Hütehunde because Shetland Sheepdogs and Old English Sheepdogs were bred in small numbers which did not warrant a club.

There was quite a lot of breeding during the fifties. Dogs with Schutzhund training were still used most often at stud. Also, sable and blue merle were crossed without hesitation or knowledge of colour inheritance. With the breed regaining its strength in Britain after the war, the huge gap of quality between German and British bred Collies widened. Nearly any Collie coming over from England was far better than the best bred in Germany. With increasing prosperity and growing interest in the breed, dogs were imported from England, namely from Ladypark and Shiel. Dogs from Switzerland with English parentage (mainly from the Birkenwald kennel), also had great influence.

Much to breeders' initial delight, the 'Lassie boom' guaranteed puppy sales. More dogs were shown and British judges invited, and the need for better dogs was obvious. By the early sixties, the best breeding in Germany came from the Dunsinane kennels, dogs and bitches. Following the lines of the current winners in Germany, the oldest only go back to those imports. The most often used stud dog was Bsg. Dean of Dunsinane, a full brother of the famous Dazzler. During the 1970s, excellent dogs were imported from the Rokeby kennels. The positive influence of World Ch. Bundessieger, Int. Ch. Response of Rokeby, brother to Royal Ace, and Int. Ch. Knightmatchmaker of Rokeby, son of the famous Ch. Ramsey of Rokeby, is still obvious today.

In an effort to improve temperaments, some breeders imported dogs from the USA, but it proved difficult to integrate the American lines into the German/English breeding. However, it was carried out with positive results in some cases. Today, a few breeders still keep to

World Ch. Bsg. and Int. Ch. Response of Rokeby, s. Dazzler of Dunsinane, d. Ch. Witchcraft of Rokeby.

Int. Ch. VDH Ch. Knightmatchmaker of Rokeby, born 1981, s. Ch. Ramsey of Rokeby, d. Ch. Witchcraft of Rokeby, br. B. Eglin.

American lines. The general improvement in the 1980s was largely due to the fact that temperament improved in England. A new generation of German Collie fanciers had grown up. Most had learnt English at school, travelling was easier, and the International Collie Handbook with its forerunner the Yorkshire Collie Club Handbook and last, but not least, the breed's own independent magazine, Collie Revue, brought the home country of the Collie closer and provided education. This resulted in imports which really enabled German-bred Collies to compete with the best of Europe and even English imports successfully.

This may well be seen from the World winners in recent years, the importance of the World show lying in its immense competition with the best of the time and the highly qualified judges. This show was first held after the war, in 1956, then again in 1965, after that bi-annually and from 1977, annually, all around the world. German-bred world champions were, in 1956, Bandit vom Tulpenhof; in 1973, Grynet vom Glockenklang; 1977, Dana von Marienhagen; 1985, Cookie vom Hause Reinhard and his daughter Rosegardens Crazy Chrissie and in 1986, Hortensie v.d. Goten, also a daughter of Cookie.

Golden Norman vd Ruhrstadt, born, 1986, s. Int. Ch. Golden Clyde vd Ruhrstadt, d. Golden Ilka vd Ruhrstadt, br. and ow. F. W. Schaumann.

71

The dog with the greatest influence during the last decade was undoubtedly Ch. Aberthorne Arrester. Due to his popularity in the UK, his offspring were much sought after by importers. Whilst breeding Collies successfully before, the import of his son, Chancellorville Aquitane, proved a great asset to his new kennel, von Hause Reinhard. Together with two bitches, Rokeby Renascent and the Dutch Lansingh's Power Pretty Girl, going back to Rokeby and Dazzler, a breeding force from which many breeders in Germany profited was established. His son, Cookie vom Hause Reinhard leads the charts of most successful sires since 1978 according to the Collie Revue pointing system. Interestingly, he and his sire were not used widely at stud. Most of today's winners trace directly back to British imports, so German Collie breeding is still as closely related to Great Britain as it was a hundred years ago.

Blue merle collies are quite popular in Germany and have an established tradition. The strongest blue merle force comes from the kennel Bienenfleis tracing back to Carramar. Currently, some geneticists are

Chancellorville Aquitane, one of Europe's most successful sires, born 1977, s. Ch. Aberthorne Arrester, d. Avaie of Arcot at Chancellorville, br. A. Hollahan, ows W. and K. Reinhard. (Photograph by Eva Maria Kramer.)

*Ch. Cookie v. Hause Reinhard, born 1981, Ger., Int. and World Ch.,
s. Chancellorville Aquitaine, d. Langsingh's Power Pretty Girl, brs and
ows Reinhard. (Photograph by Eva Maria Kramer.)*

against breeding with the merle gene at all and the popular Collie is a
welcome target. It is to be hoped that the German ruling bodies will not
find themselves forced to prohibit the breeding of blue merle Collies.
So far, the breeding of blue with blue is not allowed, to prevent defective whites, but the German Collie Club allows interbreeding of blue
and sable. It will be interesting to watch the results over a few
generations.

Dog breeding in Germany is somewhat unique in the world. We have
a Kennel Club (VDH) as a ruling body over breed clubs. However, the
power of breeding, judging etc. lies in the hands of the breed clubs as
they have their own stud books, issue pedigrees and educate their
judges. Everything is strongly controlled though not with much
success, compared with those countries who have practically no
controls at all.

Before one can breed from a dog, it has to be exhibited with good
grading, has to have hip X-rays and be 'out' with what we call 'medium'
HD (ratings are: clear, suspect, slight, medium, severe), and above all,
the Club für Britische Hütehunde requires the 'Körung' which means
a special judging for approving a dog for breeding according to the
Standard. This means a dog must not have any major faults, bite has to

Int. Ger. and Dtch Ch. Ostwind v. Hause Reinhard, born 1984, s. Int.
Ch. Cookie v. Hause Reinhard, d. Int. Ch. Carry v. Hause Reinhard.

be perfect and missing teeth are undesirable. Running a dog on until breeding age is trying and even importing is not easy – who would sell a dog who has clear eyes and hips, a full set of correctly placed teeth and is a winning Collie with excellent temperament? Also, importers often ask for eye checks. Together with the veterinary profession, the VDH promotes eye checking in all breeds and the day will come when there will be rules as a consequence.

Germany has one major all-breed show, where the CACIB winners get the title Bundessieger (Federal winner), which normally means hot competition from many countries. The titles VDH Champion and Deutscher Champion (Ge. Ch.) have to be earned with Challenge Certificates (CAC). There are about twelve international all-breed shows where the CACIB is issued, and quite a lot of club shows all round the country. 1986 saw the founding of the German Collie Club (DCC). All those who wish to get in contact with German Collie fanciers or want to buy a Collie in Germany should apply to the Club für Britische Hütehunde or the German Collie Club, whose addresses can be obtained from the VDH Westfalendamm 174, 4600 Dortmund 1, Tel. 231 592440. Please remember that the German Democratic Republic has no relation to the FCI or to dog breeding activities in the Federal Republic of Germany, which is referred to above.

Collies in Italy were not very popular until after the last war when Mr Umberto Corsiglia, a wealthy owner in Genoa started his Villa Gaia kennel. Every year he imported the two best Collies he could obtain from England and showed them intensively. They included such famous champions as Ch. Rhodelands Boy (sire of the immortal Ch. Carramar Boy Blue), Ch. Danvis Dyllorna, Ch. Danvis Drifter, Ch. Danvis Dryver, Ch. Lionheart of Ladypark, Ch. Exotic of Milburndene, Ch. Danvis Daytime and Ch. Alexander of Arcot. Unfortunately, his dogs were not at public stud and he himself bred very few litters so the influence of these dogs was not as great as might have been expected and their blood lines were to a great extent lost to the world.

On the other hand, Princess Carafa di Rocelle, who owned the Custos Collies, allowed her English imports to be used at stud. These included Frienell Fantail and the famous Ch. Laughing Lad of Ladypark. Lad was a dog of unique elegance and a lovely expression that had great influence on many Italian lines, above all on the Narciso Collies of Mr Bernini who has maintained this line and type throughout the years. Mr Bernini is an international judge of Collies who has won world-wide respect and has judged Collies in twenty-four countries to date.

It. Ch. Teresa del Narciso, born 1986, s. Int. Ch. Incredibly Blu di Cambiano, d. Ch. Saheltras Sally Sunshine of Clickam, br. L. Bernini.

75

The Devon prefix of Mrs Vera Martins had a lasting influence on Italian Collies when she imported from England one of the most beautiful tricolours ever seen, Ch. Sombre-Sextans from Shiel. He was used by most of the Italian breeders of the time and had particular influence on the Cambiano kennel of Maria Theresa Garabelli. She was only thirteen when she commenced breeding Collies but before then her mother had imported many famous English dogs including Ch. Beulah's Silver Mantilla, Ch. Tideswell Blue Prince, Beulah's Silver Don Mero and the beautiful sable Ch. Loyal of Ladypark. Reference has already been made to the loss suffered by British breeders when Libretto of Ladypark left these shores. It was interesting to learn from Mrs Garabelli that Miss Grey realised his worth too late and tried, in vain, to buy him back, as she felt he was the most significant of all the sons that Lochinvar produced.

Mrs Garabelli's success in Collies has been phenomenal and the number of champions and international champions that the Cambiano kennel has produced can scarcely be equalled. Cambiano Collies have been exported all over the world and she herself has imported Collies from as far away as the USA and Australia in an effort to improve her blood lines. It is difficult to single out any one Collie from the stream of champions she has produced but Int. Ch. Incredibly Blu di Cambiano and his sire, Int. Ch. Lupupick Blu di Cambiano, are probably the most famous. Almost every year Mrs Garabelli travels to England and takes back with her a few carefully selected Collies of the blood lines she requires. Her dedication to the breed has brought her world renown.

Other Italian breeders who have made a name for themselves include Mrs Edwige Ubiali who made a permanent contribution to the breed when she imported the great sire, Ch. Rokeby Royal Agnate, and she has consistently produced winners over the years. Franco Caselli has established a firm foundation for his Figli del Vento kennels with the importation of such good Collies as It. Chs Mybern's Melissa, Ch. Beechmere Amazing Grace, Ch. Myberns Mylenium, Ch. Myberns Mandarin and the tricolour, Ch. Pelido Midnight Scandel. The merle, Ch. Pelido Foreigner, a son of Ch. Incredibly Blu and Ch. Pelido Silver Lady, provides a unique combination of English and Italian breeding that should prove of great value to Italian fanciers.

The Della Luchesia kennel has made several importations of British dogs of whom the most successful is undoubtedly the beautiful sable bitch It. Ch. Aberthorne Angel Lace. One of the most famous Collies

It. Ch. Aberthorne Angel Lace, br. Jimmy Tate, ow. Del Pelegrino.

in Italy, at the time of writing, is Int. and It. Ch. Music Maestro di Cambiano, who won universal acclaim when he won the World Championship for his owners the Obertis. In doing so he proved that Italian Collies can hold their own successfully with any other Collie breeding country in the world.

One of the last countries to recognise the Collie was the French republic. In 1920, the Comtesse de la Poix founded the French Collie Club, but although she had several champions in her Ansville kennels, it was not until 1933 that the French Kennel Club finally recognised the breed and opened its Stud Book to Collie registrations. I am indebted to M. Michel Badie for information on the Collie in France.

All breeding ceased during the last war but after the war, Madame Andree Grellier struggled to re-establish the Collie. She imported Collies from England on a regular basis. First from the Beulah, Ladypark and Shiel lines and later from the Mywick and Rokeby kennels. Of these, Ch. Derburgh Double Diamond of Rokeby proved himself outstanding both as a show dog and sire of many French champions. Two other Rokeby imports that had great influence were the tricolours, Knight Avenger of Rokeby, a son of Ch. Asoka Clayswood Blue Venture and Knight Craftsman of Rokeby, a son of that illustrious pair Ch. Ramsey of Rokeby and Ch. Witchcraft of Rokeby.

Mallicot Home Brew, s. Mallicot Love Storm, d. Mallicot Gold Charade, br. Catliff, ow. Mrs Brussat (France).

An important addition to French blood lines came with the arrival of the lovely bitch Ch. Arranbrook Emma Peel who had a very successful career over there. Two great sires were imported in Ch. Corydon Copper Crown, a son of Sandiacre Softly-Softly, and Ch. Ardlyn Mystic Music a son of Ch. Mybern's Minstrel. The combination of these blood lines with several more recent imports has given French breeders a basis on which they can now build their own stars. The Collie goes from strength to strength in France.

Collies have always been strong in Scandinavia. The Collie is well adapted to their colder climate and revels in the snowy conditions which prevail through their long winters. The first Championship Show was held in Sweden in 1886 and although only four Collies (all bred in Britain), were exhibited, an interest in the breed was awakened that has flourished ever since. As in so many countries, a major impetus after the last war was the showing of the Lassie films which brought many new adherents to the breed. Three dogs imported from the Beulah kennel of Mrs N.K. George had an immense influence, for the good, on the heavier-headed Swedish type of Collie. Of these, the most important was Beulah's Golden

Flambeau (a sable brother of Beulah's Night Flare), by Beulah's Night Victorious out of my first Collie Beulah's Golden Fantasy. The other two were Beulah's Night Logic and Night Limit, all quality line-bred dogs. Ulla Bergh-Persson, who is well known to British and Continental Collie breeders for her Bermarks Collies, writes as follows:

In the early sixties two significant imports into Sweden came with the arrival of Int. Ch. Lethal of Ladypark and Westcarr's Wallace, both of them producing many high-class offspring. In 1965, the blue merle bitch Catriona Blue Bonnet was imported and she became one of Sweden's top winning Collies of all time. A little later, the Rokeby kennel of Mrs Betty Eglin sent over a series of beautiful Collies that established Sweden as one of the major Collie producing countries. All became international champions and included Int. Chs Recorder, Riding Light, Knight Watchman, Moss Rose, Royalist, Rangefinder and Rennet and all did a great deal to improve Swedish breeding. Three other very important sires of that period were also imported from Britain, namely Nor. Ch. Sandiacre Sweepstake, by Royal Ace, Int. Ch. Ali, by Dazzler and Int. Ch. Danvis Blue Peter by Danvis Ladyvale Blue Mist.

In recent years, there have been many further imports from Britain and of these the most successful sires have been Lynnaire All in Black

Lynaire All in Black, one of Sweden's most successful sires, born 1982, s. Ch. Karava Kornishman, d. Ch. Lynaire Chiquitita, brs Mr and Mrs Makepeace, ows M. and A. Ejerstad.

by Ch. Karava Kornishman, Abbestone Dark Invader by Ch. Abbestone Red Adair and Sylcroft Sammy Bear by Brettonpark Country Tweed. Another dog that made a great impact on Scandinavian breeding during his short stay at Mrs Eriksson's Crony kennels was Int. Ch. Incredibly Blu di Cambiano who threw many winners before returning to his native Italy.

All the reports reaching Britain remark on the great strength of blue merle and tricolour breeding in Sweden and much of this must be due to Mia Ejerstad's Steadlyn kennels, particularly with her record-breaking Int. and Nor. Ch. Blue of Blues and his daughter, Int. and Nor. Ch. Zong of Zweden. This blood, further strengthened by the combination of All in Black and Incredibly Blu breeding must give Sweden a remarkably strong foundation for future merle breeding.

It was not until 1968 that the Swedish Collie Club (SCK) was founded. It is divided into fourteen local clubs and has a total membership of about 1,400. The SCK organises shows in different parts of the country and their aim is to improve the Collie both as a show and

Int. Ch. Crony's Anniversary Maid, br. Ulla Erikson, ow. Inger Ljungberg.

a working dog. They do a great deal to organise working trials, obedience competitions and rescue dog training because they believe it is vital to preserve the Collie's working ability.

Every Swedish champion has to pass a character and temperament test before he is awarded his title. Soundness is considered of paramount importance in Sweden and all breeding stock has to be X-rayed 'clear' for HD before they can be bred from. It was their concern for soundness that first alerted British breeders to the unwelcome news that the Collie was not free from HD, as had previously been supposed, and that some of their exported stock were failing to meet the standard required by Sweden. Routine eye tests are arranged and the SCK strongly recommends that all puppies should be tested for CEA by the time they reach eight weeks.

The SCK is internationally orientated and every year a Nordic Collie Conference is arranged where ideas are exchanged, lectures are given and the problems of the breed discussed. At the conference in Oslo, in 1985, the Breed Standard was discussed in detail and it was recommended that in future, judges should place much more emphasis on movement in order that the Collie should be able to fulfil his role as a working dog.

Int. and Nor. Ch. Blue of Blues, Working Group winner five times, born, 1979, s. Int. Ch. Danvis Blue, d. Cronys Blue Sky, br. Eva Lundberg, ows M. and A. Ejerstad.

Int. and Nor. Ch. Steadlyn Zong of Zweden, Swedish Collie of the Year, 1986 and 1988, born 1980, s. Int. and Nor. Ch. Blue of Blue, d. Steadlyn Some Secret, brs and ows M. and A. Ejerstad.

In Norway the Collie has been one of the most popular breeds for some years. In 1985 the Norwegian Collie Club celebrated its 50th anniversary. It was founded by Irene Wolff Sommerfeldt who was chairman of the club for the first ten years. There was a tremendous interest in Collies at that time and new dogs were imported from Britain, Sweden, Denmark and the USA. At their first show in Oslo the Norwegian Collie Club drew an entry of thirty Collies which was regarded as very satisfactory. Most Norwegian Collies (as in Britain) are descendants of Dazzler of Dunsinane and his famous Rokeby sons as well as Sandiacre Softly-Softly. Present-day Norwegian imports include such great sires as Ch. Geoffdon Jonathan, Geoffdon Startrek, Ch. Royal Charter of Rokeby, Rokeby Royal Cavalier, Corydon Augustus Caesar and Ch. Corydon Blaze of Glory.

Nor. Ch. Milas Going in Style, a son of Am. Ch. Paradices Cloak 'n' Dagger and Am. Ch. Milas Gold in the Clouds, was imported into Norway by Kari Nylen. He is a tricolour dog whose blood appears to be mixing well with Norwegian and English stock. Norway is not a very densely populated country and travelling is impeded by mountain ranges but the Norwegians are very enthusiastic Collie breeders and determined to keep up the standard of their Collies.

Denmark built up its Collie population mostly after the end of the last war, mainly from Norwegian-bred dogs, and it now has some good-quality Collies. These have been strengthened by such importations from Britain as Int. and Danish Ch. Tavena's Tequila Sunrise, Randy Andy from Tavena and Chelborn Charlie winner of one Challenge Certificate.

The 1989 World Show is to be held in Denmark in June and Collies are likely to be strongly represented. It will make interesting viewing for members of the International Collie Society who are holding their annual week's holiday to coincide with the show and a Collie conference organised by the Danish Collie Club.

Finland has several kennels breeding high-quality Collies, notably the Black Elles kennel who have imported several good dogs, among them Ch. Corydon Knight of Glory, Corydon Be Brave and Corydon Rosie O'Grady. The majority of Finnish breeders are able to show their dogs in Norway and Sweden and take advantage of these countries' dogs at stud.

Steadlyn Striking Scoop, born 1983, s. Lynaire All in Black, d. Steadlyn Kat's Knickers, brs M. and A. Ejerstad, ow. M. Rasanen (Finland).

Several Finnish Collies have found their way into the USSR. Russia has a long tradition in Collies, thanks largely to Queen Victoria who made a present of several specimens to the Tsar. These were carefully bred together and were later found to be excellent working dogs. They were used during World War I as messenger dogs and search dogs, for which they showed great aptitude. They were considerably bigger than the modern Collie but, now, with the influence of Scandinavian Collies, they have adopted a much more uniform type. Russian Collies are expected to work but more and more shows are being held and judges from outside the USSR are being invited to judge.

Mrs Audrey Chatfield recently judged in Estonia and drew an entry of 250 Collies. (A further 200 dogs had to be turned down.) She found the dogs no bigger than ours and of very reasonable quality. Most were of Scandinavian and Czechoslovakian extraction. She was overwhelmed with the warmth of her reception and found herself quite unable to carry all the flowers with which she was presented on her arrival. Many Collie enthusiasts had travelled across Russia, even some whose entries had been turned down, just to watch the judging.

It is not possible to cover all the countries that have their own Collie clubs. They are many and varied. Unrestricted by quarantine laws breeders are able to travel freely between countries to attend the major shows. Portugal and Spain both have their share of good Collies and keen fanciers. Many of the East European countries, notably Czechoslovakia, Hungary and Yugoslavia have imported Collies from Britain and have succeeded in building up some very good kennels of high-quality Collies.

It is largely thanks to Mrs Audrey Chatfield who inaugurated the International Collie Society and who for many years has edited the brilliantly successful International Collie Handbook that the Collie Fancy is so united. Every year the Society arranges a holiday abroad that is organised by the host country. Many lasting friendships are made on these trips. English is spoken by most of the participants but as all are drawn there by their great love of the breed, there are no difficulties in comprehension – the language of the Collie is universal.

2

Pedigree

Many pet owners will tell you proudly that their dog has 'a pedigree as long as your arm' unaware that it is a totally meaningless phrase. All Collies can trace their origin to Trefoil, born in the 1870s. This involves a staggering number of generations when you consider the average breeding age of a bitch at her first litter is between eighteen months and two years. It is not the length of a pedigree that is important, but its intrinsic quality. This is something that only experience can teach you. To a breeder, a pedigree is not just a list of meaningless names. Each name will conjure up a picture of a Collie with all his faults and all his virtues and, very probably, his ability to pass them on to his progeny.

To the novice, a pedigree may appear baffling, but it is not hard to read if you realise that it is, in fact, the combination of two pedigrees – that of the sire in the upper half and that of the dam in the lower half. Very obviously, a Collie pedigree can be traced back to an infinite number of ancestors if so wished. Only lack of space confines it to the immediate three to five generations contained on the normal pedigree form. In the USA a more compact form of pedigree is used which saves a great deal of space in publication. It could be usefully employed in Great Britain.

The Kennel Club now issues three-generation computer-produced pedigrees. These not only guarantee accuracy but also reveal a considerable amount of interesting information, such as the numbers and sexes of litter mates, the numbers of previous litters produced by the dam and the colours of the ancestors. Much of this information is unavailable to ordinary breeders but many of us like to include as much information as we can, mostly in abbreviated form. A short survey of common abbreviations will not come amiss here and will help the first-time buyer to 'read' a pedigree.

D	Dog or male	CC	Challenge Certificate
B	Bitch or female	Res CC	Reserve Challenge Certificate
S & W	Sable and white	Ch.	Champion
T	Tricolour	BOB	Best of Breed
BM	Blue merle	KC	Kennel Club
JW	Junior Warrant		

A Junior Warrant is awarded by the Kennel Club to a dog or bitch that has accumulated a total of 25 points between the age of twelve and eighteen months. Points are awarded as follows. Three points for a first prize at a Championship Show and 1 point for a first prize at an Open Show, for classes confined to Rough Collies only. A class which includes Smooth Collies, Borders or Beardies counts as a Variety class.

These classes must be open to all Rough Collies subject only to age and win restrictions. For example, a first prize in a class confined to blue merles could not be counted in a Junior Warrant application. A very careful record of all eligible wins should be kept by the owner right from the outset, including class win, show name and date, judge and so on, as the Junior Warrant is not automatically awarded by the Kennel Club to whom application should be made.

There is considerable controversy about the award of Junior Warrants. It is self-evident that a long-coated breed such as ours has a much shorter show period than a short-coated breed or one that matures early. The average show period for a young Collie lasts about four months. They are seldom ready to show before seven-and-a-half months and will almost certainly have dropped their coats by eleven-and-a-half to twelve months. There is very little likelihood of them regrowing sufficient coat to make a reappearance in the ring before the disqualifying date of eighteen months is up. So to obtain a Junior Warrant with a Collie is a real achievement. Whether that justifies them being hustled round the country in the attempt is another matter.

Challenge Certificates are on offer to certain breeds but only at Championship Shows. Their allocation is carefully controlled by the Kennel Club and depends not on the number of registrations of a breed but on their number of Championship entries. This is a wise ruling as registration figures are often swollen by the large number of puppies produced for the pet market in certain breeds.

The citation is designed to make the judge think very carefully before awarding it and the judge has the power to withhold the Challenge Certificate should no dog reach the required standard. It reads as follows: 'I am clearly of the opinion that . . . is of such outstanding merit as to be worthy of the title of Champion.' Before awarding it the judge will call all his unbeaten first prize winners into the ring and compare them with each other. This is his final line-up and he may well ask them all to move again. All will have pleased him at some stage during the show but the winner of the big white card with its green lettering and border will, in his opinion, be the best Collie amongst them. That will be the champion of the show and it is a magic moment for the exhibitor. There will be a Challenge Certificate awarded to the best Collie of each sex and they will compete between each other for the privilege of representing the Collie in the Best in Show ring as Best of Breed. The official Challenge Certificate will be sent to the exhibitor by post once the Kennel Club has confirmed the award.

Reserve Challenge Certificates are awarded to the dog or bitch that stands reserve to the champion of that show. In the event of the champion's disqualification, the Reserve Challenge Certificate winner would probably, but not necessarily, be elevated to the Challenge Certificate by the Kennel Club.

Champion is a title awarded by the Kennel Club to a dog or bitch that has won three Challenge Certificates under three different judges, one of which must be won after the dog reaches twelve months of age. In certain breeds, a working certificate is also needed before a dog can obtain this title but fortunately this is not the case in Collies. It has become normal practice to write the names of the champions in red in a pedigree, as well as any other awards of interest, such as Challenge Certificates, Reserve Challenge Certificates and Junior Warrants. Less common, but of even greater value, is the growing custom of writing in the eye and hip status of the dogs in the pedigree. This is invaluable to the concerned breeder anxious to establish a strain that is free from hereditary disease. It is easy to see how useful this practice will be for future Collie breeders. The normal abbreviations appear as follows.

PRA/CEA	Clear – the dog is free from progressive retinal atrophy and collie eye anomaly and holds BVA Certificates to that effect
HD 0/0	Dog is free from hip dysplasia; other numbers indicate the hip score
BVA	British Veterinary Association

All these matters are dealt with in the section on hereditary diseases but it is as well to bear in mind that only BVA Certificates are of any value. Other abbreviations often marked on a pedigree are KCR No. and KCSB No. These stand for Kennel Club Registration Number and Kennel Club Stud Book Number respectively.

The Kennel Club is a private members club with prestigious offices at 1 Clarges Street, Piccadilly, London. Traditionally, it is a male-only preserve but it has recently admitted women as full members. It is the governing body of the dog world which it governs as a kind of benevolent autocracy. The majority of dog breeders who pay the fees which support the Kennel Club have absolutely no say in its running. The vast amount of bureaucratic work involved in such a huge organisation is carried out by paid officials but the decision making is undertaken by committee members on a voluntary basis. Every year they publish the Kennel Club Stud Book which contains a great deal of useful and interesting information covering Field and Working Trials as well as the world of dog showing.

A show dog will be awarded a Kennel Club Stud Book Number and will be entered in the Stud Book if he or she has won any of the following awards: a Challenge Certificate, a Reserve Challenge Certificate or a first, second or third prize in a Limit or Open unrestricted class at a show where Challenge Certificates were on offer for the breed. Entry into the Stud Book carries automatic qualification for entry at the Kennel Club's own show, Cruft's, so it is highly prized.

The Kennel Club also publishes their own *Kennel Gazette* monthly. It is a lively and interesting publication which carries many well written and informative articles besides a great deal of statistical information. At one time it also carried a record of all registrations, transfers, export pedigrees and so on, but this information has now become so vast that it has been transferred to a special three-monthly publication of its own – the *Breed Records Supplement*.

The Kennel Club Registration Department deals with the registrations of all pedigree dogs. Nowadays, it is all done by computer. Only the breeder can register a dog. The breeder is the owner of the dam at the time of whelping so if you are buying an in-whelp bitch, make sure you transfer her into your name before she whelps. On the reverse side of the official Registration Form you will find the 'Transfer of Ownership Form' – it is important that the breeder signs this form before handing it to the purchaser.

It is possible for the registration certificate to be endorsed by the breeder 'Not to be exhibited' or 'Not to be bred from', and this is particularly useful where a puppy carries any hereditary fault, although for some reason it is a facility which is not greatly used.

The Transfer of Ownership Form must be signed by the new owner and sent with the required fee to the Kennel Club, otherwise the dog will officially always remain the property of the breeder.

Form and Function

The original work of the Rough and Smooth Collie has now been largely taken over by the Border and Welsh Collie, but that does not release breeders from the duty of producing Collies that are still capable of performing the work for which they were evolved. If we examine the Standard in detail we can see how closely the form of the Collie is related to its function. Indeed, the very first paragraph sets the tone with the words: 'To enable the Collie to fulfil a natural bent for sheepdog work its physical structure should be on lines of strength and activity'.

Over the years, the Collie has evolved as the most efficient machine for herding livestock yet devised. From the tip of his pointed nose to the end of his long flexible tail, the Collie is aerodynamically designed to create the least wind resistance and move with the maximum speed and agility. It is worth studying the beautiful frieze on the British Collie Club's 60gn Trophy to see the Rough Collie, in action, herding sheep. Only the beauty and docile nature of the dog has lifted him out of his humble environment and transformed him into the show dog and family pet *par excellence* that he has become today.

The veterinary profession continually complain that far too large a proportion of all Breed Standards is devoted to the head of the individual breeds. Very little is said about correct conformation and even less about correct movement. Their criticism is well founded. In this chapter, I try to set out how the Standard points were evolved. I do not include the head which is fully dealt with elsewhere.

The eyes of the Collie are described as 'giving a sweet expression, full of intelligence, with a quick alert look when listening', in the original Standard. Expression is defined as the harmonious blending of the head properties, the eyes and the ear carriage, which combine to produce that 'sweet, dreamy, semi-cunning yet alert outlook which makes the perfect Collie the most beautiful of the canine race'. The Kennel Club no longer permits such a claim to be made, but every Collie owner is convinced of its truth.

At first sight, it is difficult to grasp the significance of the sweet expression or to see any possible connection with the work the dog is required to do. In fact, it is a test of character. The eyes are the mirror of the soul and just as a bad tempered human will have a bad tempered expression, so will a dog. A hard, fractious eye denotes a dog with an over-keen nature that is liable to treat his sheep antagonistically. Over the years, shepherds have learnt to select the puppy with an alert but kind eye and expression, as being the one most likely to have the patient, tractable nature so necessary in dealing with stock. At the same time the dog must have the ability to control his sheep by the 'power of his eye', so the puppy must show no timidity or lack of character. It must be pointed out here, that the Standard calls for a medium-size eye and not the tiny slit eye so beloved of some show ring judges. Such an eye is totally non-functional as the sheep would be unable to see the dog's eye, let alone be held by its power, until he was within a yard of them. The inclusion of the words, 'eyes never too small', in the 1986 Kennel Club Revised Breed Standard, inserted at the insistence of the veterinary profession, is to be welcomed.

The Collie's ears, although small in size, are admirably shaped and set to catch the least sound. Anyone who has ever walked through a flock of sheep will be familier with the almost deafening noise they make calling for their lambs. This, coupled with the noise of the wind, makes it very difficult for the working dog to distinguish his master's whistle. We are all aware that dogs are able to distinguish sounds at a much higher frequency than humans, but the actual volume of sound they hear and the distance from which they can hear it, has not been fully explored. Like a dog's power of scent or a hawk's power of sight, it is something of which humans have no conception. Suffice it to say, that the Collie has powers of hearing above that of the average dog. One of the drawbacks of the Collie for army work is that he over-reacts to loud noises. This is undoubtedly due to his very sensitive hearing rather than any basic lack of courage.

It is generally accepted that the Smooth Collie is allowed a larger ear and there are valid reasons for this. The Smooth Collie was ideally suited for the wetter warmer lowlands and did not have to face such inclement weather as his heavier coated cousin. I was once called to inspect the ears of a Smooth, who, because he loved the snow, had been allowed to stay out in it for long periods. The edges of his ears were raw and he was continually shaking his head. I diagnosed incipient frost bite. Admission to the house soon cured the problem. The smaller ear of the Rough snuggles neatly into his stand-off ruff and is well protected from the cold.

In order to overcome the problem of pricked ears, British breeders have, over the years, tended to produce large heavy ears often set too far to the side of the head. They are not as conducive to good hearing as the smaller, mobile, cupped ear that can instantly be brought to attention on the top of the head to gain maximum hearing. The Standard calls for a small ear and breeders should pay more attention to this problem.

In the 1986 Standard, the teeth are described simply as 'of a good size, scissor bite'. The provision, 'a very slight space, not to be regarded as a serious fault', has been dropped. It must be conceded that in certain breeds, such as Bulldogs and most breeds of Terrier, the teeth are of paramount importance. In a herding breed there would appear to be no such priority. The Collie that bites his sheep in a Sheepdog Trial is heavily penalised and it seems to me that a missing tooth should be regarded as a fault of no greater magnitude than any other. The Continental practice of discarding an excellent dog with a missing tooth in favour of an inferior specimen with forty-two teeth is not one that I feel should be encouraged. It seems to me self-evident that the faults that should be most heavily penalised are those that impede the Collie in his work.

The working Collie covers many miles in the course of his day and, in busy periods, is on his feet, literally from dawn till dusk. Flat, open, weak or poorly knuckled feet are not only unattractive in the ring (where they give an awkward paddling movement), but also a liability on rough ground. Here the compact, well-knuckled, thickly padded, correct oval foot gives far better protection. A well-known judge once passed on to me a piece of good advice: 'When in doubt, look at their feet.' It is a fact of life that many judges do not, yet what could be more essential in a working dog?

To enable the dog to fulfil his duties, the Collie must not only be supremely fit, he must also be well constructed. The key to good construction is a well-laid shoulder. Later on, I set out to show you what is meant by the phrase, 'shoulders sloping and well angulated'. Here, I will tell you only why they are required. It is the angulation both of the fore and hindquarters that acts as a shock absorber. The straight-shouldered and straight-hocked dog, with no flexibility in the pasterns, suffers constant jarring to the system.

It is revealing to watch a horse show-jumping and notice the astonishing amount of flexion in the front fetlocks as the full weight of the horse is taken on its front feet on landing. This is why the straight gun barrel legs ending in round cat feet required by the fox terrier are not correct in the Collie. The pasterns must not be weak but they must show flexibility and not rigidity. The 1986 Standard calls for a 'moderate amount of round bone', and this would seem correct. Round bone is considerably stronger than flat or bladed bone and the Collie must have strong legs and feet. Poor, light bone is to be strongly discouraged.

It is well known that the Collie uses his tail for balance in the constant twisting, turning and sudden changing of direction that is part of his daily work. A 'fair length of tail' is required but there seems no valid reason why the Rough Collie's tail is now much shorter than the Border Collie's. Greater length of tail would help to weight it down and eliminate some of the ugly spitz tails which create much greater wind-resistance when the dog is running at speed. The tail must be carried low if it is to be used as a rudder. Greater length of tail is something to which breeders could usefully direct their attention, as good tail carriage greatly enhances the appearance of the Collie in the ring. Inevitably, a male Collie will tend to fly his tail as he approaches other males, but this does not justify him curling it over his back.

Movement is only briefly described in the Standard but is vital to a working dog. It has been estimated that a shepherd will cover twenty miles in the course of a day's work, and his dog, probably three times as much. A good reach of stride is essential, otherwise the dog must use twice the number of steps to cover the same distance. Correct movement in the Collie requires the dog to cover the ground effortlessly. Most of his work will be done at the trot with brief spells of galloping. The trot should be tireless, graceful and flowing, the feet just clearing the ground in the approved 'daisy cutting' fashion. The dog with the upright shoulder will tend to 'hackney' in front, lifting his front legs almost to his chin – very showy and stylish but also very tiring. The short striding dog that pitter patters along is also putting in too many strides to cover the same ground and this is equally tiring. The mechanics of faulty moving are discussed elsewhere in this book, but once again, it has its roots in faulty construction.

Obviously, the correct textured coat is of great importance to a dog that has to be out in all winds and weathers. The coat must fit the outline of the body and be very dense, straight and harsh to the touch. It is a double coat and the undercoat is soft and furry and provides great warmth and insulation. It acts in the same way as a thatched roof – warm in winter and cool in summer. It is noticeable that you do not see the Rough Collie shivering in cold weather as you see many short-coated breeds, nor do they appear to suffer great distress in heat waves. The correct coat may lie flat or stand off, depending on the amount of undercoat the dog is carrying, but it will be straight, harsh and water resistant. The correct coat can easily be distinguished by the speed with which it drys when wet. It will dry literally in a couple of shakes, it does not tangle in brushwood and needs much less grooming than the soft coat. This latter type of coat, which can look very beautiful in the ring, takes longer to groom, tangles easily and is water absorbent. In wet weather it can become very heavy and take hours to dry and must be a considerable handicap on a wet hillside. Texture is, therefore, of great importance.

At first sight, colour and markings would appear to be of no great significance in a working dog, yet the Collie's characteristic markings have not emerged by accident. There are many parti-colour dogs, but only the Rough, Smooth, Border and Bearded Collie and the Shetland Sheepdog carry the white collar, front, socks and tip to the tail that are almost a uniform. Anyone who is in the habit of exercising their Collies at night will tell you what a help it is to be able to pick out their dogs in the darkness by the moving flashes of white. If you cannot see your dog you cannot control him, and a good deal of a shepherd's work during the lambing season is done through the night. Almost all guard dogs are coloured black or grey enabling them to approach an intruder almost unnoticed in the night.

The Collie is perfectly marked for complete visibility from any angle or in any weather. His dark coat stands out against snow or a light background. This is the underlying reason why 'straw or cream coloured dogs are highly undesirable', was inserted in the Standard. In poor visibility, or at night, the white blaze (still retained in Border Collies) and the white front catch the eye. From the side, the white collar and legs are conspicuous and just as a lorry driver will place a white rag at the end of a long load, so the Collie carries his white-tipped tail (or tag as the old breeders term it), to make him clearly visible as he moves away. If he were all white, the shepherd would have great difficulty in distinguishing him from the sheep but with his dark colouring and white markings, both the sheep and the shepherd can pick him out from a considerable distance.

The Breed Standard

Since the first Collie Standard was published in 1881 there have been five revisions, of which (in the opinion of many), the 1910 version was the best. It succeeded in presenting an evocative picture of the Collie that lifts the spirit to read. I quote:

> To enable the Collie to fulfil his natural bent for sheepdog work he should be built on lines of strength, activity and grace, with a shapely body and sound legs and feet. He should be lithe and active in his movements, and entirely free from cloddiness or coarseness in any part of his conformation and lastly he must be gifted with true expression.
>
> Expression is obtained by the perfect combination of head, muzzle, size, shape and colour and placement of the eye, and correct position and carriage of ears, which give the dog that sweet, dreamy, semi-cunning, yet alert outlook that makes the perfect Collie the most beautiful of the canine race.

The Kennel Club has recently drawn up a standardised format for all breeds. The Working Group set of Standards was published in 1986 and that of the Collie reads, somewhat prosaically as follows:

The Collie Standard, Collie Rough

(Reproduced by courtesy of the Kennel Club of Great Britain)

General Appearance

The Collie should instantly appeal as a dog of great beauty, standing with impassive dignity, with no part out of proportion to the whole.

Characteristics

To enable the Collie to fulfil a natural bent for sheepdog work, its physical structure should be on the lines of strength and activity, free from cloddiness and without any trace of coarseness. Expression, one of the most important points in considering relative values, is obtained by the perfect balance and combination of skull and foreface size, shape, colour and placement of eye, correct position and carriage of ears.

94

Temperament

The Collie should have a friendly disposition with no trace of nervousness or aggressiveness.

Head and Skull

The head properties are of great importance and must be considered in proportion to the size of the dog. When viewed from front or side, the head resembles a well-blunted, clean wedge, being smooth in outline. Skull flat, the sides should taper gradually and smoothly from the ears to the end of the black nose, without prominent cheekbones or pinched muzzle. Viewed in profile, the top of the skull and the top of the muzzle lie in two parallel, straight lines of equal length, divided by a slight but perceptible 'stop' or break. A mid-point between the inside corners of the eyes (which is the centre of the correctly placed 'stop'), is the centre of balance in the length of head. The end of the smooth, well-rounded muzzle is blunt, never square. The underjaw is strong, clean-cut and the depth of the skull, from the brow to the underpart of the jaw, must never be excessive (deep through). Whatever the colour of the dog, the nose must be black.

Eyes

These are a very important feature and give a sweet expression to the dog. They should be of medium size (never very small), set somewhat obliquely, of almond shape and of dark-brown colour, except in the case of blue merles when the eyes (one or both, or part of one or both), are frequently blue or blue flecked. Expression full of intelligence, with a quick alert look when listening.

Ears

These should be small and not too close together on top of the skull, nor too far apart. When in repose, they should be carried thrown back, but, when on the alert, brought forward and carried semi-erect, that is, with approximately two-thirds of the ear standing erect, the top third tipping forward naturally, below the horizontal.

Mouth

The teeth should be of good size, with scissor bite.

Neck

The neck should be muscular, powerful, of fair length and well arched.

Forequarters

The shoulder should be sloped and well angulated. The forelegs should be straight and muscular, neither in nor out at elbows, with a moderate amount of bone.

Body

The body should be slightly long compared to height, back firm with a slight rise over the loins; ribs well sprung, chest deep and fairly broad behind the shoulders.

Hindquarters

The hind legs should be muscular at the thighs, clean and sinewy below, with well-bent stifles. Hocks well let down and powerful.

Feet

These should be oval in shape with soles well padded, toes arched and close together. The hind feet slightly less arched.

Gait

Movement is a distinct characteristic of this breed. A sound dog is never out at elbow, yet it moves with its front feet comparatively close together. Plaiting, crossing or rolling are highly undesirable. The hind legs, from the hock joint to the ground, when viewed from the rear should be parallel but not too close. When viewed from the side the action is smooth. The hind legs should be powerful with plenty of drive. A reasonably long stride is desirable and this should be light and appear quite effortless.

Tail

The tail should be long with the bone reaching at least to the hock joint. To be carried low when the dog is quiet, with a slight upward swirl at the tip. It may be carried gaily when the dog is excited, but not over the back.

Coat

The coat should fit the outline of the dog and be very dense. The outer coat straight and harsh to the touch; the undercoat soft, furry and very close, almost hiding the skin. The mane and frill should be very abundant, the mask or face, smooth, also the ears at the tips, but they should carry more hair towards the base; the front legs well feathered, the hind legs above the hocks profusely so, but smooth below. Hair on the tail very profuse.

Colour

The three recognised colours are sable and white, tricolour and blue merle.

Sable   Any shade from light gold to rich mahogany or shaded sable. Light straw or cream colour is highly undesirable.

Tricolour   Predominantly black with rich tan markings about the legs and head. A rusty tinge on the top coat is highly undesirable.

Blue merle   Predominantly clear, silvery blue, splashed and marbled with black. Rich tan markings to be preferred, but their absence should not be penalised. Large black markings, slate colour, or a rusty tinge either of the top or undercoat are highly undesirable.

White markings   All the above should carry the typical white Collie markings to a greater or lesser degree. The following markings are favourable: white collar, full or part; white shirt, legs and feet; white tail tip. A blaze may be carried on muzzle or skull or both.

Size

Dogs – 22 to 24 inches (56–61cm) at shoulder.
Bitches – 20 to 22 inches (51–56cm).

Ideal weights have been deleted.

Faults

Any departure from the foregoing points should be considered a fault
and the seriousness with which the fault is regarded should be in
exact proportion to its degree.

Note

Male animals should have two apparently normal testicles descended
into the scrotum.

The written Standard of the Breed represents a word picture of the
perfect Collie. Such an animal has never existed. Yet every judge and
breeder carries in their mind their own interpretation of the Standard,
their own picture of the imaginary perfect Collie. Inevitably, they
differ slightly one from another but if you asked them all to produce
an Identikit of the perfect Collie, they would come up with a remarkably similar animal. It is only when they have to assess our imperfect
Collies that differences arise. Inevitably, one will place greater
emphasis on certain good points and denigrate certain bad points to
a differing degree. This is a matter of interpretation. It takes a long
time and considerable application to learn to evaluate a good Collie.

Many breeders will tell you ruefully, that when they showed their
first Collie they were convinced that their beloved pet was perfection
itself. When they discovered the judge did not share their opinion
they were nonplussed and convinced that the judge was either blind
or crooked. It took many months and several shows for them to
become gradually aware of the merits of the dogs that were being
placed above them. Slowly, their eyes began to adjust to the subtle differences between Collies and they began to see why their dog was so
lowly placed. Years ago, Mr and Mrs H. Cliffe, whose famous
Lyncliffe Collies had such a great influence on the immediate post-
war breeding, told me of their experience when they showed their
first Collie.

Every time they looked round the ring they were convinced that their dog was the best and they were dumbfounded when he was unplaced. Eventually, they approached a well-known Yorkshire judge and tactfully enquired if there was anything he thought they could do to improve their dog's chances. He gazed at their Collie sorrowfully for several moments. Finally he brightened: 'Aye', he said, 'you could cut t'bloody head off.' After that, although they still loved their dog just as much, they kept him at home. Judges are a bit kinder on beginners these days. When really stuck for something nice to say about a dog, I have been known to declare: 'Well, it's a lovely colour!' So much so, that friends asking my opinion on their latest puppy, will often laughingly point out that I have got to admit to the beauty of its colour, before I have time to give them my opinion! So the next time you and your champion pet leave the ring disconsolate, remember all the other breeders who have gone through this unhappy phase, who have struggled on and are now among today's top breeders.

If you wish to join them, study the Breed Standard – it is your bible. Go to the shows, sit and watch the judging. Much can be learnt from placing the winners yourself as a mental discipline. You will not always agree with the judge's decisions as he will have a different perspective on the animals in front of him, but your placings should not differ too widely. Many people have a natural eye for a good dog and this is something you should try to develop. A really good dog will always stand out from his more mediocre companions, even to the untrained eye, but only the trained eye can separate dogs that are equal in quality, whether they be good, poor or indifferent. Even then, it depends, to a large extent, on the judge's personal likes and dislikes. When making your own selection, bear in mind that although the ring is merely a beauty contest, the Collie was evolved as the herding dog *par excellence*.

The original Standard was scarcely more than a scale of points drawn up in 1880 to assist judges in evaluating the new herding breed. It was not until 1895 that the Rough Collie came to be recognised as a separate and distinct breed. There have been several changes since then, culminating in the latest 1986 standard, as modified by the Kennel Club with the assistance of the British Veterinary Association.

The American Breed Standard is based on the English Standard but goes into greater detail and has the inestimable advantage of being beautifully illustrated by Lorraine Still. All have something to teach us.

The American Kennel Club Standard
Rough Collie

(Reproduced by Courtesy of the American Kennel Club)

General Character

The Collie is a lithe, strong, responsive active dog, carrying no useless timber, standing naturally straight and firm. The deep, moderately wide chest shows strength; the sloping shoulders and well-bent hocks indicate speed and grace; the face shows high intelligence. The Collie presents an impressive, proud picture of true balance, each part being in harmonious proportion to every other part and to the whole. Except for the technical description that is essential to this Standard and without which no Standard for the guidance of breeders and judges is adequate, it could be stated simply that no part of the Collie ever seems to be out of proportion to any other part. Timidity, frailness, sullenness, viciousness, lack of animation, cumbersome appearance and lack of overall balance impair the general character.

Head

The head properties are of great importance. When considered in proportion to the size of the dog the head is inclined to lightness and never appears massive. A heavy-headed dog lacks the bright, alert, full-of-sense look that contributes so greatly to expression.

Both in front and profile view the head bears a general resemblance to a well-blunted lean wedge, being smooth and clean in outline and nicely balanced in proportion. On the sides, it tapers gradually and smoothly from the ears to the end of the black nose, without being flared out in the backskull (cheeky), or pinched in muzzle (snipey). In profile view, the top of the backskull and the top of the muzzle lie in two approximately parallel, straight planes of equal length divided by a very slight but perceptible stop or break.

A mid point between the inside corners of the eyes (which is the center of a correctly placed stop) is the center of balance in length of head.

The end of the smooth, well-rounded muzzle is blunt but not square. The underjaw is strong, clean-cut and the depth of skull from the brow to the underpart of the jaw is not excessive.

100

The teeth are of good size, meeting in a scissors bite. Overshot or undershot jaws are undesirable, the latter being more severely penalised.

There is a very slight prominence of the eyebrows. The backskull is flat, without receding either laterally or backward and the occiputal bone is not highly peaked. The proper width of backskull necessarily depends upon the combined length of skull and muzzle and the width of the backskull is less than its length. Thus the correct width varies with the individual and is dependent upon the extent to which it is supported by length of muzzle.

Because of the importance of the head characteristics, prominent head faults are severely penalised.

Eyes

Because of the combination of the flat skull, the arched eyebrows, the slight stop and the rounded muzzle, the foreface must be chiselled to form a receptacle for the eyes and they are necessarily placed obliquely to give them the required forward outlook. Except for the blue merles they are required to be matched in colour. They are almond shaped, of medium size and never properly appear to be large or prominent. The colour is dark and the eye does not show a yellow ring or a sufficiently prominent haw to affect the dog's expression.

The eyes have a clear, bright appearance, expressing intelligent inquisitiveness, particularly when the ears are drawn up and the dog is on the alert.

Ears

The ears are in proportion to the size of the head and, if they are carried properly and unquestionably 'break' naturally, are seldom too small. Large ears usually cannot be lifted correctly off the head and even if lifted they will be out of proportion to the size of the head. When in repose, the ears are folded lengthwise and thrown back into the frill. On the alert, they are drawn well up on the backskull and are carried about three-quarters erect with one-fourth of the ear tipping or 'breaking' forward. A dog with prick ears or low ears cannot show true expression and is penalised accordingly.

Neck

The neck is firm, clean, muscular, sinewy and heavily frilled. It is fairly long, is carried upright with a slight arch at the nape and imparts a proud, upstanding appearance, showing off the frill.

Body

The body is firm, hard and muscular, a trifle long in proportion to the height. The ribs are well rounded behind the well-sloped shoulders and the chest is deep, extending to the elbows. The back is strong and level, supported by powerful hips and thighs and the croup is sloped to give a well-rounded finish. The loin is powerful and slightly arched. Noticeably fat dogs, or dogs in poor flesh, or with skin disease, or with no undercoat are out of condition and moderately penalised accordingly. In grown males, the monorchid and cryptorchid are disqualified.

Legs

The forelegs are straight and muscular, with a fair amount of bone considering the size of the dog. A cumbersome appearance is undesirable. Both narrow and wide placement are penalised. The forearm is moderately fleshy and the pasterns are flexible, but without weakness. The hind legs are less fleshy, are muscular at the thighs, very sinewy, and the hocks and stifles are well bent. A cow-hocked dog or a dog with straight stifles is penalised. The comparatively small feet are approximately oval in shape. The soles are well padded and tough and the toes are well arched and close together. When the Collie is not in motion, the legs and feet are judged by allowing the dog to come to a natural stop in a standing position so that both the forelegs and the hind legs are placed well apart with the feet extending straight forward. Excessive 'posing' is undesirable.

Gait

Gait is sound. When the dog is moved at a slow trot toward an observer, his straight front legs track comparatively close together at the ground. The front legs are not out at the elbows, do not 'cross over' nor does the Collie move with a choppy, pacing or rolling gait. When viewed from the rear, the hind legs are powerful and propelling. Viewed from the side, the reasonably long 'reaching' stride is smooth and even, keeping the back line firm and level.

As the speed of the gait is increased, the Collie single tracks, bringing the front legs inward in a straight line from the shoulder toward the center line of the body. The gait suggests effortless speed combined with the dog's herding heritage, requiring it to be capable of changing its direction of travel almost instantaneously.

Tail

The tail is moderately long, the bone reaching to the hock-joint or below. It is carried low when the dog is quiet the end having an upward twist or 'swirl'. When gaited or when the dog is excited it is carried gaily, but not over the back.

Coat

The well-fitting, proper-textured coat is the crowning glory of the Rough variety of Collie. It is abundant except on the head and legs. The outer coat is straight and harsh to the touch. A soft, open outer coat or a curly outer coat is penalized, regardless of quantity. The undercoat, however, is soft, furry and so close together that it is difficult to see the skin when the hair is parted. The coat is very abundant on the mane and frill. The face or mask is smooth. The forelegs are smooth and well feathered to the back of the pasterns. The hind legs are smooth below the hock-joints. Any feathering below the hocks is removed for the show ring. The hair on the tail is very profuse and on the hips it is long and bushy. The texture, quantity and the extent to which the coat 'fits' the dog are important points.

Color

The four recognised colors are sable and white, tricolor, blue merle and white. There is no preference among them. The sable and white is predominantly sable (a fawn, sable color of varying shades from light gold to dark mahogany), with white markings usually on the chest, neck, legs, feet and tip of tail. A blaze may appear on the foreface or backskull or both. The tricolor is predominantly black, carrying white markings as in a sable and white and has tan shadings on and about the head and legs. The blue merle is a mottled or 'marbled color, predominantly blue-grey and black with white markings as in the sable and white and usually has tan shadings as in the tricolor. The white is predominantly white, with sable, tricolor or blue merle markings.

Size

Dogs are from 24 to 26 inches (61–66cm) at the shoulder and weigh from 60 to 75 pounds (27–33kg). Bitches are from 22 to 24 inches (55–60cm) at the shoulder, weighing from 50 to 65 pounds (22–27kg). An undersize or an oversize Collie is penalized according to the extent to which the dog appears to be undersize or oversize.

Expression

Expression is one of the most important points in considering the relative values of Collies. 'Expression', like the term 'character', is difficult to define in words. It is not a fixed point as in color, weight or height and it is something the uninitiated can properly understand only by optical illustration. In general, however, it may be said to be the combined product of the shape and balance of the skull and muzzle, the placement, size, shape and color of the eyes, and the position, size and carriage of the ears. An expression that shows sullenness or which is suggestive of any other breed is entirely foreign. The Collie cannot be judged properly until his expression has been carefully evaluated.

This Standard goes into such detail and is so explicit that it is difficult to see at first glance how and why the two types of Collie – the European and the American – have emerged. Both types are beautiful in their own way. The key to the difference between them lies, in my opinion, in the paragraph on expression. British breeders lay great emphasis on sweetness of expression, indeed with some judges it is considered of paramount importance. The insistence on a sweet expression has its roots in the function of the Collie as a working dog as I have already shown. In the earlier British Standard, expression is described as, 'sweet, dreamy yet alert', a description which aptly fits both the Collie's expression and his character. In the present Standard it states, 'that the eyes give a sweet expression to the dog'. Nowhere in the American Standard can the word 'sweet' be found. The expression is described in varying terms as 'bright, alert, full of sense, clear, expressing intelligent inquisitiveness and difficult to define', but never sweet. This seems to me to be a serious omission. In every other respect the American Standard seems superior to ours.

Nothing, they tell me, is ever achieved at world conferences, but now that distances have become only relative it would be of great benefit to the breed if a universal Standard could be hammered out which all countries would adopt. It is unlikely that the Americans would accept the present cryptic British Kennel Club Standard, but the next time it comes up for revision maybe we could persuade the Kennel Club to accept a fuller, more explicit version which combines the best of both Standards. That would be a definite step forward to combining the two types of Collies.

It must be stated that at the recent World Conference on just this subject, it was decided, unequivocally, that the Standard and type to be followed in all breeds was that laid down by the country of origin. So where does this leave our American friends? Not so far off as some would have us believe. The simple addition of the words, 'sweet expression to be desired', would have them producing a type of head more acceptable to European eyes in a comparatively short time. The Europeans need to move away from the Border-Collie-type heads which have crept into the breed in recent years and return to the classic head of former years; making sure that our Collies do not fall below the height laid down in the Standard. If these steps were taken, we could once again be breeding Collies that would win on either side of the Atlantic and could be successfully interbred.

There are practical advantages to be gained from interbreeding. New sets of genes could be introduced which would usefully be added to the existing pool, making it easier to combat disease. In Britain, we do not have (at the time of writing), a Collie that is genetically clear of hereditary eye disease. Such a Collie, wherever he was produced, would (if of acceptable type), be of inestimable value to the breed.

Mrs Chatfield, who has just returned from a judging trip to the USA, tells me that she was favourably impressed with USA Collies. Some were definitely oversize but a great many were perfectly acceptable. Heads lacked stop but most had superb necks and moved well. Bone was much heavier than we are used to seeing on present day Collies. All were beautifully presented and she found no evidence of artificial colouring. In the Champion class of some sixty Collies there were seven or eight that she would dearly like to have taken home.

I have long campaigned to have the American Illustrated Standard with its superb drawings by Lorraine Still accepted world-wide. It is already used in Europe and is universally acknowledged to be far superior to the British Illustrated Standard. It was published in the USA in 1966 and they now regard the Collies depicted as slightly old-fashioned. They are none the worse for that. They represent a type that both countries are in danger of losing, a Collie that is well fitted for the work it was evolved to do.

For many years I have cherished a dream that we may be one day able to set up a Collie Centre in Britain. It would consist of a house or building set in several acres of ground. The building would house historic Collie records and books and could be used for meetings and symposiums. The grounds could be used for shows and to foster obedience and agility training. A part could be set aside for Collie Rescue kennels. Sheep would be used to keep the grass in trim and sheep dog training could be introduced that would give the Collie back his rightful heritage as a herding dog, making the Collie into the dog we all know him to be, one of the most beautiful, useful, and intelligent of all breeds.

Interpreting the Standard

Head

The Collie is often described as a 'head' breed and, indeed, I know of no other breed in which the shades or nuances of measurement can so dramatically alter the quality of the dog's head. Many earlier books will tell you that great emphasis was laid on the length of head. Stud-dogs were frequently advertised as having a 'head of great length', or a 'head of eleven inches'. This is no longer true. Today, much greater importance is attached to having a well-balanced head than having a head of excessive length. The centre of balance is at a line drawn between the inside corners of the eyes and this should be exactly half-way between the end of the nose and the edge of the back skull. I have never been an advocate of the over-long head but nowadays there seems to be a danger of heads getting too short and too thick. There should be nothing heavy or cloddy about the Collie's head.

For some time, I have felt that the introduction of the word 'wedge' into the Standard was a great mistake. It implies that the head has sharp angular edges and gives no indication of the beautiful, seductive roundness of the correct Collie foreface. The word 'wedge' is no

Roman nose.

Angled head.

Straight through head.

Bumpy skull.

Dish faced head.

Nose drops off.

Stop too far down the muzzle.

Stop too deep (farm head).

Underjaw too short (shark jaw).

Deep through head.

Pricked ears.

Low-set ears.

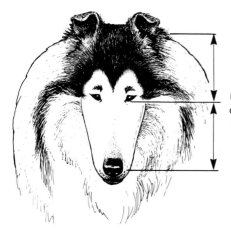

Balanced head.

mid-way balance
of the head

more useful in the description of the profile as a 'well-blunted clean wedge', as the Standard goes on to say that 'the top edge of skull and muzzle lie in two parallel straight planes of equal length, divided by a slight but perceptible stop' – a description which could scarcely be bettered. If the top of the head is, in effect, a straight line, the wedge shape must come from the bottom line. This leads inevitably to the skull being 'deep through' – a very ugly fault.

Skull

I prefer to think of the Collie's skull as a slender oblong which runs smoothly and imperceptibly into the almost cylindrical shaped muzzle. The width of the skull will depend on the size and the amount of bone carried by the dog. You will often see judges comparing width of skull on various dogs – a quite pointless exercise, in my opinion, as the Collie's head must be in proportion to the size of the dog. A small head on a six-foot man looks just as much out of proportion as a large head on a five-foot man; it is all a matter of balance. Any breeder can produce a fine skull on a fine-boned dog but it is only the exceptional dog that combines heavy bone with a lean skull in harmonious proportions.

It is essential that the skull should be as flat as possible. The whole art of the Collie breeder is directed to obtaining the very difficult fusion of a round muzzle to a flat-topped and sided skull. The foreface should run smoothly up into the skull with no marked change of width, no sudden widening of the skull or flaring of the cheeks.

113

Viewed from above, I prefer the analogy of the slender oblong to the sharp wedge, to produce the classic head.

The end of the well-rounded muzzle is described as, 'blunt but not square', with a strong underjaw. This is an important feature and should be given due weight when studying the profile, in order to avoid the ugly fault of weak or 'shark' jaw which more aptly describes it. It needs to be sufficiently strong to accommodate the roots of the teeth which will tend to fall out as the dog gets older if there is not sufficient room and depth for them.

Teeth

The top teeth should fit neatly over the bottom in a scissor bite and there should be a full complement of forty-two teeth in the adult dog. The teeth most likely to be missing are one or more of the pre-molars which are to be found immediately behind the canine or 'fang' teeth and it is not until the dog reaches seven months of age that you can be certain he will carry the full complement. Missing teeth are a hereditary fault which it is wise not to perpetuate. They should not be confused with teeth that are accidentally knocked out, usually the incisors. Missing molars are regarded by English judges as a fault, neither more nor less than any other fault, to be taken into account when making their assessment. On the Continent a missing tooth will result in the dog's disqualification from top awards and a dog with such a fault should never be exported to Europe. Whether they are right to regard this fault so seriously in a dog that is not allowed to use his teeth in his herding work, is a matter for debate.

Eyes

The Collie eye is described as being dark brown in colour, almond-shaped and medium in size. The 1986 Standard adds the words 'never too small'. There is no doubt that compared with breeds of comparable size, the Collie's eye tends to smallness but the shape and placement of the eye are of greater importance than size in producing the desired sweetness of expression.

Ears

The importance of the correctly shaped and placed ear in the Collie has already been explored in the section on form and function. The

inside of ear directly over eye

Correct ear carriage.

Flared skull.

115

Standard calls for ears that are small and not too close together nor too far apart. When in repose, they are carried thrown back into the frill, but on the alert, they are brought forward and carried semi-erect, with the top third of the ear tipping forward. I find it surprising that while the Standard calls for an eye of medium size, many breeders prefer a very small eye, yet when the Standard calls for a small ear, neither judges or breeders seem to pay much attention. The small, well-carried ear adds much to the Collie's expression and this was recognised in the original scale of points when ten points were awarded for perfect ears but only five points for perfect eyes.

When the breeder succeeds in obtaining the almost perfect head, what a revelation it is! Then the almond eye is chiselled obliquely into the skull giving maximum forward vision. The well-tipped ears are carried with the inside edge placed directly over the centre of the eye giving maximum hearing. Only when this perfect combination is obtained, can the full beauty of the Collie's expression, be revealed. Many writers have sought to define Collie expression but its beauty defies description. It is a magical combination of alertness, intelligence, sweetness and nobility that incorporates all the characteristics of the Collie's nature. It is something that once seen, makes an indelible impression on the beholder. For those who ask how to recognise true Collie expression, I will say only this: when such a Collie turns his head to look at you, you will feel your heart miss a beat and the hair rise on the back of your neck. Such is the power and sweetness of the 'Collie look'.

The Forequarters

The neck of the Collie is a distinctive feature of the breed. The proud arch and elegant reach of neck serve admirably to set off the beautiful mane and frill. The angle at which the head is set on to the arched neck is important. If the eyes are correctly chiselled into the skull, then the nose of the dog must point to the ground at an angle of approximately 45 degrees to give him forward vision.

For a correctly set on head, there will be a distinct crest in the neck bone immediately behind the ears, particularly in males. It is essential that this arched neck should be set into well-laid shoulders. The modern breeder sometimes finds it difficult to grasp the concept of the phrase 'shoulders well laid back'. Years ago, we were taught to equate the anatomy of the dog with that of a well-bred horse. That

The sweetness of Collie expression. Note the roundness of the foreface and the balance of the head. The point of balance is the inside corner of the eye, which should be exactly half-way between the tip of the nose and the back of the occiput.

117

Good front.

Front too narrow.

Front too wide.

Ballerina front.

Out at elbows.

Bowed front.

Left leg turned in.

Right leg turned in.

In-out front (knitted front).

meant that, viewed from the side, the end of the scapula or shoulder blade should be set well back from the neck and should run down to the foremost point of the shoulder at an angle of approximately 45 degrees. The shoulders will then be well sloped as in a racehorse. The shoulders are attached to the spine only by muscle and there should be a distance of approximately two fingers' width between the shoulder blades.

Straight shoulders occur when the angle between the shoulder blade and the upper arm is too steep. It should be roughly 90 degrees allowing for any curve in the bones, and can be felt at the foremost point of the shoulder. If correct, the dog is often described as having a 'good forehand'. These angles are easily disguised by a big coat and it is essential for a judge to feel them for himself. An imaginary line drawn between this forward point of the shoulder and the highest point of the withers should run at an angle of 45 degrees to the ground. This is perhaps the most important angle of all because the whole structure and movement of the dog will hinge on this correct lay-back of shoulder. Get this one angle wrong and you will get the whole dog wrong (*see* pages 121 and 128).

The forequarters of the dog carry almost three-quarters of his weight, while the hindquarters form the main method of propulsion. So it is important that the forequarters are strong and well made. A

The arched Collie neck and well-angled shoulder.

straight shoulder will be just as strong as a well-made one but will be subject to far greater strain as it is the angles that absorb shock. You have only to jump from a height without bending your knees to feel exactly what I mean. Not only is the sloping shoulder essential for the dog to carry out a hard day's work, it greatly enhances the dog's appearance in the ring.

Years ago, classes of about a dozen dogs were the norm for Collies which meant that there was plenty of room for the dog to stand well away from his handler and show naturally. An assortment of balls, brushes and bits of liver were tossed all over the ring in an attempt to catch the dog's attention, to make him arch his neck and lift his ears at the vital moment when the judge was looking at him. It was this momentary attention that won prizes. Today the dog is expected to stand with his ears up and his eyes glued to the titbit in the handler's hand for long periods of time. As there may be anything up to fifty Collies in one class, they are crowded together and there simply is not the space for the dog to stand away from the handler and show off his arched neck. Instead they stand nose-to-tail in a straight line looking up at their handlers. This stance makes them appear ewe-necked and puts the dog with a good reach of neck at a disadvantage. There is no easy solution to this problem but it is one of which judges should be aware. Nor should they be deceived by the handler who strings up his exhibit to give an impression of a good reach of neck which he does not possess. The handler should always be asked to drop the lead.

From the front, the chest of the Collie should appear only moderately wide. It must not be so narrow that both front legs appear to come out of the same hole but should not be exaggerated in width. The ribs should be well sprung allowing plenty of heart room but the rib cage is tapered towards the base into a distinct keel which can easily be felt with the hand. This allows the forelegs to swing in a free arc during movement. The barrel chest has no keel and restricts the swing of the forelegs giving the dog a shortened stride and causing him to roll as he moves. The short stride means that the dog must take three strides to every two of the correctly made dog and this must prove tiring over a long distance. As the dog moves towards you the forelegs should be straight, neither in nor out at the elbows. Out at elbow movement is not always easy to spot with today's big coats and is often easier to see as the dog moves away from you.

Body

The body should be that of a well-muscled dog – lithe and active in all his movements – as befits a working dog. It should not be short and cobby, nor should it be over-long. The length should be slightly longer than the Collie's height. Over-long backs result in weakness and if exaggerated, as in some breeds, lead to back trouble. It should not dip behind the shoulders resulting in sway or weak backs, but if correctly made, the top of the hip-joint will be placed above the spine giving a slight rise over the loin. It is this rise that gives strength to the back. This arch does not have to be as exaggerated as in the greyhound or other similar galloping breeds, but it must be there to give strength and flexibility to the Collie's movement. The phrase 'level topline' is often used by modern judges but can only accurately be used when referring to Collie movement, not to the animal in repose.

Tail Set

The croup should be well rounded and the tail low set. A high-set tail predisposes to a high tail carriage, which is a very difficult fault to breed out. The tail carriage of the male Collie has been a matter of controversy for many years. Why there should be such difficulty in producing males with long well-carried tails is not clear but it has always been so, at least in living memory. Most bitches are blessed with long, flowing, low-set tails but the dog whose tail bone reaches below the hock is a rarity. We seem to have eliminated the kinked tail which once seemed to be bred into certain strains and although tails are still short, we no longer see tails of barely seven inches (18cm) in length which were common in the immediate post-war era.

There is an in-built tendency for the young male Collie to raise his tail at the sight of another. Indeed, he will often arch his neck, fly his tail and prance in the same way as a stallion and this should be taken into account by judges in the show ring. This should not excuse the curly Spitz tail which the dog carries over his back, which has crept into the breed in recent years. This is an ugly fault which spoils the dog's outline and is caused by a fore-shortening of the tendons and is not a skeletal fault.

The length of the tail is, however, a skeletal fault. In the correct tail, there will be fifteen vertebrae; in a short tail there will be several vertebrae missing. The Collie uses his tail in his work when braking

Correct tail carriage.   *Spitz tail.*

Gay tail (acceptable).

sharply or to balance himself on a quick turn, so a good length of tail is essential. The longer the tail, the more likely it is to be carried correctly as its own weight will tend to keep it down.

Forelegs and Feet

The forelegs should carry a moderate amount of bone and be slightly heavier in the case of males. The bone should be strong and well rounded; it should not be flat or bladed. Looking at the dog from the front, the forelegs appear absolutely straight, with no turning either in or out from the knee-joint downwards. The feet are comparatively small for the size of the dog and should be oval in shape. Round or cat feet are incorrect. The toes should be well arched with thickly padded soles. Thin, flat feet with extended toes and long nails are extremely ugly and should be heavily penalised. Good, strong feet with the toes well arched and close together are a great asset both to the show and the working dog.

124

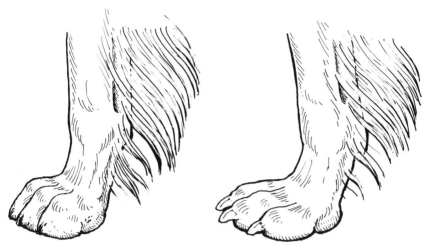

Correct foot. *Flat weak foot.*

Hindquarters

Although the forelegs carry the major part of the dog's weight, it is the hind legs that provide the propulsion. The Collie must be capable of great speed but this cannot be demonstrated in the show ring. The judge has to evaluate movement on the way the dog moves and turns on the trot. As he moves away, the dog should lift and drive from the hock. When in repose, he should stand four-square. The dog is not assisted to pose by stacking or holding up the head and tail. He must stand in a natural position.

A well-made dog will seldom put a foot wrong but a clever handler can disguise faults by manoeuvring the dog into a good position. From the rear, the hocks should form a square, equidistant from each other and the ground. (The hock is the somewhat inaccurate term used to describe the portion of the hind leg, from the foot to the first or 'heel' joint. It is also used to describe the joint itself.) There are a confusing number of terms applied to hocks:

Cow hocks	Hock-joints bowed inward and nearly touching at the joints.
Long hocks	The distance from the ground to the hock-joint is too long in comparison with the size of the dog.
Over-angulated hocks	Viewed from the side, the angle of the hock is too acute, with the foot bent underneath the body.

125

Sickle hocks	Similar to the above, but the hock is curved, causing the dog to walk on the heel or back part of the foot.
Short hocks	The distance from the ground to the hock-joint is comparatively short.
Spindle hocks	Long, poor boned hocks.
Spraddle hocks	Hocks bowed outwards and too far apart at the joints.
Sound hocks	The hocks are approximately a hand's width apart and there is no lateral movement in the joint as the dog moves.
Straight hocks	Viewed from the side, there is little angulation at the joint.
Well angled hocks	Viewed from the side, the stifle is well bent.

Over-angulated hocks and sickle hocks will be dealt with more fully later.

Good square hocks.

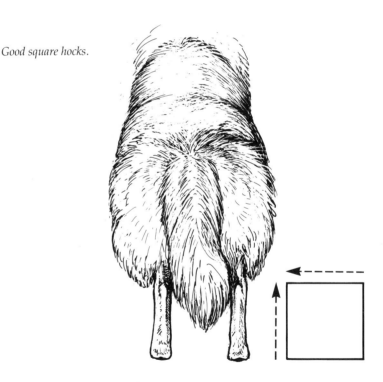

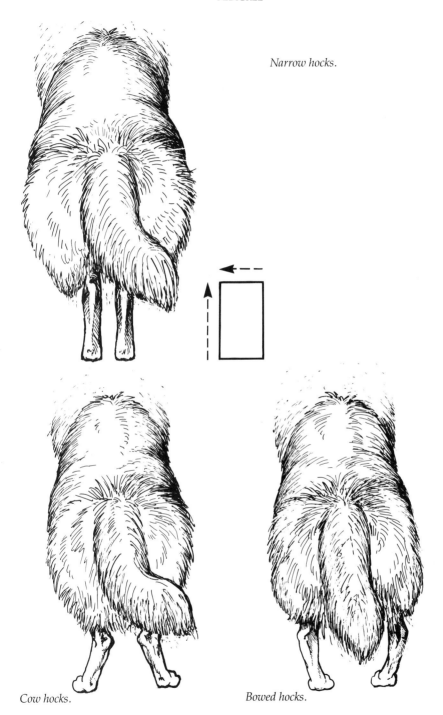

Narrow hocks.

Cow hocks.

Bowed hocks.

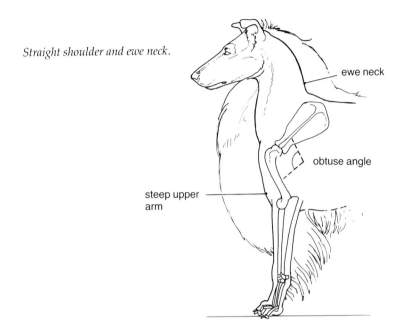

Straight shoulder and ewe neck.

ewe neck

obtuse angle

steep upper arm

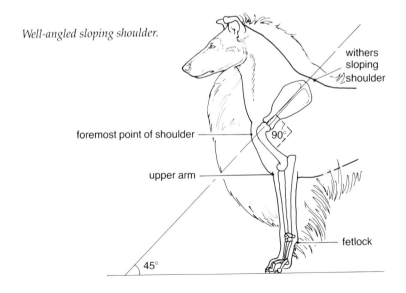

Well-angled sloping shoulder.

withers
sloping
shoulder

foremost point of shoulder

90°

upper arm

fetlock

45°

Well-angulated hock, perpendicular to the ground.

Straight hock.

Over-angulated hock.

Sickle hock.

It cannot be over-emphasised that correct hind angulation comes from the angle at which the femur or thigh-bone meets the fibula/tibia. This corresponds to the fore point of the shoulder and is in direct relation to it. If the shoulder angle is good the rear angle will also be good. If the dog has a straight shoulder he will have a straight stifle-joint. This angle will be reflected in the hock-joint. When the correctly made Collie is standing in repose his hocks will be perpendicular to the ground. The angle comes from the curve in the stifle. From the working point of view it would be better for the dog to have straight hocks than to have over-bent or sickle hocks which can virtually cripple.

Coat

I have devoted a section to the colour of a Collie's coat but for a working dog the texture of his coat is more important. The Standard states that it should be straight and harsh to the touch and judges should pay due attention to this point. The correct coat tends towards coarseness, it does not retain water and will shake dry quickly. The body coat follows the outline of the dog, thus presenting an almost impenetrable surface to the wet, while the dense furry undercoat provides wonderful thermal insulation against the cold. A great deal of criticism has been levelled at the modern coat. I believe that the almost universal practice of spraying the coat with a water-based coat cleanser has led to softer coats being regarded as the norm.

It is generally acknowledged that the golden sable has a softer coat than his tricolour, blue merle or shaded counterparts. This has always been the case but it is only in recent years that the golden sable has come to dominate the show ring, in numbers if not in quality. It seems a pity that the old-fashioned shaded sable is losing popularity. Much could be gained by making a fuller use of the tricolour in sable breeding to improve both colour and coat texture.

One thing that has improved is the length of time for which a Collie can be expected to hold his coat. When I first came into Collies you could only rely on your show dog to be at his best for about four months of the year. It would take him about eight months to shed his old coat and slowly grow a new one. Only the large kennels who had a selection of dogs to choose from were able to consistently produce dogs at their peak. The owner of a small kennel was at a distinct disad-vantage. The occasional dog that never shed his coat but always appeared in magnificent form was referred to by H.E. Packwood, in his early book on Collies, as a phenomenon to be greatly desired.

Some English breeders have been working for many years to establish this type of coat in their strain and have met with considerable success. Dogs are being bred now that do not even shed their puppy coats but are able to be shown in full coat throughout their show careers. Bitches continue to moult after they have had puppies but even they regain full coat in a remarkably short space of time. This is a great benefit to the small kennel owner, and, coupled with the increasing number of registrations, has been a great boost to show entries. Invariably, these dogs carry an immensely thick undercoat, quite impenetrable to cold and wet. It requires very little grooming to bring this type of coat to its best, but because it has such 'body' in it, it needs to be smoothed down in the final brush as otherwise it will spoil the outline of the dog.

Provided this type of coat is harsh and weather resistant I see no reason why it should be penalised in the show ring. A soft, wavy, water-absorbent coat that would be a handicap to the dog in its natural environment is undesirable.

Movement

The movement of a well-constructed Collie is a joy to watch. Easy and graceful, it seems to flow over the ground. At full gallop, the Collie moves in lithe bounds and should be capable of great speed over short distances. The well-balanced dog should be able to turn and twist with great suppleness and flexibility. From a standing start, he should be capable of moving into great speed almost instantly and equally capable of using his braking mechanism to come to an abrupt halt, should the occasion demand. All this is a question of balance.

Little of this can be discerned from the dog's appearance in the ring. The judge is limited to watching the dog move at a sedate trot. Yet much can be gleaned from this exercise, particularly if the dog is viewed from the side. It is only from this angle that freedom of reach and strength of drive can be identified. If the dog is well balanced, he will move his legs easily and rhythmically like a well-oiled machine. The shock of the pad striking the ground is absorbed by the flexing angles so that the body appears to float effortlessly along, keeping the topline level. This is in marked contrast to the badly constructed dog that has straight shoulders or barrel ribs. The short, restricted stride of such a dog requires much more effort, forcing the dog to roll in his efforts to reach a reasonable speed. Straight shoulders go with straight hocks and the combination of the two will give the dog a choppy, bouncing action. He will cover very little distance with each stride and his gait will appear stilted. Viewed both from the front and the rear, such a dog will often appear extremely sound and it is only from the side that the faulty action is revealed.

Nowadays, you seldom see the high-stepping hackney action that was once much admired. It looks spectacular but is extremely tiring and must be wrong. It is now generally recognised that the economical 'daisy cutting' style is the action that should be aimed for.

Balance in a dog is a difficult concept to grasp and is more easily recognised in humans. If you stand in a crowd and watch people walking past, you will quickly observe a great deal of difference in the way they move. Some plod along in an ungainly fashion; some roll from side to side; some put a great deal of effort into their movement. A few, a very few, move easily and gracefully, their shoulders still and all the movement coming from the hips – they move with perfect balance. So it is with Collies. A well-balanced dog will move at an easy trot that can be maintained for hours. The front right foot will reach full extension at the same moment as the rear left foot. The feet will move diagonally in perfect rhythm. If the dog moves both legs on the same side together, he is said to be pacing. This is a bad habit which you should not allow your dog to adopt, the exception being the elderly dog which often seems to prefer this form of propulsion.

It is worth spending some time watching your Collie moving at the trot and noting whether diagonal feet strike the ground at the same moment. In an unbalanced dog, the movement will be uncoordinated, the rear appearing to move independently of the front. Sometimes the rear feet will move on a different line to the front, the whole rear assembly moving to one side, when the dog will be said to be 'crabbing'. Major faults in movement which have come to the fore in recent years are sickle and over-angulated hocks. These hock-joints have very little movement in them and the dog is unable to flex his hocks, to lift and drive with them as he should. I cannot emphasise too strongly the importance of the dog standing with his hocks perpendicular to the ground when in repose, because only such a dog can have good strong driving action. The movement of the sickle-hocked dog is equivalent to that of a person walking on his heels. Not only is it ugly, it is also damaging to the tendons. These hocks are almost invariably accompanied by weak pasterns and can result in considerable pain to the dog as he gets older and the tendons become over-stretched. A dog that moves with drive will show the pads of his hind feet as he moves away.

The English Standard is not very forthcoming on movement. It does state that, 'the Collie moves with its front feet comparatively close together', but it gives little indication of the reasons for this. In fact, when the dog moves at walking pace he double tracks. This can be observed by wetting the dog's feet and moving him on a smooth surface. As the dog increases speed into a fast trot, so the tracks converge into a single line. This is called single tracking. As the dog decreases speed, the lines will again diverge. Some breeders find it very difficult to accept the concept of single tracking, claiming that the dog would overbalance if it were true. It is the momentum of the dog that enables him to retain his balance.

As your Collie comes towards you, at the trot, his front feet should converge, but the line of the leg from the shoulder to the foot should remain absolutely straight. It should not bow inwards or splay outwards. Similarly, viewed from the rear, although the hind feet will converge as speed increases, there should be no suggestion of bowed or cow hocks. It need hardly be said that the concept of single tracking does not apply to the Collie at the gallop, where the hind feet will be placed outside the front feet as they move in unison.

Size

Size in the Collie is something of a vexed question. The Standard lays down the criteria for height and (until recently) weight as follows. Dogs – height: 22–24 inches (56–61cm) at the shoulder; weight: 45–65 pounds (20–29kg). Bitches – height: 20-22 inches (51–56cm) at the shoulder; weight: 40–55 pounds (18–25kg).

Height is measured to the highest point of the shoulders. A measuring stick and not a tape-measure should always be used for maximum accuracy. The weight of a dog can be obtained by picking up the animal, stepping on to domestic scales and making a note of the combined weights. Then weigh yourself, subtract one from the other and you will have an accurate weight for your dog. This is also much the best method of weighing a wriggling puppy.

Most European countries adopt the English criteria but in Russia, where Collies have been bred from the large number of English dogs imported by the Tsar, the height is laid down as 65–69cm for dogs and 60–65cm for bitches. Their Collies are used largely as military service and messenger dogs rather than as sheep herders. Great care is taken in breeding to maintain their strength and activity which are considered of prime importance.

It seems strange that the Americans, who paid high prices for imported English show stock, have adopted a Standard differing from that of the country of origin. (Dogs – height: 24–26 inches (61–66cm); weight: 60–75 pounds (27–33kg). Bitches – height: 22-24 inches (55–60cm); weight: 50-65 pounds (22–27kg). The most likely explanation is that they were realists. They noted that almost all their expensive English imports were well above the permitted height standards and made up their own criteria to fit the dogs they were receiving. The Victorians were very sentimental over 'noble, majestic animals' and the large, heavily coated male Collie fitted the bill admirably. Size and length of head were greatly desired attributes, until fashion changed in recent years. Most of the pre-war male Beulah champions that I saw in the highly successful kennel of the late Mrs N.K. George were between 26 and 27 inches (66 and 68cm) at the shoulder with heavy bone and coat to match. Her aim, she always insisted, was to breed strong, heavily boned males with long refined heads – a very difficult combination to achieve.

Present-day males often stand barely 22 inches (56cm) at the shoulder. They carry comparatively light bone yet heads are shorter and

A well-balanced Collie, at 12 months, illustrating excellent conformation with sloping shoulders and powerful hindquarters.

wider. Curiously, these smaller, lighter boned animals do not show a corresponding increase in activity. My own Ch. Lad of Ladypark, who was born in 1946, stood 25¼ inches (64.1cm) at the shoulder. He carried much heavier bone than the average male Collie of today but was an extremely active dog. He could clear a five-bar gate without touching it and scale a six-foot fence with ease. There are not many present-day champions who could emulate him.

I would say that at the time of writing, the English Collie is smaller in size than he has been since dog shows started. There are several reasons for this. The smaller dog fits more easily into our present life-style, where space is at a premium. The demand on the pet market is for a medium-size dog. From the exhibitor's point of view, the smaller, shorter legged dog shows less daylight under him and can be presented in the ring almost three months earlier than his old-fashioned counterpart. He can start winning at six months of age (unheard of before the war), and his early success attracts breeders' attention to his possibilities as a stud dog and so the trend is perpetuated. But probably the main reason is the preference of some judges for small, feminine bitches, many of them under the Standard minimum height of 20 inches (51cm) at the shoulder. Small, fine bitches breed small, fine dogs and you have only to look round today's show rings to see how much size and majesty has been lost in today's Collies. However, fashions change and I believe that the time will come when we will once again see a stronger more active Collie dominating our rings.

Colour Inheritance

There are three recognised colours of Collies in Europe – sable, which varies between light gold and dark shaded; tricolour, which as its name implies consists of three colours (black, white and tan markings); and blue merle, described as a clear silvery blue, splashed and marbled with black. This also carries the same type of tan markings as the tricolour. All carry the characteristic markings of white collar, white front, white tail tip and white legs and feet to a greater or lesser extent.

In the USA, white Collies are recognised and shown with considerable success both in Open and in Special White classes. These are bred from white factored Collies of the ordinary colours and are not the defective whites sometimes obtained when you breed merle to merle. In Britain, whites are barred from the show ring altogether. This prejudice against a very attractive colour has its roots in the working origins of the breed. A dog that is clearly visible against all backgrounds and in all weather conditions is vital for easy control at a distance. A white dog is difficult to distinguish from sheep and is almost impossible to spot in snow. Furthermore, sheep do not react in the same way, tending to stare at an unusually coloured dog, questioning his authority in a way they would not dare to do with the more familiar tricolour or black and white.

If we adhere to the principle that we breed to a Standard in order to produce a dog best fitted for the work for which he is intended, then there can be little support for the introduction of whites into the show ring, however decorative such dogs might be. Almost all the original working dogs were tricolour or a dilution of that colour, the blue merle.

The introduction of sable colouring has been credited to one dog, Old Cockie. His antecedants are shrouded in mystery and it is quite likely that he owed his unusual colouring to a distant forebear of uncertain breed. It is likely that his reputation as a sire was entirely built on the colour that he threw, as it proved very dominant and quickly became fashionable.

Sables were an immediate success in the show ring and most of the high prices paid for Collies in that era were paid for dogs of that colour. All kinds of sables were popular but the majority were shaded or gold overlaid with black to a greater or lesser degree. Until some forty years ago, one or two tricolours could be expected in every litter. If you had suggested to a breeder in the immediate post-war era that it would be possible to completely eliminate the tricolour from sable breeding, he would have looked over your shoulder for the man in the white coat. Such a theory would have been dismissed as the product of an irrational mind. Yet today you can look round the ring and see up to fifty golden sable Collies in one class and scarcely a tricolour or shaded sable amongst them. This transformation is due entirely to one dog, Int. Ch. Lochinvar of Ladypark.

Born in 1947, Lochinvar was a big golden sable with a well-placed almond eye and a sweet expression. He was a lovely natured dog and breeders flocked to use him. He bred pure for sable, i.e. whether the bitch was tricolour or shaded sable, Lochinvar sired only sable puppies. This was all the more remarkable because both his parents, Eden Examine and Ch. Beulah's Golden Flora were shaded sables and he had one tricolour and three shaded sable grandparents. His brother, Ch. Lad of Ladypark, was about as dark a shaded sable as it was possible to get and sired many tricolours. Lochinvar, then, was a 'sport' – one of those curious quirks of nature that revolutionises plant and animal breeding from time to time.

Golden sable was Miss Grey's favourite colour and by judicious line breeding to Lochinvar she was able to establish a strain of sable Collies that never produced a tricolour. Several of them inherited Lochinvar's genes for breeding pure for sable and, thus, the post-war dominance of golden sables in the ring, was established. There are several strains of Collies that breed only sables today. In fact, many of the golden sables border on the 'cream or straw coloured' dogs mentioned in the Standard as being undesirable.

It is a great pity that we see so few of the heavily coated shaded sables that used to dominate the ring in pre-war days. The texture of the shaded sable's coat is, generally speaking, much harsher and carries a sheen that is lacking in the ubiquitous golden sable. The most beautiful of all sable colouring has virtually disappeared altogether. This is the glorious fire-gold or fox-red sable whose red gold coat seems to catch fire in the sunshine. Mrs George of the famous Beulah Collies had several of this colour of which she was very proud. I myself still have two 'old-timers' whose colouring is remarked on by all who see them but, unfortunately, have nothing to carry on the line. This colour is easy to distinguish at eight weeks. The bright red hairs are clearly visible amongst the puppy fluff if you run your hands through the coat. If you find such a puppy in your next litter that otherwise pleases you, hang on to him – he may prove to be another Lochinvar and produce generations of fire-golds.

You can improve the colour of your sables by careful selection. All things being equal, pick the puppy with the richest coloured mask. He will never give you washed out sables. Neither the fire-gold nor the shaded sable can be produced without some tricolour blood in the background, but if you are going to use a tricolour to improve sable colouring, be careful to pick a really black tricolour with rich orange tan markings. A rusty tricolour with pale tan will do more harm than good.

My research into colour breeding has convinced me of one thing – the key to all colour breeding lies with the tricolour. Whether you are endeavouring to breed richer sables or clearer blue merles, you must start with a tricolour, and a tricolour of good colouring himself. Many breeders are under the misconception that if you breed tricolour to tricolour (which incidentally can only produce tricolours), you will improve the density of black in the progeny. This is not necessarily so.

Whether or not they produce good coloured tricolours will depend entirely on their colour genes. Tricolour is a recessive colour so there must be two tricolour genes present for the dog to be a tricolour. There will be four if you mate tricolour to tricolour. You will probably have noticed, as you look round the ring, how much the density of black varies from tricolour to tricolour. The true jet black coat that never rusts out however much it is exposed to sun, sea and salt air, is rare. If you have such a Collie, treasure him as he will be invaluable for colour breeding. The majority of Collies are a good black for most of the year but tend to rust out in high summer or when moulting. The third type is the really rusty tricolour, which is a horrible colour. In the first case, both tricolour genes are blue-black, in the second, there may be one black gene and one rust gene and in the last, there may well be two rust genes.

The easiest time to pick your tricolour for his colour is in the nest when the coat is at its shortest. It is surprising the variation in colour that can occur in a litter of tricolours. At that time it is easily discernible. Most breeders seem to believe that the rusty tricolour is the result of too much sable breeding. You will often hear ring siders pointing out a rusty tricolour and stating just this opinion. They are totally

Bermarks Barley Sugar illustrating a well-bent stifle and perpendicular hocks.

wrong. Unless the sable is an homozygous sable (such as Lochinvar), he will be carrying one sable gene and one tricolour gene. A sable parent's sable gene cannot affect the tricolour's colour, only his tricolour gene can do that. It follows, therefore, that two sables, both carrying the jet black tricolour gene will produce better colour tricolours than two tricolours mated together that are carrying rust genes.

The difficulty here is to pick out the sables that are carrying the true black genes. You must look not only at colouring (usually shaded), but also at the richness of the mask. Just as the blue-black tricolour carries rich tan face markings, so the sable will carry a richly coloured mask. It will also be necessary to consider both parents and progeny. If one of the parents is a true black or the dog has produced at least one litter of true black puppies, then it is highly likely that he will carry the true black gene. He will be a far better proposition than a rusty tricolour.

You might think that the production of a jet black tricolour would be an end in itself. Indeed, there are few more attractive sights than the gleaming black tricolour, with his dazzling white ruff and rich tan markings contrasted against the sunlit grass of the show ring. But the production of a good-coloured tricolour has more far-reaching importance. He holds the key to the production of possibly the most beautiful of all colours – the clear silvery blue merle.

Ever since I can remember, breeders have been brainwashed into believing that only blue-bred tricolours were capable of producing this lovely colour. Sable-bred tricolours, we have been told repeatedly, will give us nothing but muddy blues. Consequently, many breeders have regarded merle breeding as something of a mystique that only blue merle specialists were capable of fathoming. Only they could run on the generations of blue-bred tricolours necessary for success. At the risk of being branded a heretic, I would like to state that, in my opinion, nothing is further from the truth. Rusty tricolours (carrying two rust genes), will produce rusty or muddy coloured blues, no matter how noble their blue breeding. A jet black tricolour that is sable-bred will, on the other hand, (if bred to a silvery blue merle), produce the same colour. The important thing to remember is that it is the jet black tricolour, carrying two black genes (whether sable-bred, tricolour-bred or blue-bred), that will give you beautiful coloured blues.

If you follow this argument to its logical conclusion, you will be forced to admit that the breeding of a sable carrying the jet black genes to a silvery blue merle will also result in beautifully coloured merles. The practice has been widely adopted in the USA, with striking results, but has always been considered taboo in England. The worry is that it will result in blue-eyed sables. The chances of this are greatly reduced if the merle has been bred from dark-eyed merles and not wall- or blue-eyed merles.

One of the loveliest sable bitches ever bred was the very dark-eyed Ch. Lena of Ladypark, daughter of the shaded sable, Lucky of Ladypark and the dark-eyed merle Lilac of Ladypark. It is not a project to be undertaken by the novice and should never be attempted between a golden sable and a merle. Such a union would almost certainly result in sable merles and blue-eyed sables. Sable merles can be distinguished in the nest by their rather pretty beige colouring with darker marbled markings. These markings often fade with adulthood and the sable merle is almost indistinguishable from a golden sable. It is only when you breed from one that their true status is revealed.

Another way to obtain instant success (or sometimes instant disaster) is to breed a clear silvery blue to another of the same colour. It must be stressed that this colour need not be all over. Some of the best merles have been produced from merles very heavily marked with black. It is the actual colour of blue that is important. Equally important is that black splotches, however heavy, are a true black and not a rusty black. This is not a mating that can be recommended to the novice as it may well result in the birth of one or more defective whites.

In Germany, where dog breeding is strictly controlled by the breed clubs, such a mating is forbidden, because of this danger. So far, this prohibition has not spread to other parts of Europe although the German viewpoint has been widely campaigned. In England, experience leads us to believe that there is no reason to suppress the merle to merle mating if due care is taken. It is essential, however, that at least one of the grandparents be a tricolour. The defective whites will be pure white in appearance possibly with a few merle spots. Pigmentation on eyelids, nose, mouth and pads will be almost completely lacking. Eyes, if present, and often they are not, will be pale blue. Almost certainly they will be deaf, and have very poor eyesight. Such animals are commonly destroyed at birth.

Breeders usually resort to mating their merle bitch to a merle dog, risking the appearance of defective whites, because they think that this will improve their chances of obtaining more merles than tricolours in the resulting litter. I believe this to be a fallacy. During the time that Int. Ch. Incredibly Blu di Cambiano was at stud with me in England, I kept careful records of his progeny. From six merle-to-merle matings he sired eighteen merles, twenty tricolours and seven defective whites. From ten merle-to-tricolour matings he sired twenty-seven merles, twenty-nine tricolours and no whites, of course. One of the merle-to-merle matings produced five tricolours only. The chances of producing more merles than tricolours are very slightly enhanced by using a tricolour as one of the parents. Some tricolours are particularly good at throwing a high proportion of merles in their offspring and it is worth making enquiries on this subject before deciding on the right dog for your bitch.

Very rarely will you get a white puppy born from merle parents that has sufficient merling on the head to prevent it from being blind and deaf. He will still lack pigmentation on his eyelids, lips and nose but otherwise will be perfectly normal. Such a dog is likely to produce excellent colour merles and has the added advantage that, bred to a tricolour, he will produce only merle puppies. It will not be possible to show him, of course, and it is only the bigger breeders who can afford to run him on. It is sometimes worth enquiring as to whether there is such a dog available at stud when visiting a kennel.

Homozygous white merle. (Photograph by Eva Maria Kramer.)

All the different colours have their adherents. Some judges are known to have strong preferences and it is seldom worthwhile showing a merle under a judge who is known not to care for them. Many judges are prejudiced against white blazes on the head which are said to spoil the expression, so much so that the blaze has almost disappeared from the show ring. I think this is a pity. A dog that carries a blaze is almost certainly carrying the white factor. This is easy to distinguish because a white factored dog will have an unbroken white line from under the chin, down the chest under the belly and down the inside of the hind leg till it joins the white hock and foot. It is worth considering keeping such a puppy, all other things being equal, as he will invariably produce better marked puppies than a non-white-factored Collie. Originally, nearly all Collies had a white blaze on the face, just as in the present Border Collie, but it has gradually been bred out. Many of us remember nostalgically the old upstanding Collie carrying a white star on his forehead and a huge shawl collar – a truly spectacular animal.

3

Buying a Collie

Before you decide on the breed most suitable for your purposes you should consider very carefully indeed your reasons for wanting a dog. There are many advantages to dog owning. A dog is, or should be, a much loved member of the family. He is always pleased to see you and ready to welcome you home with shining eyes and wagging tail. You will never have a more loyal friend and companion. You need never feel alone when you have a dog. However, there are some drawbacks – the hairs on your best suit, the muddy feet on your clean floor, the additional cost to your budget of his food and vet bills. A dog has to be fed and exercised daily. Regular walks will keep both you and your dog fit and can be an enjoyable experience for you both but unless you have a very large garden you must be prepared to take him out in all winds and weathers and in the British climate it is no good waiting for the sun to shine before you start your walk! Holidays must be considered. A dog is an undoubted tie and unless arrangements can be made for a reliable dog-sitter then a booking must be made, well in advance, at a well-run, secure boarding kennel. It is a recipe for disaster to rely on friends to look after your dog while you are away, especially if your dog is a Collie with a highly developed homing instinct. Finally, you must face the fact that a dog's life is comparatively short. Losing a much loved pet can be a traumatic experience and over the years I have had many letters from Collie owners proving just this point. Kipling put it rather well:

> Brothers and Sisters, I bid you beware
> Of giving your heart to a dog to tear

If, in spite of all this, you decide you want a dog then you must consider carefully whether the Collie is the right breed for you.

If you are looking for a medium-sized, sweet-natured, easily trained, companion dog then in many respects the Collie would seem ideal. Nevertheless, the breed has its drawbacks (as do all breeds), and these must be taken into consideration. Due to his long association with man in his shepherding work, the Collie craves human companionship and hates to be left alone. He is certainly not the breed for you if you are out at work all day. He may well bark in your absence and cause a nuisance. A puppy left on his own may even prove destructive through boredom.

The heavy coat the Collie carries is not a problem for most of the year. Unlike some breeds with shaggy coats, it does not tangle or knot. As a result, the Collie always enjoys being groomed and his coat can be kept immaculate with a routine weekly groom. Most Collies will commence moulting around their first birthday and it is advisable to increase the number of grooming sessions to once daily until all the old coat has been removed. As soon as the new coat comes through, you will be over the worst and can revert to grooming once a week. This puppy moult is the worst. Adult moults, with the exception of a bitch after a litter, are not so severe. Nevertheless, it is something which has to be taken into consideration. If you or any member of your household are fanatically house-proud then perhaps you should think twice about having a Collie, or even a dog at all. It is most unfair to banish your Collie to an outhouse for reasons which he cannot understand. It is as well to start as you mean to go on, so do not allow him on the furniture (however cute he may look, curled up on the settee). Provide him with his own rug in a secluded place, well away from the fire. Collies are not fire spaniels and most prefer a cool place away from direct heat.

Before making a final decision that the Collie is the breed for you, you must carefully consider his temperament. Breeds are as different in temperament as they are in looks. A great many are bred to work, either to hunt or to kill vermin or to act as guard dogs. The Collie was the shepherd's dog, his herder, his protector and often his only companion. As a result, the Collie has an almost telepathic relationship with his owner and I have been told many tales of Collies communicating with their owners without a word being spoken. I have one friend who swears that she has only to think about taking her two Collies for a walk for them to rise to their feet and go expectantly to the door waiting for her to get their leads. I have another friend whose husband habitually takes his Collie to the pub with him. When she feels that they have been out long enough my friend communicates her thoughts to the dog who promptly catches hold of her husband's sleeve and insists that they return home.

Some years ago I sold a tricolour Collie to a home in the country where he became the constant guard and companion of two young girls. Every day he waited at the end of the lane for them to come home from school. Each year when the children went on their annual fortnight's holiday the dog remained at home pining, scarcely eating, until the day they were due to return. On that day he got up a different dog, ate his breakfast eagerly and trotted down the lane to wait patiently till they returned. They were never able to discover how he knew but he invariably did and they firmly believed it was by telepathy. I think that something in the household preparations may have triggered off his reaction but one cannot be sure.

One of our old champion bitches who was noted more for the sweetness of her nature than the brilliance of her intelligence, always knew of my husband's return some ten minutes before he appeared. She would get up, tail waving, and go to the gate to meet him. The most likely explanation was that she could pick out the sound of his car, at some distance, and before the other dogs, but we could never be certain. It could not have been a matter of timing (although most Collies have a very well developed sense of time), because his return was always irregular.

One of her granddaughters, that I sold as a puppy, was instrumental in saving a life when she was only nine months old. Her owner was attracted by her barking and running backwards and forwards between the kitchen window and the fence at the bottom of the garden. It was a six-foot (2m) solid wood fence but as she was obviously trying to attract her owner's attention the lady went to investigate. Peeping over, she found her neighbour lying on the ground unconscious, still attached to the live cable of her electric lawnmower. If the victim had not been wearing rubber boots at the time the accident might well have proved fatal. As it was, the puppy's owner was able to switch off the current and call an ambulance in time. The puppy was rewarded with a large bone and a piece in the local newspaper but no one could understand how she knew about the accident on the other side of a fence which she was unable to see through. Perhaps it was just instinct that told her there was something wrong and she needed to get help.

All Collies hate violence as it is not part of their nature, but they will spring to the defence of their owner with quite astonishing speed if they sense a threat. Many an owner has been amazed at how quickly his gentle affectionate Collie has been transformed into a protective guard dog on occasions. He will not need an order; he works by telepathy. I have myself experienced this on a couple of occasions and each time the dog came from nowhere, launched himself at the intruder, knocked him down and dared him to get up again.

I once sold an eight-week-old puppy that grew up into a very friendly sensible dog and was the constant companion of the young son of the family, Paul. One day, Paul was watching his Collie playing with another dog in the distance when two older boys came up and started to bully him. There was no sound, just a flurry of golden fur as Prince launched himself through the air. The next instant one boy was running away while the other was lying on the ground, being dragged away by his ankle. This is typical protective action by a Collie. They may not have the ferocity of a guarding breed but they will instinctively try to push or, in this case, pull danger away from you. Never think that your gentle, docile Collie would be useless to defend you. The speed with which he reacts is quite breath-taking.

The Collie's dislike of violence often spills over into the nursery. They hate the sound of children quarrelling and will often push between squabbling children in order to separate them. The other day, two strapping young men told me that their Collie ruled them with a rod of iron even after they were grown up! Even friendly wrestling was forbidden. Lassie wanted a peaceful home and she made sure she got it!

Once you have finally made up your mind that the Collie is the dog for you, it is as well to consider your own life-style and to decide whether a puppy or an adult Collie would be most suitable for you. Have you got the facilities to cope with an exuberant, not yet house-trained puppy? Whether you choose an adult or a puppy, you will need either a totally enclosed garden or a well-fenced area where your Collie can remain in safety. You will find that very few people who come to your door, delivering goods or leaflets will close the garden gate behind them, so beware. If your Collie has free run of the garden it is only too easy for him to slip unnoticed through the open gate, with dire results. Most of the hardened 'latch key' dogs have a highly developed road sense. It is more often the beloved family pet that is killed on the road.

Nowadays, veterinary advice is geared to advising the public to buy a puppy at six weeks of age, so that he bonds to his owner more firmly. This may well be advisable in a guarding breed but in a breed that becomes as firmly attached to its owner as the Collie I think that eight weeks is quite early enough for a puppy to leave home. Puppies have much to learn in those last two weeks and six weeks is a very difficult age at which to start house-training.

Collies are very good with children!

Whether you should buy a puppy or an adult is a question that needs careful consideration. In most cases where young children are involved it will be better to buy a puppy that can grow up with them. I usually advise families who have small children that a bitch has more mothering instinct and will probably watch over them with more patience and tolerance than a dog. If, on the other hand, the children of the family are older and more energetic and need a dog to play ball and hide-and-seek, and act as a companion/guard on their outings, then usually a dog would be more suitable. In either case, I stress very strongly that a puppy needs plenty of sleep and must have his own quiet place to rest.

While there is an almost irresistible temptation to buy a gorgeous fluffy eight-week-old puppy and watch him grow through the leggy teenage stage into glamorous adulthood, there are many cogent reasons why an adult might be more suited to your particular lifestyle. An adult Collie can make a very loving, sensible companion and it is often possible to obtain a well behaved adult through your veterinary surgeon or local newspaper, that, through no fault of his own, is seeking a new home. I do not think it matters a great deal whether you choose a dog or a bitch. Both can be equally affectionate and the problem of a bitch coming into season can be overcome by the use of proprietary deodorant tablets.

A breeder may have just the Collie you are seeking, which may not have quite fulfilled his early promise in the show ring or may be a non-breeder, which the breeder will be very happy to part with, for a reasonable sum, in order to secure for him a loving permanent home. Occasionally, an adult that has been badly treated or neglected can be obtained from a Collie Rescue kennel, but it must be emphasised that such a dog could have lost his faith in human nature and will require much patient loving care. It takes a very special kind of person to take in a Rescue Collie, but I have heard some heart-warming tales of the reward it brings to both dog and owner.

Finally, you must decide which colour Collie you prefer. Sable and white is the most popular, largely because of the tremendous influence that the 'Lassie' films have had, but both tricolour and blue merle have their adherents and are equally beautiful. The colour is really immaterial, for the Collie character transcends such external trappings. The love and devotion of your Collie will shine through his eyes, no matter what his colour may be.

How to Approach the Breeder for a Show Puppy

Let us suppose that you have spent some time studying books and photos, you have attended one or two shows and watched the Collie judging, you have decided on the type you like and you are ready to approach your chosen breeder with your requirements. It is not advisable to quote the Standard and demand a puppy that is perfect in every department. The breeder has spent a lifetime trying to breed just such a puppy! All Collies have faults but if there are some that you find unacceptable then it as well to say so and such puppies can be eliminated from those offered to you.

The sort of letter that any breeder is delighted to receive is one that says something about yourself and the conditions under which you propose to keep the puppy. No breeder worth his salt is going to part with one of his treasured pups to someone who is out at work all day and proposes to keep a puppy by himself in a kennel.

The ideal purchaser, from the breeder's point of view, is one who is prepared to wait for the right puppy and for whom colour and sex are less important than show quality. That gives the breeder the chance to mull over his stock and possibly place something with you that he had originally planned to keep himself. While it is advisable to start with a bitch, it is often easier to obtain a show-quality dog puppy. Competition is not quite so keen in dogs and a dog puppy has more coat which he will hold longer than a bitch. He will give you a lot of fun in the ring while you are learning the ropes and before you are ready to breed your first litter. A top-quality puppy will always cost money, but price is not the main consideration for a reputable breeder. He will be looking for someone who is willing to listen and act on good advice, who will rear the puppy and produce him in the show ring at the right time and in top condition. Nothing is more heart-breaking for a breeder than to sell a good show prospect and see him brought into the ring some months later, all legs and wings with no body and no coat simply because he has been incorrectly reared. Equally infuriating is to see a pet puppy who was sold as a pet being brought into the ring, when the breeder would have sold the owner a show-quality puppy if they had been honest with him.

Be frank with your breeder. If you want a pet say so, but if you want to show your puppy make sure the breeder is aware of that fact. Only then will he produce his top-quality puppies destined for the show ring. Even then, I would advise you to rely on the breeder's choice. I stress this point as only he knows how his line is likely to develop. Believe me, he will be as anxious for his most promising puppy for sale to go to a good show home as you will be to have him. So often I hear novices proudly announce that they selected their own puppy against the advice of the breeder who wanted them to have a different one. They seem to think the breeder was trying to palm them off with a poor puppy and they were clever enough to outwit him. This is far from the truth. The breeder wants you to take a puppy into the ring that will do both you and his kennel justice. After all, it will be carrying his prefix, as under Kennel Club rules only the breeder can register a puppy.

It is quite probable that the puppies that the breeder has been running on for himself will be of varying ages. He may offer you one of his four- to five-month-old puppies that is going through the ugly stage. Such a puppy may look too long in the head with a receding skull and a bump instead of a depression between the eyes. His legs may seem to be uncontrollable when he moves. His puppy fluff will have disappeared leaving no coat and his ears will be so heavy it seems impossible that they will ever go up. He will be nothing like the kind of Collie you had in mind. Now you are in a quandary. Should

149

you trust the breeder when he says this puppy will make a nice Collie or would it be better to go up the road and buy one of those adorable fluffy puppies that another breeder is advertising as certain champions? You tell him you will think about it and walk away. Some months later you see the ugly duckling in the ring and you cannot believe your eyes. His skull has levelled up, his ears are perfect, he has a gorgeous coat and moves smoothly and soundly round the ring. Now he is exactly what you wanted and you kick yourself for not having bought him when you had the chance.

The moral is, trust your breeder. Only he knows how his line is going to finish. He will be carrying, in his mind's eye, a picture of almost every dog in the puppy's pedigree, many of them he will have had in his own kennel, and will have watched them develop from puppy to adulthood. Looking at the ungainly youngster in his kennel you will see only the ugly duckling, he will see the swan, though sometimes it takes longer than even he expects for the transformation to take place.

A few years ago I bought a bitch puppy from a famous line. I was particularly anxious to have her because she was descended, in tail-female line, from one of my old champions. I saw her at eight weeks and liked her. I took her home. Head, expression, coat conformation, movement, temperament – she had it all. I was delighted with her. At five months I began to have misgivings, at six months I had grave doubts and at eight months, when she should have been coming right, she looked like every breeder's nightmare. This was confirmed by her breeders when they saw her.

They were appalled. They apologised profusely for selling me such a poor specimen and offered to exchange her. I refused their kind offer because I wanted to retain that particular blood line. I bred a very nice litter from her and, almost immediately, she began to blossom into the kind of bitch we had all expected her to be. She was well on the way to her title when her breeders saw her again. They could not believe the transformation.

Show Puppy Selection

If you ask a dozen breeders at what age they like to choose their puppies, you are likely to get a dozen different answers. A surprising number will say, 'at birth', or, 'I like to pick my puppies while they are still wet'. Others will opt for five or eight weeks. The cynical will say, 'at twelve months precisely, because it is not till a puppy passes into adulthood that one can make an accurate assessment of his chances in the Puppy ring.' I personally like to make my choice out of a litter at eight weeks but every line is different and experienced breeders know what to look for at certain ages in their own line.

Not everyone is an experienced breeder and one of the questions I am most frequently asked is how to select the best puppy in a litter. I can only tell them what I look for in my own puppies. Basic head shape does not change with age. I look for a good oblong-shape head with the muzzle almost as wide as the skull and I discard the pointed foreface which is noticeably narrower than the skull. I like to see a well-finished blunt ended muzzle with a good underjaw, which will be apparent from the earliest stages. I do not worry if the nose appears to drop off at the end as this will correct itself as cartilage turns to bone. Really good heads have a smooth look even at this stage; the apple-headed puppy will never have a classic head. A good stop will be apparent even at this age by a certain cleanness between the eyes.

Games in the snow at the du Clos kennels of M. Castronovo, Belgium.

151

The ears, which are sealed for the first fortnight, lie flat against the skull and should be small and not too far down the side of the head. I find that eyes which open early, at about ten days, are always the roundest. Good almond eyes often take till fourteen days to open.

Take time to watch your puppies when they are nursing. You will quickly single out the puppy with the best arch and length to the neck and spring of ribs can also be evaluated at this stage. When all the tails are wagging in unison at the milk bar, from three days onward, you can spot the desired long, thin whippy tails. Short, thick otter tails are prone to end up carried too high over the back. Good strong round bone cannot be mistaken in the nest. This is particularly important in a dog puppy and if he combines it with an oblong head and a good reach of neck you have a puppy that will be worth watching.

At a fortnight, eyes can be given their first assessment. The puppies with round eyes and the puppies with good almond eyes will be immediately apparent. At this stage, they will be blue and colour can only be determined at a much later date. Unfortunately, some Collies have eyes which tend to lighten with age and what appears to be a lovely dark almond eye in a puppy may end up almost yellow in a yearling. This is not common but it does tend to run in families and only the breeder will know whether it is a point to worry about or not. All puppies have a third eyelid or haw across the inside corner of the eye. Usually, this is dark and virtually invisible but sometimes, one or both will be white and they tend to spoil the expression. If very small, they will virtually disappear with age but if they are really prominent at fourteen days of age, they are likely to remain so. They are more common in blue merles where they are considered acceptable, probably because they blend in with the colour of the dog and are not so noticeable.

At about six weeks, you can usually pick out the puppies with the best conformation. I look for a good reach of neck as this is almost always coupled with well-laid shoulders. Almost invariably, such a puppy will have good angulation at the rear end. Make sure this angulation is coming from the femur and not from the hocks being bent under the body. To the uninitiated these may look like beautifully angulated hocks but they will end up as sickle hocks which place great strain on the joints and prevent the puppy from ever moving with drive. I like a puppy to have a nice square back end and move away with a reasonable amount of space between the hind legs. Most puppies are a bit wobbly at this age and you should not pay too much attention to movement. Look instead for good conformation. The puppy that appears sound at this age may well be the one that ends up with straight hocks.

Good shoulder placement is the key to good conformation and good conformation is the key to good movement. If you really are at a loss, pick the puppy with the best reach of neck and you will not go far wrong. A lot can be learned by watching puppies at play. The attentive, inquisitive puppy that is interested in everything and is able to concentrate for several minutes on end, is likely to be a better show prospect than the bored, inattentive puppy.

I would never advise anyone to make their final selection until eight weeks. I am a firm believer in the adage, 'What you see at eight weeks is what you will get at eight months'. Occasionally, you have to wait a bit longer than eight months for a puppy to mature, but if you are patient he should return to the quality you saw at eight weeks. One thing that is difficult to assess at eight weeks is coat. Coats vary tremendously from line to line. Sometimes a litter of big fluffy-coated puppies turns out with flat outer coats and little or no undercoats. Look particularly for density of undercoat. The only reliable tip I can give you is one I use myself. A good coated Collie will have noticeably thick and quite long feathering on his front legs even at such a young age as eight weeks. Puppies with little or no feathering at this age will be, at best, late maturers and, at worst, permanent no-coaters.

All puppies tend to curl their tails in play, but they should put them down when they come to such serious business as eating. Beware of the puppy that curls his tail over his back while at the dish, particularly if the tail is short and thick.

Much of the appeal of a Collie puppy lies in his expression and at eight weeks the expression should be there for all to see – impossible to describe but unmistakable when you meet it – a combination of sweetness and mischief. Avoid the puppy with a hard expression, it will remain hard. All other things being equal, choose the puppy with the sweetest expression. You will not regret it.

If you have learnt a little about Collies you will have some idea what you are looking for. Avoid choosing your puppy before eight weeks if you are seeing the litter for the first time. Take your time. Stand back and look at them through the wire if possible. Make a mental note of any puppy that makes an immediate impact. Ask the breeder to remove any that are not available or are the wrong sex. Examine the remainder in detail.

First the head. Take a puppy's head gently between your hands, talking to him all the while, and look at it from the front. Is the muzzle full, smooth and rounded; does it taper smoothly into the skull in an unbroken line? Is the skull reasonably flat? A perfect flat skull cannot be expected at this age but you should avoid a pup with a bump like an egg as it will never completely flatten.

Examine the head from above. Is it balanced? In other words, does the length of the muzzle, measured from the tip to the inside corner of the eye, equal the length of the skull measured from the same corner to the back of the skull? This measurement may change as the puppy grows in stages but it should finish up with the same proportions it had at eight weeks. Pull back the puppy fluff over the ears and examine the profile. Look for the two parallel planes of skull and muzzle, with just a small break at the stop. Make certain the stop is in the right place, between the eyes and not half-way down the muzzle. Only a slight depression is needed but it must be there. A rise between the eyes indicates that the head may never come right.

Examine the profile carefully and note if the muzzle has a blunt well-finished end supported by a strong underjaw. Avoid a puppy with a weak or shark underjaw. Check that the teeth meet in a scissor bite but do not worry unduly if the puppy is slightly overshot at this stage. This will correct itself in time. Check for veins in the foreface. These tend to come up if a puppy is excited which he is bound to be at his first few shows. Many puppies develop lumps, bumps and veins as they are teething. If you are looking at an older puppy, remember that large teeth coming through cause bumps and missing teeth cause dents, so take this into account.

Eyes, as the Standard tells us, are a very important feature. Look for an almond eye in preference to a round eye. The shape of the eye will never alter but as the head lengthens, so the setting of the eye will become more oblique. Unless you are looking at a blue merle with wall eyes, the colour should be as dark as possible as eye colour on many Collies tends to lighten with age. Look for the puppy that seems to be smiling at you with his eyes.

Ears are difficult to judge at this stage, but neat, small, correctly set ears are usually well cupped at the set on. There seems to be an increasing tendency for some strains to have ears set half-way down the skull, which makes the foreface appear overlong. They should be set not too far apart at the top of the skull. A puppy with perfectly set, small, mobile ears is a joy but he is also a rarity. Large, floppy ears are impossible to gauge at this early age. If they are correctly set, they should go up eventually but some strains are known to have ears which do not go up until nine months of age.

Having decided which puppy has the best head and expression, check the other points I have already mentioned. Note the puppy with the longest neck, a good spring of ribs, a good curve to the femur and the shortest hocks. Check for tail length and setting. The bone of the tail must reach at least to the hocks but it is just as important that it should be set well down the croup and not level with the back line. Watch the puppies move. Even at this early stage you can see the puppy that reaches out with his front feet. You can expect a bit of wobble on the joints but there should be no real unsoundness. Very seldom will you come across a puppy that excels in all departments. It is usually a question of making up your mind which faults you can live with and which ones you cannot live with. Pick your puppy accordingly.

4

Puppy Management and Training

When you collect your puppy from the breeder it is as well to take a cardboard box with plenty of newspaper to make a warm bed inside. Your passenger can then hold the box and gently play with the puppy on the way home without fear of him being sick over them. The human contact will reassure the puppy who has suddenly been removed from his familiar surroundings and make the journey a less alarming experience. If the puppy enjoys his first car journey he will always be a good traveller.

You will receive from the breeder, a diet sheet which should be strictly adhered to for the first few weeks of the puppy's life. If possible, obtain a week's supply of the food the puppy has been reared on so that the puppy will not be upset by a change in diet. It is not possible to give an exact diet to suit every puppy but basically it will consist of four meals a day plus a drink of milk. A suitable and convenient diet would consist of:

Breakfast – two Weetabix in warm milk.
Lunch – 6oz (170g) chopped meat or tripe with a little soaked biscuit meal.
Tea – scrambled egg on toast or grated cheese on brown bread.
Supper – as lunch.
Hot milky bedtime drink.

Once a day, add a little powdered bonemeal to the food, and if you are feeding tripe be sure to add a teaspoonful of vegetable oil every day.

Increase the quantities gradually as the puppy grows bigger but decrease the number of feeds. By the time the puppy is four months old he will need only three meals a day and this number can be decreased to two at the age of six months. The puppy will be growing so quickly at this stage that he will need far more food to satisfy his energy requirements than he will need when he reaches adulthood.

By the time you receive your puppy, he will (if you bought from a reputable breeder), have been wormed at least twice. He will need regular worming after that and it is as well to consult your veterinary surgeon on this matter when your puppy has his inoculations.

A great deal can be done by the breeder to ensure that his puppies leave the home kennel well equipped to deal confidently with any problems they may encounter in the outside world. It will be difficult for a puppy that was kennel-bred and never saw a human being, apart from his breeder, not to be a little overawed when he is taken out into the world for the very first time, so I like to accustom my puppies to human noises and experiences from the very earliest age. My puppies are programmed from birth to become used to human hands picking them up and stroking them lovingly. Although their ears are sealed until they are a fortnight old, they can feel from the first. By the time their eyes are open, they are beginning to respond to voice and touch and before long they wag their tails as soon as they are picked up.

I never object to visitors seeing my puppies from an early age because I believe that the benefits the puppies derive from contact with strangers far outweigh the risk of infection. If children wish to pick up a puppy, I insist they sit on the ground first. Puppies are wriggly creatures and can easily be dropped and children should never be left alone with them. Children and puppies have a natural affinity and the Collie that establishes a bond at an early age will grow up to love children all his life.

It is a good idea to bring individual puppies into the house for an hour or two each day. This will accustom them to strange machines such as vacuum cleaners and washing machines so that when they enter their new homes, they will do so with confidence.

It is also possible to instil the rudiments of house-training at the same time. If your puppies get used to going on newspaper in their kennel the battle is already half-won. A good method of house-training is to put the puppy to sleep on a blanket inside one of the folding metal cages that are available at all the major shows. The puppy will be most anxious not to soil his bed and if you put him out in the garden every time he wakes up, he will quickly get the message. Alternatively, you can place a piece of turf in his cage.

These cages are excellent for leaving puppies in, either in the car or when you go out. If you place a blanket over them they form a nice draught-free 'cave' which the puppy will quickly learn to accept as his home. He can sleep there at night or whenever he has to be left on his own. Make sure he has his toys with him and you can leave him for short periods during the day without having to worry about your furniture. Most puppies go through a 'chewy' stage while they are teething and these cages really are the answer to destructive puppies.

Even if you do not invest in a cage, you should still find your Collie easy to house-train. I put down newspaper in one corner of my puppies' run, as far away from their kennel as possible. They soon learn to use this corner. When they leave for their new homes, I advise owners to put down newspaper for the first few nights, not near their beds but by the back door. It is then a simple matter of moving the newspaper outside and gradually to the spot they wish him to use. I always stress that puppies are like babies at that age – they have very little control over their bodily functions, and constant watchfulness is the key to a successful house-training. You should always put your puppy outside immediately after feeding.

Watch for the puppy to wake up. The first thing he will do is yawn, then he will stretch and after he has walked a few paces he will spend a penny, so before he has the chance, scoop him up and put him outside. If he does have an accident, scold him gently and put him outside. Never, never smack your puppy. Human hands are for patting and caressing, not for punishing, a lesson it is vital for him to learn when it comes to show ring training – he will need all the confidence he can get when strange judges start to feel him all over. If you must punish your puppy, then take him by the scruff of the neck and give him a little shake, just as his mother would. He will hate it but he will respect you.

The Collie is a very sensitive animal. The very fact that you are displeased with him will be enough to reduce most Collies to a state of abject misery. His sole object in life is to please you so a severe talking to will be all that is necessary if he has misbehaved.

Before taking a puppy out it is wise to accustom him to wearing a collar. When he is used to this, attach his lead to it and practise walking with him until he is happy to move with you. A Collie is, by nature, obedient and you should have no difficulty in teaching him to come when called. Do not make the mistake of only calling him when you want to put his lead on or put him away in his kennel. If necessary, carry a few titbits in your pocket. Call him from time to time and every time he comes, praise him and give him a titbit.

One of the easiest things to teach a Collie is to walk to heel because they have a natural instinct to do just that. If you keep your Collie on the left-hand side and keep him walking between you and a wall there is nowhere he can go other than forward or backward. If he pulls in front, tap him lightly on the nose with a folded newspaper. He will quickly learn that his place is by your side. The Collie is not a natural retriever, so if you aim to work him in obedience then you must encourage him from an early age to retrieve. This is quite easy to do by playing ball with him or throwing his toys for him to fetch. Do not worry if he will not part with them at first or drops them at your feet, the main thing is to teach him to enjoy retrieving. The polish can be put on later.

It is a pity that more people do not train their Collie for obedience. Most Collies have a natural aptitude for it. So much so that there seems scarcely any need to give them any training. Dog training classes are full of undisciplined problem dogs but it is from such unpromising material that future obedience stars are often drawn. The Collie is so amenable to discipline and so eager to please his master that there often seems little point in subjecting him to formal obedience training. This is a pity as a tremendous amount of fun can be had in the obedience sphere both for the owner and the dog. I would urge anyone who owns a young Collie to join their local Dog Training class. He will probably find his dog is a 'natural'.

One problem with Rough Collies is that some of them have a phobia about slippery floors. It helps to cut out the hair between the pads of their feet and there are varying non-slip substances which can be bought to rub on the pads which are helpful. This is a problem that affects show Collies just as much as obedience dogs. Many a promising Collie has thrown away his chance by refusing to move on a slippery floor, much to the chagrin of his handler. There is no easy answer to this problem in the adult Collie as the habit is obviously well established. However, much can be done in a young puppy to stop the habit ever materialising. The secret lies in the three Ps – practice, play and praise. Start your puppy off at eight weeks by bringing him into the kitchen. Make the floor really wet and slippery and put him in the middle. Play with him gently and praise him excessively. Do this every day for a short period and the chances are that he will associate slippery floors with play and you will never have any trouble.

The other, almost insoluble, problem that some owners come across in obedience training has already been mentioned. Unlike most gundogs, the Collie has absolutely no instinct to retrieve. It is, therefore, vital to instil in a puppy the rudiments of retrieving. It is frustrating to have a Collie whose work is excellent in every respect who refuses point-blank to pick up the retrieve article. I have never had much luck with the 'put it in his mouth and make him hold it' method advocated by most Dog Trainers. The look of disdain your Collie gives you as he spits out the article can be quite withering. I use a much quicker and simpler method – bribery. I find it almost fool-proof.

Collect a box of your Collie's favourite titbits. You can use liver if you like but I find liver flavoured cat Munchies equally effective. Rattle your box and get the dog's attention. Place the retrieve article in his mouth. Almost instantly, withdraw it and replace it with a titbit. Do this about twenty times for the first lesson. You can break in your dog gently by using a favourite toy but I prefer to start as I mean to go on and use the dumb-bell.

Next day, repeat the lesson making him hold it a little longer. The next stage is to place the dumb-bell on a chair by his side. He has only to turn his head and pick it up to receive his reward. The first time he does it, you have won the battle. Gradually, you can place it on the floor at greater distances. Make the whole thing into a game. Try hiding the article and praise him as soon as he goes near it. He will have great fun finding it and it will teach him to use his nose – an invaluable lesson when he comes to scent discrimination.

Only when you are confident he will bring back the article from wherever you have placed it, should you begin to throw it for him and tell him to 'fetch'. Most Collies hate loud noises so always throw on grass or a carpet. You can graduate to hard surfaces later. A fortnight from commencing this training, you should have a Collie that will retrieve any article you care to throw. He will already be familiar with a Recall, Sit, Heel routine, which he will have learnt at his training classes, so now all you have to do is to get him to sit in front of you before he hands over the article in exchange for a reward. I know purists will throw up their hands in horror at this method, believing that a dog should work for the love of it, but Collies regard the retrieve as a singularly pointless exercise and quickly lose their enthusiasm without some motivation.

I would like to see Obedience classes at all Collie shows in order to encourage owners to train their dogs. The Border Collie is, of course, the Einstein of the canine race but Roughs and Smooths can more than hold their own with other breeds. In the USA, where Borders are scarcely known, almost one-third of Collies, including show champ-ions, have the letters CD or CDX after their name, indicating that they have reached quite a high level in their obedience training. They are all bred from English imported stock so it is hard to believe that they are any more intelligent than our Collies. They are simply better educated.

The new craze for Agility is sweeping the country and Agility clubs are springing up everywhere. It is unwise to allow your Collie to participate fully until he is at least fourteen months old. Jumping and climbing can seriously damage young joints but some of the ground exercises can be taught with great success. Almost all dogs will benefit from a previous course in obedience as instant reaction to a command may make all the difference in the heat of the moment.

The sport originated as a fun pastime to fill in spaces in the big horse show programmes while the jumps were being changed. It began as a series of jumps for dogs, taken against the clock, and it proved so popular that various obstacles, such as the see-saw, the weave poles and the tunnel, were introduced to make the competition more difficult. The Collies that I have seen participating have been very successful and it keeps both them and their owners fit.

Agility can be very exciting to watch, especially when the competition is keen. When teams are competing against each other the noise can be deafening! The Kennel Club has a special section for Agility and every year the top Agility teams in the country compete in the

Agility over the long jump.

final at Cruft's. It is one of the most popular sections of the show and holds the large audience enthralled. It is difficult to know who enjoys it most – the dogs, who obviously love every moment, the handlers, who must be extremely fit, or the spectators.

One lesson that you yourself must learn (and this is true whether you own one dog or several), is that you are the boss. The dog is, by nature, a pack animal, he is programmed to obey a leader and you are that leader. You must not allow him to challenge your authority and win or you will lose respect in his eyes. Fortunately, this position is not difficult to secure with Collies. All that is needed is firmness.

If and when you add to your pack you will need both tact and leadership to maintain harmony. When you bring home a gorgeous bundle of fluff there will be a great temptation to completely spoil him to the exclusion of others. An older dog will feel hurt and resentful but when he shows his displeasure he will be further punished by being put outside. It is only human nature to try and support the underdog (in this case the new puppy), against the older and stronger one. This is exactly what you must not do. Think of your older dog as your second-in-command which is exactly how your new puppy will see him. Support his authority, make a special fuss of your older dog. Let him be the one that sits next to your chair, make sure that you put his plate down first and do not allow the puppy to go near him when he is feeding. If he snaps at the puppy do not scold him. The puppy must learn his place.

Before long, your older dog will be feeling quite pleased at the new addition to the pack. After all his own status has definitely improved. The puppy has already learnt to accept the authority of his mother and will accept his place in the hierarchy without question. Thus, the two will build up a happy relationship which will last a lifetime.

Trouble is more likely to arise if you introduce an older dog into your home and the same procedure must be followed. Occasionally, you will introduce a dog of such dominance that nothing will induce him to submit to another dog. At such times you have little alternative but to support the new dog against the old. Otherwise you will have a lifelong feud on your hands. It should go without saying that you only meet this trouble when the Collies are both of the same sex. A dog will welcome any bitch into his home. In fact, he will probably be highly delighted at the intrusion. Bitches are not quite so welcoming to a member of the opposite sex but after they have laid down some ground rules they will usually accept a dog happily enough.

Most groups of dogs seem to run on a matriarchal system. It is usually a bitch that is top dog. You should feed a bitch first in acknow-ledgement of her position, but if you feed all your dogs together, always watch her or the rest will stand back and let her take their food, particularly the males. A little observation will tell you the exact pecking order in your pack and by supporting those in the higher echelons against the lower, every time there is a squabble, you will quickly establish harmony in your kennel. There is no greater joy than watching your Collies running free, happily playing together or fol-lowing at your heels in their daily walks.

Housing Your Collie

Many people start their breeding activities with one bitch, purchased as a pet. When the time comes for her to have a litter, she and her pups fit snugly into a corner of the kitchen. All goes well for the first few weeks until the puppies start scrambling out of the nest and the situa-tion becomes chaotic. All too often a kennel is bought as quickly and cheaply as possible and the mother and pups are moved outside. As the interest in Collies grows, so does the number of kennels and you can quickly end up with a shanty town of ill-assorted and badly main-tained sheds. It is better to plan well ahead.

A great deal of thought and planning goes into the production of a well designed and easily maintained kennel complex. There are three requirements to be satisfied – it must be as pleasant and comfortable as possible for the dogs, it must be as easily and efficiently worked as possible for the owner and it must cause the least possible nuisance and inconvenience to his neighbours. Right from the start, a decision has to be made on whether to house your Collies singly or in small groups. Single kennelling is more expensive but has the advantage of avoiding squabbles and the subsequent scarring which often mars a Collie's appearance in the ring. On the other hand, the dog is a pack animal and is probably happier with companions. Provided he knows his place in the pecking order you should have little trouble, although it must be emphasised that dogs should never be left alone at feeding times. Probably the ideal arrangement is for a dog and a bitch to share their quarters, thus avoiding kennel jealousy.

If you decide to use wooden kennelling, make sure that the sides and roof are lined with hardboard and insulated between the skins. Otherwise wooden kennels will prove too hot in summer and too cold in winter. They have other disadvantages. They are an undoubted fire risk and are eminently chewable. Once chewed, they become very difficult to clean and even more difficult to render escape-proof. Also, they will require constant maintenance, in the form of painting or wood treatment and attention to their felt roofs, if they are to maintain their efficiency and their attractive appearance.

The modern concrete kennelling which comes in kit form is very efficient but somewhat ugly in appearance. Most firms are prepared both to deliver and erect if required. They will lay out the complete complex, lay on water, electricity and drainage as well as the kennelling and runs. These runs tend to be very small but can be sited to lead into a large exercise run. Kennels are a standard six-foot (2m) in height for ease of cleaning. Paving stones make an attractive alternative to concrete for both paths and runs and have the advantage that you can take them with you should you decide to change properties.

Runs must be adequate in size, easily cleanable and sloped slightly away from the kennel for drainage. Unless they are close enough to the house, they will require their own water supply. Drains must be properly sited to carry away surplus water and access to main drainage is the ideal solution to the waste product problem. An outside light is essential for winter nights and electricity will need to be supplied to each kennel for lighting and heating, unless you have made arrangements for central heating to be run from the house.

It is a matter of debate whether or not Rough Collies require heated kennels. Some hold the view that they will grow thicker coats to help them withstand the cold in unheated kennels. Mrs George of the Beulah Collies always maintained the reverse. In her view, the dogs in unheated kennels used up so much nutrient energy keeping themselves warm that there was less available for growing coats. Certainly, her theory was supported by her dogs' fabulous coats. My own view is that some form of heating, however slight, keeps the dogs' quarters dry and comfortable and makes working conditions for their attendant much more pleasant. This in turn leads to more human companionship for the dogs during the dark winter months, from which they will greatly benefit.

It is well worth sitting down with paper and pencil and jotting down the routine tasks for the day. This will give you a much better idea of the facilities you will require and the best place to site them. Finally, draw up a plan of your ideal kennel complex, incorporating all these ideas. Apart from housing the dogs you will need a grooming room, which can double as a stud work area, and will need facilities for bathing and drying dogs. Also, a dog kitchen with hot and cold water, storage space for dog food and space near an electric plug for a large freezer. A cupboard in which to store buckets, cleaning and feeding equipment is another essential all too easily overlooked.

Ease of access is vital. All too often kennel and run doors are badly hung. A correctly hung door will swing gently back to the closed position enabling the bolt to slide home easily. The attendant should not have to put down everything that he is carrying in order to free two hands – one to lift the gate and the other to slide the bolt. This is time consuming and apart from being irritating it is extremely ineffi-cient.

There is one other vitally important consideration to be taken into account before you embark upon the large outlay needed to set up an efficient working kennel area. That is, will it be worth it from a finan-cial point of view? In other words, will you get your money back on your investment? On a large commercial or boarding kennel the answer is probably, yes. On a small hobby kennel the answer is prob-ably, no. In fact, it may have an adverse effect and restrict the number of potential purchasers of your property.

Before you make your final decision, consider instead the conver-sion of a garage or outhouse or even an extension to your home. The latter would require planning permission but would form a valuable asset when the time came to sell. Such a conversion could easily double as a utility room, with a downstairs cloakroom and its own access to the garden. A large wash-basin could be used for washing dog dishes and a large tiled shower area would be ideal for bathing dogs. A 'stable' connecting door would enable you to keep an eye on the dogs at all times.

My ideal small kennel would consist of a large room completely tiled with ceramic tiles on the walls and thermoplastic tiles on the floor which would have rounded edges for ease of cleaning. The advantage of bringing up Collies on a tiled floor is that they never suffer from the phobias against slippery floors which seem to afflict so many promising youngsters. The room would be adequately heated by radiators and the large windows would be double glazed for warmth and, more importantly, sound-proofing. The ceiling would be insulated and sound-proofed.

Kennelling would be a matter of choice. It could consist of tiled or wooden partitions but these might be difficult to remove when the time came to sell. Indoor kennels would fit the bill adequately or you could consider the folding cages that are now so popular. These are variously described by their advertisers as 'folding indoor kennels' or 'collapsible dog cages'. This latter description always fills me with alarm but, in fact, they are extremely strong and very versatile. Made of bright steel, they are virtually chew-proof and fold up easily for ease of carrying. Used as a kennel, they can be covered with a blanket at night and make a warm and very acceptable home for any dog. They can be used in estate cars or hatchbacks *in lieu* of dog guards and are ideal for keeping your dog safe and out of harm's way at shows where benching is not available.

The ideal covering for the plastic tray that covers the bottom of the cage would be one of the fleecy Vet or Dry Beds that are advertised in all the dog papers. These virtually indestructible fabric beds can be bought in various sizes and are easily washed in the washing machine. Initially, they are expensive but their long life and hygienic properties make them an excellent investment. They are equally valuable as bedding in more orthodox kennels and are rapidly superseding the old favourite, straw.

Straw is warm and cosy and has always been popular with the dogs themselves but has the twin disadvantages of making the place look untidy and of harbouring insects. Wood shavings make very acceptable bedding but are expensive and not easily obtainable. Shredded white paper is rapidly growing in popularity. Newspaper is warm and cheap but the print comes off on the dogs, giving them a permanent grey tinge to their coats. You can solve this problem by laying white paper over the newspaper and this makes effective and easily replaceable bedding that is especially suitable for puppies.

Extra heating for whelping bitches and young puppies can be supplied by an electric pad under the bedding or an overhead lamp. With a properly made whelping box, as described in the whelping section, this would be no problem and would not affect the room temperature for other dogs.

Whatever the size of your grounds or garden, you must make certain that the part used by the dogs is escape-proof. It is difficult to better chain-link fencing supported by angle iron posts. Unless you are particularly good with your hands it is advisable to get your fences erected by professionals. If you are living in a built-up area, there is one great disadvantage to the use of chain-link for your perimeter fence, however, and that is that you can see through it. Outsiders can see in, and worse still, your dogs can see out. You have only to get one dog barking at passers-by for the rest to join in and soon you will have a kennel of fence runners and complaints from your neighbours.

More and more suburban dwellers are turning to dog showing and finding it an absorbing hobby. The days are long gone when dog breeding was a hobby of the rich who maintained large kennels of up to a hundred dogs in their own grounds. There are few kennels in England today which keep more than a dozen adult Collies at one time. Even so, if you live in a built-up area, neighbours tend to object if you keep more than three or four dogs. The Breeding of Dogs Act, 1973 precludes you from keeping more than two bitches of breeding age without a Breeder's Licence, though it places no restriction on the number of male dogs you may keep. Most breeders like to keep their old favourites to the end of their lives and numbers soon mount up. Ninety-five per cent of all complaints are caused by the barking of dogs reaching an unacceptable noise level, so it is vital that barking is kept to a minimum.

In order to do this, there are several noise prevention precautions that you can take. Firstly, fence in your garden or dog enclosure with solid wooden six-foot-high (2m) fencing. Your dogs will be unable to see anything going on outside to bark at and passers-by will be unable to see in. Wooden fencing comes in panels and with the aid of metal post sockets is not too difficult to erect. It is expensive but permanent; it looks attractive and will give you complete seclusion – a decided asset to your property.

The closer your dogs are to the house, the easier it will be to keep their barking under control. If they are housed in your utility room or garage, you should have little problem. If they are housed some distance away, you will have to resort to voice control. A useful tip is to keep a small pile of pebbles handy and hurl one at the offender's kennel the moment he starts up. If you do this accurately he will be shocked into silence. Puppies should learn from an early age not to start up at the first light of dawn, a habit which is not calculated to endear them to the most tolerant of neighbours. A few noisy whacks to the inside of their kennel with a folded newspaper works wonders, but prevention is always better than cure. Impose a strict black out. Cover all windows with opaque material and seal all cracks, ensure that they have one of their main meals as late as possible to see them through the night and you should have no trouble.

If you should receive a complaint from one of your neighbours, it is as well to know where you stand as regards the law. The whole of the Law of Nuisance is concerned with the attempt to balance the right of one neighbour to use his property, as he thinks fits, with the right of the other to the quiet enjoyment of his neighbouring property. It is important to take the matter seriously right from the start. The first time your neighbour rings up to complain, listen to what he has to say, apologise and give your explanation. Very often, if you can convince your neighbour that the noise is caused by a visiting bitch or some temporary problem that will quickly resolve itself, he will be satisfied and you will hear no more about it. At all costs you must resist the temptation to tell him his parents were unmarried, and that he is a malicious neurotic with over-developed hearing! Remember that the law is on his side. All he has to do is to send a letter of complaint to the Local Authority and you are in serious trouble. They are bound by law to investigate and if they are satisfied that his complaint is justified, they will serve a Noise Abatement notice on you.

If the noise continues unabated, then the Local Authority will lay a complaint before the Magistrates. You will be obliged to attend Court and state your case in mitigation. It will be a great help if you can persuade other neighbours to give evidence that they are not disturbed by the barking of your dogs. Magistrates like to come to a compromise that will suit both parties if they possibly can. There is, unfortunately, no real defence to an action for nuisance. Nor is it a defence to claim that your neighbour came to live near an already existing kennel, i.e. you were there first. It is true that twenty years' uninterrupted use will legalise the position, but this period does not commence to run until the nuisance is known to exist by the complainant.

So if you are served with an Injunction by the Magistrates' Court, what are you to do? Nothing will induce you to part with your beloved Collies, but you can and must do something to mitigate the nuisance and lower the noise level. You can sound-proof your kennel or re-site them further from your neighbour. In some countries, particularly the USA, a debarking operation is commonly carried out which completely solves the problem of noisy dogs. In Britain, this operation is rare and considered somewhat unethical. The essential thing is to be able to show that you have taken steps to comply with the Magistrates' Order.

If you keep more than two bitches of breeding age that have not been spayed you must apply to the local authority for a licence in order to comply with the provisions of the Breeding of Dogs Act, 1973. The conditions on which this licence is granted and the fees charged, vary considerably from authority to authority and it is advisable to settle these details before you purchase or set up a new kennel. The Act was designed to prevent the notorious 'Puppy Farms' which it has signally failed to do and for that reason there are no restrictions on the number of male dogs you may keep.

5

Showing

Grooming Your Collie for the Show Ring

Even if you only have one Collie as a pet and have no intention of having any more, it is well worth investing in the right grooming kit. Just as in any job or trade, the work is made much easier if the right tools are available. A good brush and comb will last you a lifetime so it is worth buying the best you can afford. You will also need a pair of sharp scissors, and a toothbrush and if you want to make a really professional job then you will require a pair of thinning shears and some nail clippers. Pet shops do not always stock the right kind of brush to get through the thick Collie coat. A dandy brush is worse than useless as it does not penetrate and separate the hairs. A wire brush will do this successfully but it will break the hair and drag out most of the undercoat. By far the best brush on the market is the Mason Pearson woman's hair brush obtainable from most chemists but any rubber based bristle brush will do the job successfully. All good pet shops stock the steel combs that are needed and those with a bone handle are easier to manage. Choose a fairly wide gauge as it will tease out the old coat better. A fine steel comb is only needed for the wispy hair round the ears.

A grooming table is an optional extra. It will certainly save a lot of backache over the years. There are many such tables on the market. Most of them fold up and can be carried. All have one thing in common – they are expensive. A perfectly good grooming table can be made from an old wooden table with the legs sawn off to the required height and a hinged ramp attached to it so that the dog can walk safely up and down. Puppies should be taught this from an early age and never be allowed to jump off on to a hard surface, which can easily damage youthful joints and ligaments. To my mind, the ideal grooming table is made from a large box with a hinged lid. It can be used for storing dog food or grooming equipment and the lid forms the working surface which should be covered with rubber matting or carpet to make a secure foothold for the dog. The ramp can be a permanent fixture or can be hinged to the box and folded across the top when not in use.

Young puppies need virtually no grooming but it is essential that they become familiar with the routine from an early age. It is surprising the number of pet owners of all breeds who complain that their dog will not allow them to groom his tail or some other part of his anatomy or to clip his nails. All this should have been part of a puppy's early training. Teach your puppy to lie on his back while you brush the underparts as this will be a great aid to thorough grooming when he grows his adult coat. Grooming should be a pleasure to both Collie and owner, so rolling your puppy over and tickling his tummy while you brush him is all part of the fun.

A lot of people like to groom their Collie daily and during the moulting period this is to be highly recommended. Indeed, there is no reason why the pet Collie should not enjoy his daily groom throughout his life, but if you plan to show your Collie, then weekly grooming only is advisable. A Collie that is groomed daily will never grow as heavy a coat as he would otherwise. Some kennel Collies are only groomed when they go to shows as their breeders believe that this method produces the heaviest coats of all. I like to groom my dogs weekly, and they queue up, waiting for their turn with every sign of enjoyment.

There are many sweet-smelling sprays on the market for grooming long-haired dogs. Most are excellent but they all tend to be expensive. A perfectly adequate grooming spray can be mixed at home in a plastic garden spray bottle. The ingredients are:

> 1 teaspoonful surgical spirit
> 1 tablespoonful floral disinfectant
> Top up of rain water

Spray the coat all over, thoroughly massaging it in and then brush through the coat in the usual way. Frequent bathing of your Collie is not advisable but it is still the quickest way to get rid of an old coat and leave space for the new one to come through. This is the stage at which I like to give my dogs their annual bath in a good insecticidal shampoo. It cleans out the old coat and the dogs seem to appreciate their new squeaky-clean image.

If your Collie comes in from his walk covered in mud, then remove the worst of it by rubbing with newspapers. Wring out a cloth in hot water and rub over the muddy parts again. Leave the dog in a warm place to dry and the remaining mud will literally disappear. Most Collies are very fastidious and will spend some time cleaning their paws with their tongue, just like a cat, till they are sparkling white again.

If you decide to show your Collie, then you must be prepared for some hard work. The Collie that is groomed to perfection for the show ring is a work of art and there is no short cut to producing the desired result. Every breeder has their own method of preparation but most tasks are fundamental. It is a matter of individual taste in which order they are performed. I like to start with nail clipping and get that particular chore out of the way.

Nails

If your Collie is exercised regularly on hard pavements there will be very little need to clip his nails in daily life, but for the show ring, neatly trimmed nails make a great difference to the shape and neatness of the feet. If the nail is pink and transparent the quick will be easily visible and the nail clippers can be positioned to avoid it. If the nail is black the quick will not be discernible and great care should be taken – it is best to clip just a little at a time. If you cut the quick it will bleed profusely and a clotting agent should be on hand. It is painful for the dog and he will always dislike having his nails clipped in future. If your Collie has become accustomed to having his nails manicured from the time he was a puppy then he will have confidence in your ability to do the job without hurting him. If you are clipping the nails of a strange dog it may be advisable to lightly muzzle him in case he has had an unfortunate experience in the past. If you prefer, the nails can be filed down, but this is a tedious process and most breeders prefer to use a file merely to round off the edges of the clipped nails.

Teeth

As a judge, I am always saddened by the number of quite young dogs who come into the ring with dirty teeth. The problem will only get worse as they get older. The tartar deposits will accumulate giving the dog gum problems and bad breath. The tartar can be cracked with a dentist's probe or even a sharp, pointed knife working from the gum line. Once cracked, the scaly deposit will flake off but it would be much better if it had never been allowed to develop. Hard biscuits or marrowbones to chew will help to prevent the tartar from building up but the easiest method of prevention is to clean your Collie's teeth during grooming sessions. Use an ordinary dentifrice powder and toothbrush and brush the gums as well as the teeth. Do not forget the back teeth. Start a teeth cleaning routine as soon as your puppy's permanent teeth appear and he will have sparkling white teeth throughout his life.

Head and Ear Trimming

Years ago a great deal of head and ear trimming was required before a Collie was considered fit to enter the show ring. Whiskers were cut off close to the skin and the throat, cheeks and stop were cleaned out, first with thinning shears and then with sandpaper or the edge of a matchbox. The fluffy hair round the ears was stripped out and the edge of the ears neatened with scissors. Fashions change and now scarcely any trimming is done to the head and ears as it is deemed to harden the expression – even the whiskers are left on these days. The picture is very different in the USA and an immense amount of time and effort is devoted to head sculpturing and trimming. In England, just a little of the excess hair round the ears is removed by finger and thumb or with the discrete use of the thinning shears.

Feet and Leg Trimming

I do not bath my Collies before a show but the night before I wash their legs and feet and before they are completely dry I trim their feet using the following method. First trim away the excess hair beneath the pads. Then turn your attention to the feet themselves. Push the damp hair on the toes upwards and with the thinning shears trim the long hairs on the foot to a uniform length. The aim is to neaten the feet and give the impression of well-arched, close-together toes. I do not like to clean between the toes as this tends to give an ugly, flat, separated appearance as opposed to the rounded, compact look you are seeking to achieve. The rear feet should be trimmed in exactly the same way and the long straggly hair on the hocks neatly trimmed.

To do this, comb the damp hair on the rear pasterns, backwards and upwards, then, with sharp scissors, cut straight down from the hock to the floor. Do not trim too close to the leg or it will give the dog a

Untrimmed front foot.

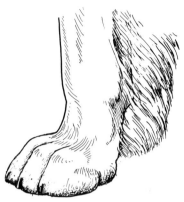

Trimmed front foot.

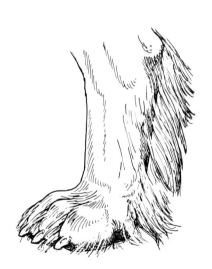

Untrimmed hock.

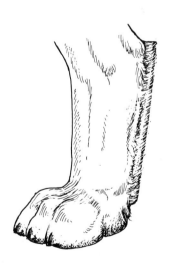

Trimmed hock.

spindle-hocked look. Normally, the cut should be perpendicular to the floor but if your dog is a bit straight in the stifle, then angle the cut away from the hock slightly to give the dog the appearance of well-angled hocks. If, on the other hand, he suffers from over-angled hocks then the cut should be closer at the hock-joint and further away from the heel to give the illusion of perpendicular hocks. Comb out and stand back to study your handiwork. If you are satisfied that you have created the effect you require then all that needs to be done is to round off with the thinning shears. The aim is to make the trimmed hair appear to be part of the rounded bone of the leg.

Bathing

If you live in the country your Collie will probably not need bathing, but if you live in the town he will have picked up a certain amount of dirt and smog in his coat that only bathing will remove. Bath him at least two days before the show to allow time for his coat to settle. Use a good-quality dog shampoo and rinse his coat out thoroughly. Dry with a hair dryer, brushing the coat straight as it dries. Beware of bathing your Collie if he is about to lose his coat and you are anxious to preserve it for a few weeks – bathing will make the loose coat fly out. In fact, it is much the fastest way to get rid of an old coat and leave space for a new coat to come through.

There are two methods of preparing your dog for show without bathing him – dry shampoos and sprays. Using powdered chalk or talcum powder as a dry shampoo, you can sprinkle it throughout the coat and brush it out. This will leave the coat clean and slightly harsher to the touch than if you use a spray. It is not advisable for tricolours who need to have their black coats presented with as brilliant a sheen as possible. This is best achieved by polishing with a piece of silk, working always with the lay of the coat.

If you decide to use one of the many sprays that are on the market, or your own made-up one, then use the following method of brushing. The technique is simple but cannot be hurried. First, brush all the coat towards the head. Then, starting from the rear, brush the coat in sections. Hold back the hair against the lay of the coat with one hand, and, with the other, spray the section down to the skin. Then, using your bristle brush, gradually brush out the coat from under the hand, brushing towards the tail. Continue this process, spraying as you go, until you have dealt with the whole coat. When you have finished and while the coat is still damp, chalk the white parts. Separate the hair into layers and sift magnesium carbonate, powdered chalk or talcum powder into the coat, getting the whitening agent right down to the skin. Continue down the legs and featherings. Chalk the legs while they are still damp and then dip each foot into a plastic bag containing powdered chalk. Most breeders prefer to complete this work the night before.

When you reach the show, brush your dog again, using the same technique. Lay a towel or blanket on the floor and get your dog to lie down and roll over. Thoroughly brush the underparts, starting with the rear legs, carefully brush the long hair between them and work along the stomach up to the chin in the usual way. Stand the dog up and repeat the process, starting at the hocks and working back up the dog, layering the hair as you go until every inch of the coat has been thoroughly brushed. Most breeders use a spray when working on their dog's coat at a show but this is entirely a matter of personal choice. It is against Kennel Club rules to apply chalk to a dog at the show and any chalk already in the coat must be brushed out before entering the ring.

Finally, comb round the ears with a curry-comb, fluffing up the hair to give a softer look. Settle his show collar into his ruff and lightly smooth over the top of his coat with a comb to make the coat fit the outline of the dog. As a finishing touch, smooth a little Vaseline into the dog's nose to make it black and shiny. Having completed his show preparation, you can enter the ring, head held high, knowing that your Collie has been groomed to perfection and is looking his best.

Types of Show

All dog shows are held under licence from the Kennel Club and are subject to Kennel Club rules with the exception of Exemption Shows. These rules are very strict and anyone who seriously transgresses against them is liable to be banned for life from exhibiting or judging at a Kennel Club show. This would almost certainly happen to anyone caught exhibiting at a show not licensed by the Kennel Club, so it would perhaps be as well to give a brief description of the different types of shows available.

The Kennel Club run the most prestigious dog show in the world – Cruft's. At one time anyone could show their dog at Cruft's provided he was registered at the Kennel Club. This led to such large entries of pet dogs that the Kennel Club was forced to introduce a qualifying system. It is not easy to qualify in a breed which has such large entries as ours, but it has succeeded in raising the standard of the dogs shown. Sadly, of course, many of the Collies that qualify for Cruft's are out of coat by the time the show comes round. Entry is restricted to dogs who have won at Championship Shows. It is constantly under review but from 1991 onwards those eligible to enter are:

1. A dog that, in the previous year, has won a first, second or third prize in Minor Puppy, Puppy, Junior or Post Graduate class at any Championship Show at which Challenge Certificates are on offer to the breed.
2. A dog that has won a first prize at Cruft's the previous year.
3. Any dog entered in the Kennel Cub Stud Book by the closing date for entries.
4. A dog that has won a five point Green Star in the Republic of Ireland under Irish Kennel Club rules.
5. Any dog that is a Champion, Show Champion, Field Trial Champion, Working Trial Champion or Obedience Champion.

These qualifications have remained standard for several years and as Cruft's entries remain high it seems unlikely they will be relaxed for some time to come.

It seems that the Kennel Club is about to move the venue from Earl's Court Exhibition Centre in central London to Birmingham NEC which has better accommodation and adequate parking for the exhibitors so that it may be possible to allow an increase in entries. It would be particularly useful if more young stock could be exhibited as it is the puppies and juniors that most fanciers from abroad come to see. They are often disappointed to find their numbers so few, and those that are exhibited often lack coat because of the time of the year.

There is no doubt that in the mind of the public, both in Britain and abroad, the name, Cruft's, conjures up a special magic, yet to serious breeders a win at one of the big speciality shows is of equal merit. There are, at present, some fourteen Collie Clubs in Great Britain. Of these the most prestigious must be the British Collie Club closely followed by the younger Collie Association. Both these clubs cater for fanciers from all over the country. The other clubs cater for more local interests although membership is not restricted to any locality. Most, but not all, have been granted Championship status for one show a year and will also hold at least one Open Show a year. At the time of writing there are some thirty Championship Shows held each year by all breed societies which offer Challenge Certificates for Rough Collies. A further sixteen sets of Challenge Certificates are available at the breed shows. These are not limited in any way. They are open to all exhibitors, and champions can be shown in any class for which they are eligible.

Open Shows

These may be held by single breed and all-breed societies alike. There are no Challenge Certificates on offer but champions can be exhibited.

Limited and Sanction Shows

These shows are confined to members of that society and champions are excluded.

Primary Shows

Primary Shows are confined to members and restricted to novice dogs.

Matches

Matches are held under Kennel Club rules. They do not schedule classes but are run as a competition between two dogs on a knockout basis. The winners then go forward to the next round until one dog is finally left as overall match winner. They are often run as a competition between two or more clubs and members enjoy the team-work involved. It is usually a lot of fun and matches have enlivened many a dull Annual General Meeting.

Exemption Shows

The Exemption Show is the odd one out. It is, as its title would suggest, exempt from Kennel Club rules, to the extent that the Kennel Club grants permission for a show to be held, restricted to no more than four pedigree dog classes. The remainder of the classes are thrown open to non-pedigree dogs who have various attributes, such as the waggiest tail or the most appealing eyes. These shows are almost invariably held for charity and a great deal of money has been raised through them for various good causes. They are often the public's first introduction to dog shows and many a serious exhibitor has come from such humble beginnings. They are also useful ground for the general ring training of young puppies and a good way of getting them used to the atmosphere of dog shows. They should not be used by seasoned exhibitors for promoting well-known dogs.

Entering a Show

There are many excellent Collies who live out their lives without ever seeing the inside of the show ring. The ratio of show Collies to pet Collies is quite small, yet there is a good deal of fun to be had out of showing. Man is a competitive animal and there is a great deal of pleasure to be gained when your beautiful Collie on whom you have lavished many hours of training and grooming is rewarded with a prize. It can be an enjoyable day out for both of you. You will make new friends and most Collies thoroughly enjoy showing, particularly kennel Collies for whom it provides a welcome day out in their owner's company. They love all the trimming and brushing and being at the centre of attention.

To become a successful breeder requires hard work and dedication but it becomes a way of life. It will be a life full of interest, sometimes rewarding, sometimes heart-breaking but never ever dull. It is not for everyone. Only you can decide whether it is for you. I well remember attending my first open-air all-breeds show as a teenager just after the war. There were many new breeds that I had never seen before and there were many regional and foreign accents that I had never previously heard. I was filled with an overwhelming sense of excitement. This was my world and I felt at home in it.

So how do you enter this world of dogs? You can watch out for news of local dog shows in your newspaper but you may find that Collies are not scheduled. If you only enter Variety classes you may find the judge knows little about Collies and that other Collie breeders have not entered under him. You will go home, probably unplaced having learned nothing.

By far the best method would be to join your local Collie club. A list of them is included at the end of this book and you can write or telephone the Secretary for details of how to become a member. Most clubs hold two or three shows a year confined to Collies. Usually they try to vary the venues so that all members have at least one show in their area. Many include special classes for beginners which give complete novices the chance to compete on equal terms and possibly go home with a prize. Paid-up members will automatically receive a schedule for each show. At first sight, an entry form can be confusing but if you get your dog's registration form and start filling the entry form in, from left to right, you will find it set out quite logically.

If you know your dog's name but his registration certificate has not come through, add NAF (name applied for), after his name, or TAF (transfer applied for) if you are still waiting for his transfer certificate. Study the definition of classes in the schedule and enter your Collie only in classes for which he is eligible. Many classes carry restrictions as to age, colour, previous wins etc. It is most important that you sign the declaration on the bottom left-hand side of the form confirming that your dog has not been in contact with any contagious disease for the six weeks prior to exhibition. Without this signed declaration, the Secretary cannot accept your entry. All that is left to do then is to fill in your name and address and send the form off with the entrance fee in good time before the closing date. This will be at least four weeks before the date of the show and, in the case of a Championship Show, may be as much as eight weeks.

This time lapse works against the long-coated breeds and can prove expensive. Many a Collie is looking his best at the time of entries closing but can lose nearly all his coat by the time the show date arrives. If this misfortune happens to you, then by all means go to the show and watch the proceedings but leave your semi-bald Collie at home. It is not fair to expect him to compete against other Collies in glamorous full coat. It is quite a good idea for you to visit one or two shows before you enter the exhibiting world in order to absorb the atmosphere, so that when you and your Collie attend your first show, it will not be a totally alien world to one of you at least.

Show Training

The four- to eight-week lapse between the closing date for entries and the actual show can be invaluable to you to complete your dog's show training. Some Collies are natural showmen. They have the ability to enter a ring, stand four-square, arch their neck and bring their ears together on top of their head with a panache that draws all eyes. Such Collies are few and far between. Most of the excellent showmen you will see in the ring are made, not born, and by a lot of hard work on the part of both dog and handler.

The best time to begin show training your puppy is at eight weeks. Utilise his main interest in life – food. Show him a titbit and catch his interest. It is unlikely that he will be able to get his ears right up at that tender age but every effort should be made to get him to lift his ears as far as he can, even if it is only momentarily. Gently restrain him so that he is not leaping about all over the place in his efforts to get at the food. He will soon realise that he is expected to stand quietly, giving you his undivided attention before he receives his reward. A few seconds at a time is sufficient to begin with but as he gets older and his attention span increases, so can the length of time that he is expected to stand and 'show'!

The next step is to slip a loose slip-collar over his neck (never a choke chain which will damage his coat), and hold the end of the lead in your left hand. If he has learnt his first lesson well, he should scarcely notice the introduction of the lead.

I have already dealt with the best method of teaching your Collie to walk to heel. Usually it is a lesson swiftly learnt as the Collie instinctively knows that his place is at your side. Quite often, the Rough Collie will adopt the age-old position of the working sheepdog, weaving from side to side behind you, never coming more forward than your knee. This, of course, is not what you want in the show ring. You want your Collie to move smoothly and easily at your left side in a controlled, steady trot. A well-constructed dog should be capable of breaking into a trot from a standing start but this needs practice. Do not let him walk or pace, i.e. move both legs on the same side at the same time, nor let him break into a gallop. Above all, do not let him pull, as it is impossible for a judge to assess his movement if he is pulling against the lead. Practise walking straight up and down and in an anti-clockwise triangle, always keeping your dog on your left-hand side between you and the judge. Get a friend to advise you on the most suitable speed for your dog.

Do not neglect his road work. Serious road work should not begin before a puppy reaches the age of eight months, but your puppy can begin training as soon as he has finished his inoculations. Very short periods of from ten to fifteen minutes are sufficient at first, and much of this time can be spent in letting him get used to traffic and meeting other dogs and people. Socialising is the 'in' word at the moment but it is a very important part of any puppy's training, and the confidence it gives him will stand him in good stead all his life.

As he grows older the length of time he spends on the road can be increased to about half an hour. Serious muscle building work can only be done at the trot and this is the natural pace of the Collie. He is not designed as a galloping dog but as a trotting dog that should be able to move at a steady, easy, effortless trot for mile after mile. I am not suggesting that you exercise your Collie as much as a true working dog, but at least three miles a day should be the norm. If you are the energetic sort then a three-mile jog will do you nothing but good, provided that you build up to it slowly and you will get as much benefit from the exercise as the dog. Years ago I used to do most road work on a bicycle with the dog trotting along by the side. It is almost impossible now to find a traffic-free road but if you have a hard surfaced area where you can safely ride a bike, then this is the ideal method of getting your dog to move at a steady controlled trot. It is advisable to give the dog a short break after each mile so that no strain is put on his muscles.

There is no substitute for road work to put muscle on a dog. There will be a pronounced improvement in his general fitness; his heart-rate will slow and his lung capacity increase. It may take up to twelve months to build up his muscle and reach peak fitness but at the end of that time you will have a free moving dog that will gait tirelessly round the ring or up and down as the judge requires. The benefits do not stop there. There is nothing like road work to bring up weak pasterns or correct wobbly hocks. Part of the reason why many present-day Collies move so badly is that they are never given any road work. It will strengthen pads, improve flat feet and shorten nails better than any nail-clippers.

You may think all this work is unnecessary, indeed you may think your Collie is so beautiful that any judge worth his salt is bound to place him first. You would be wrong. It is easy to look at your Collie, at home, as he stands to attention, neck arched, eyes riveted on some distant object, and be lost in admiration at his beauty. Sadly, this is not how he will appear in the ring. It is against Kennel Club rules to have your dog's attention attracted from outside the ring (a practice known as double handling), and you are liable to have your dog disqualified and a complaint upheld against you if you attempt it. On the Continent, different rules prevail and double handling is common practice. People resort to all sorts of ruses in an effort to get the dogs' attention and to ensure they are looking their best whenever the judge glances in their direction. In Britain, it is left to the handler to get the best out of his dog – something which is unlikely to happen without considerable prior training.

The best place to learn all this is at ringcraft classes. These are usually advertised at local veterinary surgeries and both puppies that have received their final inoculations and adults are welcomed. A stand-in judge will examine your puppy's mouth, run his hands over his conformation and finally watch him move in the usual way. This is the ideal preparation for the show ring as it will accustom him to meeting other dogs and he will not be overawed when his big moment comes and he enters the show ring for the first time. If there are no ringcraft classes in your area then it would be helpful to take him to your local obedience class and just let him sit and watch. It will be too confusing for him to learn obedience work until he has mastered his show training, but he will accustom himself to the noise and bustle and being surrounded by strange dogs. Leave it to a later date to start his obedience training.

Continue your show training at home. Just a few minutes at a time is sufficient, right up to the date of the show, until you are satisfied that your dog will stand four-square and use his ears when required. By this time he should be moving easily and freely on a loose lead at your left-hand side in whichever direction is required of him. Very occasionally, a judge may ask you to perform a manoeuvre that will

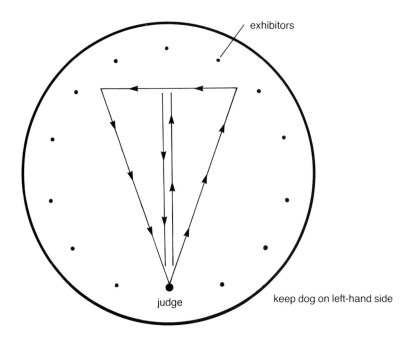

Ring manoeuvre.

require your dog to move on your right. This will involve you changing the lead into your right hand so it is as well to practise this in advance. The golden rule is to remember to always keep your dog between you and the judge so that his view of your dog is never obscured. For this training, use a light nylon or fine leather show lead similar to the one that you will use in the ring, so that your Collie learns to respond to the lighter touch. Practise the more common ring manoeuvres which are usually the triangle or 'T' shape.

Last Minute Preparations

The night before the show, pack your show bag with everything you will need. Minimum requirements are grooming equipment, brushes, combs, spray, scissors, show lead and a towel, as well as a benching chain and benching rug if the show is benched. Do not forget your dog's water bowl. Although water is on tap at all shows it is wiser to take a bottle from home. Many fastidious Collies will not drink strange water, however thirsty they become. Make sure you have packed your entry tickets to the show if it is a Championship Show. If you place your cooked liver titbits in the fridge overnight, remember to pack them in the morning.

Wear comfortable but inconspicuous clothing. You do not want to distract attention from your dog. It is advisable to wear constrasting rather than matching colours. You want the dog to stand out rather than blend into you. Comfortable shoes in which you can walk quickly or run to keep up with the natural speed of your dog, are essential. You can buy special aprons which include pockets which will accommodate all you need to take into the ring but if not, make sure you have a titbit pocket in the right-hand side of your skirt or trousers. British weather is so unpredictable that, at an outdoor show, it is as well to go equipped for all weathers, particularly rain. All shows have wet-weather accommodation but there are a few judges who insist on staying outside as long as possible. Layers of clothing that you can don or discard, according to the conditions, are probably the best answer. Finally, pin your ring-clip (or large safety-pin if you have not yet acquired one), to your outside garment before leaving home. Nothing is more annoying for ringsiders trying to mark the winners in their catalogue than to find that the handler's number is invisible.

Somewhere in your schedule you should find a map or directions to the show. Study it the night before. If you are travelling a long distance then it is a good plan to write down the main routes, exit numbers from motorways and places you are passing through *en route*. You may be travelling on your own or your companion may not be a very good navigator and you could well miss your classes if you get lost.

Arrive at the show in good time. Buy a catalogue, look for your breed section and find your name in the list of exhibitors. There will be a number against your name. This will be your number both in the ring and of your bench, if it is a benched show. If it is, then make your way to your bench, get out your dog's benching chain and his rug and settle him on his bench. If not, find a quiet corner to spread out his rug and settle your dog on this. Study your catalogue to find the number of the Collie ring and the order in which the classes are to be judged.

The major part of your grooming preparation should have been done at home. All the chalk should have been brushed out of his coat before arriving at the venue. A light spray on his coat and a thorough brush through should be all that is required on the day. Check that his feet are clean and that you have made a neat job of trimming his hocks and nails. If there is any shaping to be done such as flattening an over-prominent rump or fluffing up a sway back, then the time to do this is just before you enter the ring. The judge's first impression is most important. If there are two identical numbers on your bench then take one with you, it will be your ring number. It is harassing to get into the ring and find you have left your number on your bench at some distant part of the showground. In most cases your ring number will be handed out to you in the ring by the steward.

Make your way to the ringside in good time for your first class and spend some time studying the procedure. Every judge will vary in his methods. Most All-Rounders will ask the exhibitors to circle the ring in an anti-clockwise direction but this is seldom done today by Collie specialist judges. The majority of Collie judges will simply prefer to walk round the ring making a preliminary study of each dog in the class before calling them out individually for examination.

He will then stand back and observe the dog from all angles before examining in detail. He will approach the dog from the front and examine his head, first from the front and then in profile, running his fingers over the roundness of his muzzle and feeling the bumpiness or flatness of his skull and the cleanness of his stop. He will scrutinise the mouth, checking to see whether your dog has a scissor bite, is not overshot (I have yet to come across an undershot Collie), and making sure he has no missing molars on either side. Often, he will cup your dog's head in his hands, bringing his ears up into the desired position so that he can verify the alignment of eyes and ears.

A good judge will compare the width of the skull with the dog's bone, as the combination of a fine skull and good bone is not easy to achieve. Gradually, his hand will move down the dog's neck, feeling for length and arch of neck. He will check the amount of forehand and the angle of the shoulder by placing one hand on the dog's withers and the other on the foremost part of the shoulder blade seeking the desired angle of 45 degrees. He will run both hands over the dog's rib-cage noting both depth and spring of rib. Light pressure along the dog's back will reveal a possible sway back and the strength or other-wise of loin. The hand will continue sweeping down over the hip to investigate the curve of the stifle, the angle of the hock-joint and the muscle-tone of the hindquarters.

Whether the tail is high-set or low-set is important to the correct tail carriage and this can often only be discovered by feeling for the place where the base of the tail joins the body. A judge's hands will often be working independently. With one hand, he will test whether the tip of the tail reaches the hock, while with the other, he investigates the strength and roundness of the bone in the foreleg. If you have a dog, the judge must make sure that he is entire and is not a monorchid or cryptorchid. Feet are a most important item in a working dog and strong, well-arched, tight feet can be approved by observation but a judge will often pick up one fore-paw to examine it more carefully.

A big coat frequently hides a multitude of faults and I do not believe that you can correctly assess a Collie's conformation without 'laying on hands'. It is true that movement is the test of conformation and after he has completed his examination, the judge will ask you to move your dog, sometimes in a triangle, sometimes straight up and down, occasionally in a 'T' shape. On his return to the judge, the handler must bring his dog to attention so that the judge gets a last favourable impression of the dog's outline and expression.

You should observe all this from outside the ring so that by the time you enter it you will know what is expected from you. You will have noted whether the judge likes the handler to return to his original place or whether he prefers some other procedure. If it is a very large class, as is frequently the case with Collies, the judge may call out some eight or ten dogs from which he will make his final selection. The rest will be asked to leave the ring to make more room for the remaining exhibits. The judge will already have made a detailed examination of these dogs but he may want to refresh his memory as to the movement of a few individuals and check out one or two other points. This period is known, irreverently, in the dog fraternity as 'make your mind up time', and does not last long.

Very soon, the judge will call out his winners, placing them from left to right in the centre of the ring in the order in which he wishes to make his awards. If you are lucky enough to be in the final line-up then do not relax. Keep your dog alert and looking his best, as the judge may yet change his placings before he finally marks his judging book.

You may have been one of the less fortunate ones who left the ring early. All is not lost if you have entered your dog in more than one class. It could be a class for which the previous winners are not eligible and the judge may prefer your dog to the new exhibits presented to him. All is never lost until the cards are handed out. If you go home without a card do not despair. You and your dog will have learnt a great deal from the experience and your next show may prove a very different story.

Your first show can be a nerve-racking experience. Even seasoned exhibitors can suffer from nerves when there is a lot at stake. It is important that you take things calmly. I have already written of the telepathic abilities of the Collie and if you communicate your nerves to your dog he will immediately think that there is something to be worried about and his well-learned lessons in showmanship will be forgotten. Many an experienced handler has had the chagrin of finding his dog refusing to show in the ring but returning to his usual high standard of showmanship as soon as the tense situation has been resolved and he is once again outside the ring. It is the handler who has lost the day through nerves, not the dog. He is only there in order to please you, so try and make it a happy occasion for him and, win or lose, give him an appreciative pat when he leaves the ring – not just when he wins a prize. When you get home in the evening, remember that he is just the same dog that you took out with such high hopes in the morning. You may be thrilled with his wins or you may be downcast but he has done his best to please you and you are his whole world. So feed him, exercise him and give him a cuddle before he settles down for the night. There is always another day.

Barnville Country Squire, Britain's top veteran.

Ears

The Collie puppy who has small, genuinely natural ears that come up into the perfect position at eight weeks and never vary from that day on, is a rarity. We have all had such puppies and what a joy they are. Neither teething, nor cold, windy weather make any difference – their ear carriage remains perfect. Most puppies have very erratic ear carriage. Nearly all have some problem during teething and all sorts of remedies are suggested to the bewildered novice. So many promising puppies have had their show careers ruined by prick ears that breeders are now tending to err in the opposite direction. Large, heavy ears set on the side of the head now seem to be the order of the day. If only half the attention was paid to breeding for the perfect ear as is paid to breeding for the perfect eye, then a great many ear problems would be solved.

Many puppies fly one or other of their ears when they are teething and if left unchecked for more than a few days, this may become permanent, so you cannot afford to ignore it. I am not a great believer in greasing the ear. Although effective in warm weather, I find that in cold weather, it worsens the problem and, believe me, pricked greasy ears look even worse than ungreased pricked ears. Kaolin poultice is still the best remedy. The secret of its successful application is to apply it sparingly over a matter of days. Large dollops which are sufficient to weight the ears down immediately will only be shaken off, with disastrous results to your wallpaper. Spread it thinly on the inside tip of the ear only. Do not apply any more until it is completely dry. Continue until the weight is sufficient to bring the ear over into the correct position. Reapply when necessary. A little vegetable oil massaged into the inside fold of the ear is helpful, provided the weather is not cold, as it will help to keep the ear supple.

The really persistant prick ear is very difficult to bring down and unless your puppy is a very good specimen in every other respect, I would not recommend that you breed from him. In any case, great perseverance will be needed. The advantage of using kaolin is that it can be removed, without trace, prior to entering the show ring and so has an immense advantage over chewing gum, plasticine, half-sucked fruit gums or any other of the means of weighting ears to which desperate owners resort.

At present, more trouble seems to be encountered trying to get low ears up rather than pricked ears down. Many puppies have just one 'soft' ear. It is advisable to leave well alone until the puppy is over four months but if the trouble persists, it is worth examining the ear. Very often you will find that it is the outside edge of the ear only that is weak. If you straighten this edge with your fingers, the ears will fall naturally into the perfect position. It will be obvious to you that if the weak muscle could be artificially strengthened for a time, the problem might be solved. It is comparatively simple to achieve this by the following method.

Clip the hair from the inside edge of the ear with a pair of sharp scissors. Make sure the ear is clean and dry, and apply about two inches (5 cm) of adhesive draught excluder to the clipped surface. Most puppies tolerate this treatment very well but it is advisable to keep them apart from other puppies who will delight in removing your handiwork in the shortest possible time. The strip should be left on for about three weeks or until it comes off naturally. Usually the muscles will have taken over the work by then. Sometimes, the ear will remain up for a week or more and then collapse. In this case the treatment must be repeated until success is achieved.

Low-set, heavy ears can also be improved by supporting them in the correct position until the muscles take over. There are several methods of doing this but the one that I prefer is as follows. You will require:

Insulating tape
Safety razor
Sharp scissors
Surgical spirit
Cotton wool
Chiropodist's foam

The latter can be obtained from most chemists under the trade name of Dr Scholl's Molefoam (or Moleskin if you prefer to use a lighter material). The support must be tailored to fit each individual dog and, before cutting out your foam, I suggest that you cut out a pattern and try it out until satisfied that you have the right size to bring your dog's ears into the correct position.

1. Get someone to hold your dog's head steady.
2. Shave the lower two-thirds of the inside of both ears. Make sure that you do not remove any hair from the top one-third as this will affect the ear tipping over correctly.
3. Clean the shaved part with cotton wool and surgical spirit. This will remove all grease.
4. Remove backing on ear support and place carefully in each ear in the desired position. Press carefully into place.
5. Cut a strip of insulating tape sufficient to go round both ears twice. Press one end against the Molefoam and wind round both ears to protect the support. If necessary, weight the tips of the ears with tape or kaolin.
6. Check that the dog is comfortable, that there are no trapped hairs and that you have not wound the insulating tape too tightly.

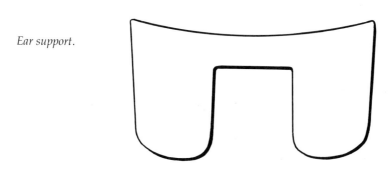

Ear support.

The ear supports should be left on for about three weeks, by which time the dog should be quite accustomed to wearing them. It is important to check from time to time to make sure that no irritation has set up. The chances of keeping the supports intact will be greatly enhanced if the puppy or dog is kept on his own for this period.

Occasionally you get Collies with over-tipped ears that break at the half-way stage instead of at two-thirds. Very often, they are well set on the top of the head but the expression is completely spoiled. This is the most difficult fault of all to correct and very little can be done, other than thinning out the hair on the skull to give an appearance of lift and training the dog to look up in your face in the ring.

6

Judging

After a few years of consistent showing and breeding you may achieve such success that you find other breeders value your opinion on their dogs and your thoughts turn to judging. It is as well to do your homework first, so that, should the opportunity arise and you are offered an appointment, you will feel sufficiently confident in your own abilities to accept.

Every aspiring judge should study the anatomy of the dog and have a good understanding of his moving parts and how they work. There are several ways in which you can do this. You can work from books, you can study some of the excellent video films on dogs and their movement that exist, or you can embark on one of the professional dog judging courses that will give you a thorough training in anatomy and movement as well as judging procedure. These courses are not cheap but I am told they give excellent value for money. Some of the breed clubs hold judging 'talk-ins' from time to time. An experienced judge will give a lecture (usually with the help of a Collie to illustrate certain points), and answer questions put by the audience. After a break for lunch, a small competition may be arranged where aspiring judges are asked to place four Collies in order of merit and give their reasons. This gives them good experience in both the theory and practice of judging the Collie. Anyone who shows a flair for judging will be noted and may be asked to put their name down on the lower rungs of the club's judging list.

All breed clubs have an 'A' list of Championship Show judges, already approved by the Kennel Club, to judge at Championship Show level, a 'B' list of Open Show judges, and usually a 'C' list of judges who have some experience and aspire to becoming Open Show judges, and a 'D' list of novice judges. From this last list, the club may select a judge for a club match. This is a very good way to start judging as it is a knock-out competition and you only have two Collies of similar age and sex to compare together. From there you can progress to judging Collies locally at a few shows.

All the Collie breed clubs submit their list of judges to the Rough Collie Breed Council annually. This is a body representing all the breed clubs in the country, and they compile one overall list of judges for the Kennel Club. Of course, the Kennel Club is a law unto itself and from time to time approves judges to judge at Championship Shows who are not on the Breed Council list, much to the Breed Council's chagrin. Not a great deal can be done about this as the Kennel Club reserve to themselves the right to approve whom they like to award Challenge Certificates.

Before being approved for this honour, the aspiring Championship Show judge must fill out a questionnaire giving full details of any of his stock that have been awarded a Stud Book Number or won any other recognised award such as a Junior Warrant. They will also need to know the date, show and number of Collie classes that you have previously judged so be very careful to keep accurate records of any judging engagements that you fulfil, right from the first. There are heavy penalties for submitting inaccurate or 'puffed up' claims to the number of classes a person has judged. The Judges Selection Committee at the Kennel Club consider very carefully the qualities of any candidate to award Challenge Certificates and must be satisfied of the judge's integrity. At one time, any person who handled dogs professionally or traded in dog equipment was precluded from judging at any show. Things are a little more democratic these days, but it is still regarded as a great honour to be accepted by the Kennel Club to award Challenge Certificates.

All this will seem a long way away when you arrive at the show to fulfil your first judging engagement. Your first duty will be to report to the Secretary who will be grateful if you arrive in good time. All shows have to be run against the clock and a judge who is late in starting can throw the whole show out of gear. You will be introduced to your stewards, who will take care of the award cards, and be handed your judging book, pen and judge's rosette. There will be very little space for your notes on the winners in the standard judging book so it is often better to take a small notebook for this purpose. Arriving in good time will allow you to have a relaxing cup of tea or coffee and a quick wash and brush-up before making your way to your ring. If it is your first engagement, you are bound to be a little nervous but once you start to concentrate on the dogs, you will find your nerves disappear.

While one of your stewards is handing out ring numbers and checking that each dog is entered in the class, take the time to observe the dogs coming into the ring – it can be very revealing. Take the opportunity to sit down. You may be on your feet all day judging a large entry, walking about and examining dogs from all angles and it can be very tiring. Comfortable shoes are essential as is wet-weather gear. While you are waiting you can explain to the other steward how you intend to move the dogs and agree on the best place for your line-up. Remember that other exhibitors will be very interested in the results so try to give the spectators as good a view as possible.

A good steward is invaluable to the smooth running of your ring and will line up your winners of a previous class in the right order amongst the 'seen' dogs. Most stewards work on a purely voluntary basis and are entitled to be treated with the utmost courtesy. If you 'break' for lunch, make sure they accompany you – it is small enough reward for standing around in all winds and weathers watching someone else judge. It is, of course, one of the best methods of entering the exalted ranks of the judges, as much can be learned from watching an experienced judge at work and a steward who is already familiar with the inside of the ring has a head start. Show Secretaries are always grateful for all the stewarding help they can get and are usually sympathetic to you stewarding in your own breed.

When your steward finally reports that all is ready, ask him to move the dogs round the ring. This can be very revealing on such matters as reach of stride and tail carriage and will be invaluable as a breathing space for you to steady your nerves and get your 'eye in'. If the class is too large for this manoeuvre to be performed satisfactorily, then wait until you have made your final selection of some eight to ten Collies before you ask them to move round. Almost all judges like to walk round, taking a preliminary look at each exhibit before commencing a detailed examination of each dog.

If time and space permits, move each dog in a triangle and then up and down. If a mat is provided on a slippery floor that permits only up and down movement, then you will need to move to the side on the return journey to assess sideways movement. Make a final tour of the ring to decide which dogs you would like to see again (preferably not more than eight), and indicate to your steward that you would like the others to leave the ring. If you have any doubts on movement ask some of the eight to move again before making your final selection. Line up your winners from left to right in the previously agreed place and call for your judging book.

Some judges like to juggle the dogs about and change their minds at the last moment but this is seldom advisable. Write your notes about the winners – first only for an Open Show, first and second for a Championship Show, as clearly as possible. It is surprising how illegible your notes can be when later you try to write your report! A tape recorder can be a boon here but check your batteries to make sure it is working before you arrive and take great care not to wipe the tape clean before you have written your report. Your steward will ensure that you sign each slip in your judging book, but I like to sign the book throughout while I am waiting for the first class to come in. It saves valuable time later. While I am writing my report, I like the stewards to be assembling the next class and checking numbers so that there is very little time lapse between each class.

Only the new dogs will need to be examined in your next class. Your previous winners will have been lined up by your steward according to your placings and it is as well to check these over with him when you have finished your examinations of the new dogs. Try and rely on your own memory as far as possible – not all stewards are infallible, particularly those who are not familiar with the breed.

While judging, handle the dogs gently, especially puppies, and treat each dog as you would like your own Collie to be treated. It is easy to put a timid dog off showing for life, whereas a reassuring judge can make showing a pleasurable experience that he will come to enjoy. Be methodical in your ways so that both stewards and exhibitors can follow your system of judging.

You have spent years learning about the Collie, you know the type you like, so judge to it. Pick the dogs you would most like to take home, in descending order, and you will not go far wrong. You cannot please everyone so do not try. It is your day, it is your opinion they have come to seek and if you judge with honesty and integrity you will go home happy and content in the knowledge that you have judged to the best of your ability.

7

Breeding

At the present time, when there are so many unwanted dogs in rescue kennels and charity dogs' homes, everyone who wants to breed a litter must carefully consider the consequences. It is too late once the litter has arrived and homes are being desperately sought, regardless of their suitability. For some reason, many pet owners are convinced that their pet bitch should have at least one litter for the sake of her health. Even veterinary surgeons sometimes concur with this theory, which to me seems nonsensical. I have yet to hear medical opinion suggest that a maiden lady should give birth to a child for the sake of her own health! Why then should it be thought beneficial for a bitch to produce a litter?

I firmly believe that only if a pet bitch is of high quality and has been tested free from heriditary diseases should any consideration be given to mating her. Collies have comparatively large litters and a pet owner is unlikely to have the waiting-list for puppies that the established breeder will have. Rearing litters is hard work and time consuming. Puppies cannot be left on their own, but need constant supervision. In my opinion, breeding is better left to those intent on improving their strains and the breed, and who are prepared to dedicate many years to this cause. I include this chapter for them.

The Brood Bitch

Your whole future in the breed may depend on your choice of a good brood bitch. Its importance cannot be overestimated. Years ago, there used to be an oft-quoted saying, 'Your stud-dog is half your kennel'. I rather side with the Irishman who replied, with all the logic of his country, 'Well if me dog is half me kennel then me bitches are the other three-quarters'. How right he was.

You may be lucky enough to obtain a top-flight bitch puppy at eight weeks but the odds will be stacked against you. No breeder will part with what they believe to be a future champion. If any good at all, the pick of the litter will stay at home. The only way you can be certain of getting the pick of a litter, is to breed your own. For that you will need to buy, borrow or otherwise acquire the services of a good brood bitch. Take great care in her selection. Go to as many shows as you can, study the Collies in the ring, decide on the type you like and note the kennels that are producing that type. Pay attention to temperaments as well as show points. Poor temperaments are all too easily inherited, so ask questions and not only from the breeder. No breeder will ever admit to having poor temperaments in his strain. All his Collies have good temperaments and are sweet natured, he will tell you. Indeed, he is telling you the truth. It is the dog's behaviour with strangers and not with his owners that is the giveaway.

The average Collie bitch will produce three litters in her lifetime, sometimes four, but rarely more. As the bitch gets older, whelping complications become more frequent so it is advisable to get a bitch who has had no more than one litter. Beware of the three- or four-year-old bitch that has never had a litter. She may be barren and the breeder may be trying to off-load her to a good home. Make enquiries about the mother and grandmother. Were they easy whelpers and good mothers? Did they lose many puppies? Did they have plenty of milk? These things run in strains. I have in my kennel the fifth generation of an easy whelping, good lactating, prolific bitch. She herself produced four litters, her daughter three, her granddaughter two, so far, and her great-granddaughter has just reared her first litter. Not one of these bitches has ever lost a puppy, even though a few were very small when born. On the other hand, I also have a particularly well-bred bitch that I bought as a puppy. She has produced two litters with only one puppy surviving from each litter and this only by fostering and great care and attention. As far as I am concerned, this is not a line worth preserving. In nature it would rapidly die out.

My experience keeping records for a pedigree herd of Guernseys some years ago, led me to some interesting conclusions. I noticed that the best milkers that produced up to ten calves in a lifetime and gave very high milk yields were confined to two families. Outside those two families, the lives of the other cows were comparatively short and unproductive. There is an immense difference between cows, not only in the amount they each give during a lactation but in the speed with which they let down their milk. Some are easy milkers and some hard milkers. I believe that just such a variation can be found in bitches. Some litters seem to spend all their time asleep, occasionally waking for a short suckle before nodding off again in contentment. Others seem to be constantly struggling and butting their mothers in an attempt to extract the milk. They appear to be getting milk but they use up so much energy in extracting it that when they fall asleep, it is with exhaustion rather than with contentment. They do not thrive as well as the sleepy puppies who, paradoxically, seem to be seldom at the milk bar. Such an easy milking mother is worth her weight in gold.

It goes without saying that your bitch must be well bred. I personally do not like to see too much inbreeding in a pedigree. By inbreeding, I mean father to daughter, mother to son or brother to sister mating. The laws of the land on incest have been wisely drawn up. Its practice leads to desperate problems in both physical and mental health, which is why it has been outlawed. It is difficult to believe that dogs can be any different. On the other hand, line breeding, where the pedigree blends together using different animals of the same line, is highly successful. Matings of proved excellence are a bitch to her grandfather, a dog to his grandmother, uncle to niece, nephew to aunt and, if you can vouch for their temperaments, half-brother to half-sister. This matching of pedigrees is known as breeding for genotype.

Many old-time professionals practised a very different method. They maintained that by breeding like to like they would come up with something to beat the most carefully line-bred dog. This is look-alike breeding or breeding for phenotype. My own thoughts on this method are that, with Collies at least, you seldom get look-alikes unless they are from the same line.

A third method, which seems to be meeting with some success, is to mix pedigrees but only using highly successful specimens. The thinking behind this is that whatever throw backs you get, they are bound to be good because there are no weak links in the pedigree. The drawback is that the litters are so much more uneven than line-bred litters. All this should be borne in mind when choosing a mate for your bitch. If you feel you need to out cross to obtain some particular point, it is wise to return to the same line at the next mating.

The ideal brood bitch, that has won well in the show ring, from a well-bred line and that has proved herself a good whelper, is likely to be expensive. Buy the best you can afford but if she is beyond your means then consider one who for some reason or another has not had a glittering show career. If she is bred from the line you like and fulfils your other criteria then accept her gratefully. Many an undistinguished bitch has produced better progeny than her more glamorous sister.

I strongly advocate patience if you are waiting for your bitch to come into season. Collie bitches are a law unto themselves in this respect. It is rare for a Collie to be on a six-month cycle. Nine to ten months is more usual but it is not uncommon for a gap of eighteen months to elapse between seasons. No matter how long the wait, I would not advise you to have her brought into season artificially. Over-reliance on this method will lead to sterility as more than one famous kennel has found to its cost. If she is definitely overdue then the safest way to bring her in is to run her with a bitch in full season. This usually has the desired effect and is known amongst breeders as the 'me too syndrome'. No logical explanation has been found but it certainly works in many cases. If a bitch is on a regular yearly cycle it can sometimes be altered to a twice-yearly cycle by this method.

Fertility varies from both bitch to bitch and from strain to strain. Years ago, such strains as Mrs Newbury's Alphington Collies consistently produced bitches who bred between ten and thirteen puppies in a litter. Between five and seven is the average these days and quite enough for a bitch to rear well. However, some bitches seem to produce only between one and three puppies in a litter. To increase fertility in such bitches it is worth taking a leaf out of the farmer's book and to try 'flushing' your bitch before mating. This is a practice common amongst sheep and pig breeders and has proved highly successful.

As soon as your bitch comes in season, increase her food intake considerably. Double her meat or protein ration and introduce a milk-based breakfast. The logic behind this is that nature is fooled into thinking there is a plentiful supply of food available and responds accordingly. Naturalists will tell you that in a good spring the number of young animals and fledglings produced is significantly higher than in a cold spring when food is short. It is important to return the bitch to her usual rations immediately after mating for the next three to four weeks.

Care of the Brood Bitch

Let us suppose that you have now acquired your brood bitch and are eagerly waiting for her to come into season. If she has been acquired on breeding terms then it is almost certain that the breeder will have reserved the right to choose the stud-dog. He may well be at a considerable distance from you and you will be expected to pay the stud fee. Breeding terms vary considerably. Most breeders will want the pick of the litter and one or more of the other puppies. Try to retain at least the second pick of the litter as this will allow you to keep either the pick of the dogs or the pick of the bitches for yourself. The Kennel Club issues a 'Loan or Use of Bitch' contract on which breeding terms can be recorded. It is not widely used, but is available.

Some breeders will give you a free service if they own a suitable dog but are usually happy if you prefer to use a more famous dog and are prepared to pay the fee. If the choice of sire has been left to you, then try and get to as many shows as you can. Look at the dogs, note their lines and study photographs of their forebears in the handbooks and elsewhere. Look carefully at the progeny of the dogs in the ring. Read the show reports as much can be gleaned from this source of information. When you have made your final decision, make a firm booking with the owner. The first day the bitch comes into season, phone with this information so that he will have a rough idea when to expect you and can arrange his bookings accordingly. Never leave it till the day your bitch is ready and casually ring up to inform the dog's owner. If you do, you are liable to receive a sharp reply!

The owner may require you to take a vaginal culture from your bitch and possibly a brucellosis test before accepting her. Such a request is not commonplace but the practice is growing. Brucellosis can cause a pregnant bitch to abort before full term. It is spread in the same way as venereal disease. There is some evidence that it is increasing, so do not be offended if the owner asks you to have such a test done. He is naturally anxious to protect his dog.

Every breeder has their own method of telling when a bitch is ready to accept the dog. It will normally be somewhere between the tenth and fourteenth day but bitches vary tremendously. The amount of swelling of the vulva also varies and seems to get progressively less as the bitch becomes older. The more the swelling, the greater the hormone activity. If the bitch never swells then she may have a fertility problem and such bitches are difficult to get in whelp. It is worth taking her to your vet for a hormone injection if all else fails. When the swelling begins to go down and the colour changes from bright red to a transparent pink, the bitch is most ready to accept the dog. In their anxiety not to leave it too late, far too many novice owners bring the bitch too early. This makes the mating unnecessarily difficult and lessens the likelihood of conception.

Most bitches will accept a dog for four or five days after the change of colour. Sometimes I have found this to be as late as the seventeenth day and I know of one champion bitch who after several failures, triumphantly produced her first litter when she was mated on the twenty-first day! The change in colour is a more reliable guide than sticking to any preconceived notion of the right day to breed. If necessary, you can take her to your vet for an ovulation test to make sure you choose the right day.

If you have had difficulty previously in getting your bitch in whelp then you should try to arrange for her to have two services. You have no right to this as a matter of course but most breeders will agree to it unless the dog is very booked up. If the mating is normal and the bitch was ready, there is usually no need for a second mating unless the dog has not been used for some considerable time. In such a case two matings are preferable. Many experienced stud-dogs know well enough when the mating has been successful and will refuse to mate her a second time.

So now you have your lady-in-waiting at home. Continue normal feeding for the first four weeks. It is important not to overfeed at this time as you do not want to make her overweight and the embryos are absorbing very little at this time. Continue steady exercise as muscle tone is important. All breeders have their pet theory on how to tell whether a bitch is in whelp. Some rely on seeing a watery discharge about ten days after mating, some say the skin round the nipples turns purplish as pregnancy advances, others that the hair on her flanks curls upwards by six weeks! The only certain way is to feel the number of heads through her abdomen. They can be counted between the twenty-first and twenty-eighth day but it requires considerable experience. Most vets rely on this method unless they have a scanning machine.

At a later date the whelps disappear up the horns of the uterus and cannot be felt. Sometimes it seems that the bitch is putting on weight but you cannot be certain whether this is due to her extra food intake or to her pregnancy. It is worth trying the tape-measure test. Every week from the fifth week measure round her waist, just where the rib-cage ends, and note the measurement. You will soon discover whether her increased size is an optical illusion or not. Many in-whelp bitches start to experience discomfort in the fourth week of pregnancy, they go off their food and suffer from 'morning sickness' or periodical vomiting. This usually only lasts about a week and from then onwards her appetite rapidly increases.

If she is carrying a large number of embryos then she may experience difficulty in retaining large quantities of food. It is better to give her small meals at least three times a day. She will need a higher protein level (up to 28 per cent of her total diet should be protein), as the rapid growth of the puppies places a tremendous demand on her body from which they extract the protein and minerals they need. Many anxious breeders overdose with mineral and vitamin supplements, and they can do more harm than good as research into Greyhound feeding has revealed. It has been proved that the addition of too much calcium has a deleterious effect on bone and joints, and causes a significant increase in hip dysplasia.

If you feed one of the fortified complete diets for whelping bitches, no additions should be made, but not all ladies-in-waiting appreciate these complete foods. I myself prefer to continue my ordinary feeding of soaked biscuit meal but to increase meat rations and milky feeds. The meat feeds are mixed with some mashed green vegetables and a spoonful of corn oil and a little bone meal sprinkled on top. Hard-boiled eggs are a palatable extra form of protein and most Collies enjoy some cheese grated over their food. It must be remembered that two-thirds of the puppies birth weight will be gained in the last three weeks of pregnancy. The nutritional demand placed on the mother at this time is enormous and must be met from her food intake.

Throughout the pregnancy, stress must be avoided. This is particularly important between the third and fifth week. If you relate one week of a bitch's nine-week pregnancy to one month of the human mother's nine-month pregnancy, you will realise that between three and five weeks is the most likely time for the bitch to miscarry or re-absorb her puppies. She must take things very quietly during this time, she should not be shown or taken on long and tiring journeys and she certainly should not be wormed at this stage. She should have been wormed prior to mating but if not, it is better to worm her gently a fortnight before whelping, for roundworms only. All bitches will infect their puppies with roundworm larvae to a greater or lesser degree. Every dog retains roundworms in his body in a state of suspended animation. In a male, they will remain dormant throughout life. In a female, they awake to the hormone stimulus of pregnancy and will be passed to her puppies through the umbilical cord in the womb and through her milk after birth. Each bitch carries enough of these dormant larvae in her body to affect every litter she produces to a diminishing extent. Her first litter will be the most heavily infested, a phenomenon which many breeders have observed for themselves.

Whelping Preparations

A great deal of money can be spent on the right equipment for whelping, from lamps and whelping boxes to expensive kennels and puppy runs. Gone are the days when a bitch was allowed to run loose, dig a hole under a tree and produce her litter in the open air. Infant mortality was high in those days. Only the strongest survived. Nowadays, we pamper our bitches and struggle to rear the whole litter.

If your bitch is a house pet then you cannot expect her to take willingly to a kennel when she becomes a mother. It is best to find some secluded spot for her where she will be away from the general traffic of the house but will still feel she is part of the family. You should have all your equipment ready, well before the date she is due. There are still breeders who prefer to use a covered box with a door in one end and a flap of material to cover the opening. This is as close as you can get to nature. Obviously there is no room for a lamp – the bitch's body heat supplies all the warmth required. It may well be that there will be a revival of this type of natural rearing method but at present most breeders seem to prefer the open whelping box where mother and puppies can be monitored constantly.

A good, strong whelping box is essential and it is worth having one constructed if you are not a DIY enthusiast. It will give many years of service and is, we hope, destined to become the birthplace of your future champions. A box approximately 3×4ft (1×1.25m) is suitable. The sides should be at least 1½ft (0.5m) high and preferably hinged for easy storage. A small door for the bitch to enter is advisable and this can be closed when she leaves the box to prevent the puppies following her once they can walk. Remember not to use carbolic if you are disinfecting it after previous use. A strong solution of household bleach has been found to be the best germicide for parvo and other infections, but in this case should be followed, a few hours later, with copious rinsing with fresh water.

Warmth is vital and can be provided by an infra-red lamp suspended from above. It does not have to be a very powerful bulb for a Rough Collie. Smooth Collies would require slightly higher wattage as they do not have the advantage of a thick coat for the puppies to snuggle into. I would suggest 250W for a Rough and 350W for a Smooth, if your bitch is in the house; rather more if she is in a kennel and there is no other form of heating. Always use a dull emitter. A bright emitter will disturb the mother's rest if left on day and night and will not be good for the puppies' eyes once they open.

The ideal floor covering for the whelping box would be the warm shaggy man-made fabrics that are freely advertised in the canine press. These can be put in the washing machine and dry quickly. They not only provide warmth, their rough surface is ideal for the puppies to get a grip with their hind feet to enable them to nurse easily. The new heating pads that are finding favour with breeders can be placed under one of these rugs and they eliminate the need for an overhead lamp. These electrically heated pads cover only a small area of the box but the puppies seem to have no difficulty in congregating on one while the mother lies in the cooler part of the box. If you use one, you must remember to get a hole bored in the box to take the cable.

The average gestation period of the bitch is 63 days or exactly nine weeks. Make sure that you have everything in readiness well in advance. I have had bitches whelp a week before their due date, and you do not want to be caught unprepared. As the time draws near, you will find your excitement mounting. You will probably have spent hours studying pedigrees and photographs and possibly travelled many miles in your search for the right sire. Now all your plans are coming to fruition. Most Collie bitches are easy whelpers. The Collie pup is shaped like nature's own torpedo with his long nose and narrow head – the best possible shape for easy whelping – so try not to worry. A calm and confident approach will communicate itself to your bitch. Always notify your vet in advance, in case an emergency should arise.

Introduce your bitch to her whelping box, although she will probably refuse to go into it until the time comes. Wash her nipples in warm soapy water taking care to rinse and dry them well. If you are certain she is not having a false pregnancy it is advisable to cut away the hair round her nipples and her skirts. Otherwise puppies can get entangled in the long hair, sometimes with disastrous results. Prepare your midwife's bag which should contain:

Veterinary thermometer. (Unless you are a trained nurse I would suggest you buy one of the digital thermometers that are enclosed in a plastic case – they are virtually unbreakable and ideal for the purpose.)
Covered hot-water bottle or covered heating pad
Antiseptic
Sharp, blunt-ended scissors
Jar in which they can be disinfected
Cardboard box in which the puppies can be placed on top of the hot-

water bottle or pad
At least two clean rough towels
Roll of kitchen paper
The stack of newspapers that you and your neighbours have been saving for months
Miniature bottle of brandy

The only sure indication that your bitch is close to whelping is her temperature. Take her temperature regularly for at least a week beforehand. If you have not done this before ask your vet to show you how it is done. Her normal temperature of 101.5 °F (39 °C) will drop dramatically to between 97 and 99 °F (36.5 and 37 °C) prior to whelping and is a sure sign that something is about to happen. The refusal of food is another indication but one upon which you cannot always rely. I have had bitches that produced puppies in the middle of supper and calmly finished their food before turning their attention to the indignant puppy on the floor!

Not long after her temperature has dropped, you will notice a change in her behaviour. She will start to pant, sometimes tremble and her eyes will assume a strained 'wild-eyed' look with her ears laid back. This is the first stage of labour and will last for anything up to twelve hours. She will become restless and start scratching up the floor covering. Try to get her to stay in her whelping box but leave the door open. If she does not want to stay, do not insist. She may wish to make several trips outside to urinate. During this time the cervix will slowly dilate and a clear watery discharge is usually apparant. Whenever she goes outside, accompany her. She may be seeking an outside whelping spot, or she may simply drop a puppy unobserved, so follow behind so that you can catch the puppy in a folded towel.

This first stage can last a long time and it can stop and start again several hours later. Bitches seem to be able to control the whelping mechanism in some way and if strangers arrive, whelping can be interrupted. It is surprising the number of people who will ask if they, or even their children, can watch the whelping process. You must be firm about this. Your bitch needs complete privacy. She will be grateful if you stay with her throughout but she will not want an audience any more than a human mother would in similar circumstances.

This first stage can last a long time. Calm your rising panic by checking over your midwife's bag, making sure that all is in readiness. Inform your vet that whelping has started. Newspapers are quite the best material for a bitch to whelp on. They rapidly absorb fluid and fresh ones can be inserted under the bitch as whelping proceeds. Bitches vary tremendously in the amount of fluid they produce. Some are very messy whelpers and the box will be awash; others will have almost dry whelpings.

After what may seem to be an interminable time, you will observe a muscular ripple passing along the bitch's back – her contractions have begun. At first, there will be fifteen to twenty minute intervals between them but they will gradually become stronger and more frequent. When you see the bitch arch her back and hold her breath while she 'pushes' you will know that the first birth is imminent. Most bitches whelp lying down, but some prefer to stand so allow her to choose her own position. Most puppies are born in the water bag which allows them to slip out easily, but in some cases the water bag will have already broken and the puppy will be delivered dry.

There are often considerable differences in the behaviour of kennel and house bitches in their reaction to their first-born. Kennel-bred bitches usually remove the sac, clean the puppy vigorously with their tongue, chew through the cord and devour the afterbirth in no time at all. House pets behave rather differently. They view their first-born with a look of absolute horror, convinced they have had an unfortunate 'accident' and dire punishment will follow. If the puppy does not move or cry, nothing will induce the mother to go near it. This is why it is so essential for you to be on hand at this time to calm the mother and to remove the membranes from the puppy's mouth and nose. If he shows no sign of life, do not attempt to give him the kiss of life; this will only push mucus down into the lungs. Shake the puppy gently, head downwards, to free the air passages and rub it quite roughly with your towel. Persevere with your efforts and a seemingly dead puppy may be revived. Once it starts to cry and move, the mother will instinctively take over. If she still shows no sign of having any maternal instincts, put the revived puppy in your heated box and let her get on with the whelping. By the time she has got to the third puppy, she will have got over her initial shock and all will be well.

Make sure that a placenta is passed with each puppy. Normally, the bitch will devour them so quickly that you will have difficulty in counting them. She will chew through the cord and eat the afterbirth in almost one movement. It may appear that she is about to eat the puppy at the same time but rest assured – she will not make that mistake. If, for any reason, she does not cut the cord, you must do this for her, but it is very seldom necessary. Cut through the cord cleanly, about two inches (5cm) from the puppy's body with your sharp, disinfected scissors and dab the severed cord with antiseptic.

Eating the afterbirth is nature's way of stimulating milk production. It also cleans up the nest and provides nourishment for the bitch at a time when she is unable to go hunting. If you have a large litter it may be wiser to remove the last few afterbirths if your bitch has a delicate stomach. Over-distension will make her sick. If, on the other hand, she is one of your 'dustbin dogs' that will eat literally anything without ill effect she can be safely left to carry on as nature intended.

Very occasionally, a bitch will seem to have difficulty producing a puppy. This may be an extra large one or may be a breech or backwards presentation. Usually, she will stand up in her efforts to expel the puppy, but if she is not making much progress you must examine her. If part of the head is out but it disappears up the birth canal and reappears as she strains, then you can help her. Scrub your hands thoroughly and roll back the lips of the vulva. Do not attempt to catch hold of the puppy by the head. Instead, place the tips of the fingers of each hand on either side of the body of the puppy, which you can feel quite easily through the mother's body. Next time she strains, squeeze gently from the back and the puppy's head will pop out. Continue gently squeezing from the back each time the bitch strains and soon the shoulders will appear. Once they are through, the puppy will pop out like a pea from a pod.

The same method can be used for a bitch in difficulty with a breech presentation but you must be careful not to apply pressure internally on the puppy's head. I have found this method to be invaluable when a bitch has been straining unproductively for some time. If this should fail and a couple of hours have passed since she started straining, you will need to call your vet in case a puppy is sideways on. If inertia sets in, he will give her an injection to stimulate her contractions. Such complications are rare in Collies but it is as well to be prepared.

Most labours progress without incident, puppies following each other at fifteen to twenty minute intervals. Very often there is a pause when one horn of the uterus is emptied and the other horn takes over. Often the bitch appears to have finished whelping and has settled down with her litter when one final puppy makes his appearance several hours later.

If the whelping is prolonged, a drink of cold milk, with a couple of egg yolks and a little sugar or glucose beaten up in it, will give her renewed energy, assuming you can persuade her to take it. I like to place my puppies in a box, as already indicated, until the bitch has finished whelping, for fear she might injure one. Other breeders prefer to let the puppies attempt to suckle throughout the whelping, claiming that it stimulates milk production. Indeed, this is the more natural process and if she seems to be distressed at having the puppies put in a box by her side, it is wiser to let her have them, in turn, to clean and caress. When she appears to have finished the whelping, try and coax her outside for a few moments to relieve herself. During this time you can remove the soggy newspapers and have her puppies neatly arranged on their warm bed by the time she returns.

Now is the time to open that miniature bottle of brandy. Your bitch will be settled in with her new family, tired but happy. You, on the other hand will feel completely exhausted. A celebratory drink while you watch that loveliest of all sights – a Collie proudly nursing her babies – will be no more than you deserve.

Rearing Problems

One of the hardest lessons a breeder has to learn is when to accept that nature knows best and to give up the battle to preserve a life that would not survive on its own. Unlike man, nature does not struggle to bring up her defectives. The world is a tough place and only the fittest will survive to become the progenitors of the next generation. We have all, at some time or another, stayed up all night or slept on the settee with a box of orphan puppies by our side and an alarm clock set to wake us at two-hourly feed intervals. It is one thing to bring up a litter whose mother is no longer able to feed them; it is quite another to bring up a weak or sickly puppy that is unable to make it on his own. I am not talking about the small, lively puppy that, in a large litter, tends to get pushed out by his stronger siblings – it is quite legitimate to make sure that he gets a protected place at the milk bar to enable him to survive.

Experience leads me to suggest that we are often mistaken in trying to rear weakly puppies. By 'weakly' I mean the constantly crying puppy, the puppy with the bubbling throat cry or the puppy that always seems cold even under the lamp. Puppies that are born with dead white skin on their pads, nose and mouth instead of a healthy pink are seldom worth resuscitating and struggling to keep alive. If a mother constantly rejects a puppy by pushing him to one side or by hiding him under the rug, she has good reason. I once had a devoted mother who, after a fortnight, carried her largest strongest puppy into the house and laid him on the hearthrug. Every time we returned him to the box, she carried him back into the house as if asking us to take care of him. We did our best to bottle feed him, but he died anyway. We never found out why, possibly a weak heart, but something made her discard him with such quiet persistance.

There are times when you will have no choice but to hand rear a litter. The mother may have died or had an infection or simply be unable to produce any milk. It is not a task to be lightly undertaken. By far the best and easiest method is to obtain the services of a foster mother.

Years ago these were readily available and advertised weekly in the canine press but nowadays they are more difficult to locate. It is worth contacting your vet who will have a list of recent whelpings. Your best bet is probably a notice in your local shop, as it is the owners of mongrel bitches who are most likely to be able to help you. For a small financial inducement they will often allow you to borrow her or even substitute some of your aristocratic puppies for some of her own. In this case, it is only humane for you to take the unwanted puppies to your vet for euthanasia. The mother, provided she is allowed to keep a couple of her own, will happily accept the newcomers. A bitch that is going through a false pregnancy will often be delighted with her ready-made family, produce copious supplies of milk and settle down to be an exemplary mother. Even a very maternal bitch without milk will make a better job of it than you can hope to do on your own. You will have to feed them, by hand, but she will provide warmth, love and will clean them with great vigour and efficiency. If you are offered a bitch at a later date, accept her gratefully, but meanwhile you must get on with hand rearing.

Breeders do not always appreciate the value of the colostrum or first milk. This is immensely valuable as it provides an immunity to many infections that beset small puppies. Even hard-headed farmers allow their calves to run with their mothers and take the first milk before the cows return to the milking herd and the calves are taken to be reared on milk substitute. So valuable is this commodity, that I would advise you to set up a colostrum bank to be used in emergencies. This is quite simple to do if you draw off a small quantity from your bitch in the first day after whelping. Put it in a small, labelled, plastic bag and place in your deep-freeze. Add to it every time you have a bitch whelping and soon you will have a respectable quantity of frozen colostrum. This can be warmed and fed from a dropper to orphan puppies in their first few days of life and will dramatically improve their chances of warding off infection. This is equally important for puppies placed on a foster mother, whose own babies are more than two days old, as it is for those you intend to hand rear.

There are several products that claim to be a complete substitute for bitches' milk. None of them are totally satisfactory. I cannot speak for other breeds, but these products are known to produce nutritional cataracts in Collies. I first came upon this problem nearly forty years ago when an orphan puppy that I had proudly reared from birth was found to be almost totally blind. I noticed that by the time he was six months old the cataracts had disappeared and his sight was perfect. He went on to win many prizes and sired three champions, none of whom had or produced any progeny with eye troubles. Present-day eye specialists confirm that nutritional cataracts in hand-reared Collie puppies are not heriditary and are reversible. There is a parallel to be found in the vitamin deficiency blindness in Third World children which can be reversed, and finally cured, by the addition of vitamins to the diet. It would be advisable to add a vitamin supplement to any commercial feed you use. A perfectly adequate feed for emergency use could be made up at home as follows:

> 1 cup warm boiled milk
> 1 teaspoon of vegetable or corn oil
> 2 egg yolks
> 2 teaspoons of glucose, honey or sugar
> 1 pinch salt
> 2 drops liquid children's vitamins

It is labour conserving to make up double the quantity and keep it frozen until you need it. Similarly, night feeds can be kept in a thermos at the required heat to save you warming them up separately. Make sure you have, to hand, the facilities for disinfecting your utensils. Vets advise feeding every two hours but I have always found three-hourly intervals to be sufficient, at night at any rate.

Tube feeding is quicker and less time consuming when you have a large litter but I prefer to use it only when puppies are too weak or too small to suckle from the bottle. To use this method, you will need a catheter tube and a syringe obtainable from your vet or a chemist. Sterilise them before use. To measure the tube, lay it against the side of the puppy and mark on it the distance between the puppy's mouth and his last rib. This is the distance you will need to push the tube down the puppy's throat to reach his stomach. Draw up sufficient of the milk mixture and place the tube on the nozzle of the syringe. Lay the puppy on a rough towel with his front feet extended in the nursing position and gently insert the tube into his mouth, over the tongue and down the back of the throat, until you reach the marker on the tube. Very gently, press the syringe so that you are slowly injecting the fluid into the stomach. When you are finished, withdraw the tube gently.

I must emphasise that where the puppy is strong enough to nurse from the bottle, this method is to be preferred as it encourages the sucking reflex. The best results can be obtained by using a premature baby bottle with a soft nipple. Whether you use the tube or bottle method the puppy must be cleaned afterwards with damp cotton wool and stimulated to defecate and urinate. Always remember that the mother will do this quite roughly with her tongue. If she is able to do this although not capable of producing milk, it is far better to give the puppy back to her to complete his toilet.

The litter that is born fighting fit, all puppies latching on to the milk bar like limpets and growing fatter by the day, is an absolute joy. There is no more pleasurable sight than a litter of puppies with their front feet firmly braced against their mother's body, their little tails wagging in unison as they suckle. The only sound to be heard is the noise of the milk gurgling down their throats, or the little contented grunts they emit. Very different is the sound that all breeders dread – the persistant mewing cry of the sick puppy. Usually, the puppy refuses to suckle and sometimes the abdomen appears swollen. If this is the case, he may be suffering from colic and a couple of drops of baby Gripe Water may relieve the symptoms.

It quite frequently happens that a puppy crawls away from his mother and becomes chilled. When you pick him up he will feel limp, cold and almost lifeless. Do not make the mistake of trying to feed such a puppy. His digestive system will have temporarily packed up and it will be incapable of absorbing food. Various ways of warming a chilled puppy back to life have been suggested, such as placing him inside your clothes next to your skin, placing him in a warm oven or even under the grill! In my experience, by far the best method is to treat him as you would a human being suffering from hypothermia – immerse him in hot water. Run a bowl of hand-hot water, test it with your elbow and, keeping his head clear of the water, lower the puppy into it. Let him try and swim if he can – the exercise will help to warm him. When the puppy is sufficiently recovered, take him out and dry him carefully with a hair dryer. Before returning him to the mother, wrap him in cotton wool and encase him in tin foil, leaving both ends free so that the mother can clean his face and bottom.

Every now and again, strong healthy puppies will die, one after the other, in quick succession, for no apparent reason. This is the dreaded 'fading puppy syndrome'. It has been likened to cot deaths and is equally inexplicable. My research and the considerable correspondence I have had on this subject lead me to believe that many deaths attributed to this syndrome are, in fact, due to other causes. Hypothermia is an obvious one. Overheating is another not quite so obvious cause. A weak heart or simple failure to suckle accounts for many deaths. Occasionally, puppies appear to be suckling strongly but the mother, through shock or some other reason, is withholding her milk. If you suspect this may be the case, put the mother on to tranquillisers and all will be well. I once had a bitch who produced nine puppies the first three of which were born dead. She was inconsolable and took very little notice of the live ones. She seemed to have plenty of milk and the puppies nursed strongly but did not thrive. At first the vet diagnosed fading puppy syndrome, but when she was put on tranquillisers there was a dramatic improvement in the condition of the survivors.

A mother might clean her puppies so diligently that it completely masks the fact that they are suffering from tummy upset or diarrhoea. This is the cause of many deaths as dehydration quickly sets in. If a puppy has lost his fat, round appearance, seems thin and stringy and lacks energy, dehydration should be suspected. Pinch the skin and if it does not spring back to normal immediately but remains pinched, your worst suspicions will be confirmed.

Make up a solution of one cup of boiled water, two tablespoonfuls of glucose or honey or sugar and one teaspoonful of salt. Give one dropperful of this fortified warm water every half-hour until the puppy is fully recovered. Monitor his progress carefully as you will only have cured the symptoms, not the cause.

There appears to be an established link between kennel cough and fading puppy syndrome. A remedy is available on the Continent which seems to be extremely effective in preventing both diseases. Unfortunately, it has not been tested in Britain and it is illegal to import this drug. Nevertheless, it is obviously wise to take extreme precautions if you know that kennel cough is in the area. Further research may reveal that fading puppy syndrome is, as many breeders suspect, linked with breathing problems.

The Stud-Dog

Selection

For those considering keeping a stud-dog for the first time, one is tempted to offer them the cynical advice so often proffered to those contemplating marriage – 'don't'. It is certainly not the easy path to riches that most novices believe. There are a great many male show Collies but few that can be accurately described as stud-dogs of value to the breed. Not only must such a dog be an excellent specimen himself, with good breeding behind him, he must also have the ability to pass on these good qualities. A good dog should be able to improve on the bitch. A great dog will not only do this but he will put his unmistakable stamp on every litter he produces, no matter what the bitch or her breeding. Very often this is handed down for several generations and his stamp can clearly be seen in his descendants long after he is dead.

At the time of writing, Collie stud fees are exceptionally low. When I first came into the breed they corresponded to the price of a puppy. On top of that you would have to send the bitch, in a basket, by rail and possibly pay for her keep while she stayed with the owner of the stud-dog. Nowadays, the average stud fee for a champion is less than half the price of a puppy, a level which owners of other breeds find unbelievably low, particularly as the Collie breed is not noted for the smallness of its litters. It costs a great deal of time and money to make up a champion and the owner should be at least entitled to recoup his expenditure. In the long term, it is not to the advantage of the breed that stud fees should be kept at their present artificially low level. While they are, it behoves the novice to take advantage of them. There is nothing to be gained by using your own, or a nearby mediocre, dog when the best champions are available at low cost and only a motorway trip away. If you make your selection carefully, the results will be incomparably better.

So what are the considerations to be taken into account when choosing a suitable consort for your pride and joy? Firstly, you should have studied the breed sufficiently well to know the type of Collie you are aiming to produce. It is no good just saying 'the correct type'. Even if all breeders started with the same bitch, they would still evolve strains of differing types. Over the generations they would be selecting and discarding for different characteristics. All great breeders have their own interpretation of the Standard. There are some traits which for them are a must and some on which they are prepared to compromise. For instance, some will insist on a full rounded muzzle with a good underjaw and will not worry too much about stops. Others will select their puppies chiefly on eye and expression and will not be too concerned about high tail carriage. Some will place conformation above all else and will forgive an over-sensitive temperament. Of course, all breeders want to own the perfect Collie but such an animal has not yet been born. It is better to choose a Collie with several minor faults than one major fault which cannot be overlooked.

More important than the dog himself is the type of progeny he is siring. This you can only learn by attending shows or studying show reports. Note the faults and virtues that he is passing on to his offspring. Think carefully before you make a decision. Decide which faults you can live with and which faults you cannot live with. Consider the various strains, their strengths and their weaknesses and try to think ahead and not just to the results of the first mating. You will diminish your chances of success if you jump from blood line to blood line. In endeavouring to obtain the best points from each you will be liable to end up with the worst points from all of them. Once you have established your own blood line it will be perfectly feasible for you to make the occasional out cross to obtain some special characteristic.

Finally, you must consider the question of heriditary diseases. The day has not yet dawned when all Collie breeders have their stock tested for these diseases, though I firmly believe that day will come. Make sure you choose a stud-dog which is physically healthy and sound in temperament. It is wise to ask to see the dog's BVA certificates for freedom from eye disease and hip dysplasia; if he has them, his owner will be only too pleased to show you them. Do not be put off by a breeder's protestations that he does not have his dogs examined because he has never had any problems. At present, there are no strains which are free from hereditary eye and hip disease although some are significantly better than others.

All these points must also be borne in mind when the time comes for you to select a puppy as your own future stud-dog. Financially, it will seldom be worth your while but like all aspects of Collie breeding, money is not the only criterion. There is no doubt that a good male Collie is a magnificent animal and a great deal of pleasure can be gained from breeding and showing such a specimen. If he also passes on his best characteristics it is almost equally satisfying to be able to watch the success of his progeny in the ring. It is a great temptation, having carefully selected the most suitable sire for your bitch, to keep a dog puppy from your first litter. You have to be realistic about this. It is so easy to be convinced that one of your puppies is a certain champion, simply because he looks better than his brothers and sisters. Only an experienced breeder can tell you whether he has really got what it takes or whether he is simply the best out of a mediocre litter. It is possible to breed a champion in your first litter, but it doesn't happen very often. If you do keep him you will have a problem finding a good bitch to use him on. Unless he is phenomenally successful in the ring few breeders will be interested in his services. They will want to see what he produces before deciding whether he can usefully be incorporated into their breeding programme. A few pet Collie owners may ask to use him but this will do him more harm than good in the quality stakes.

It is far better to wait for a second generation before you decide to keep a dog puppy. You will probably still have his grandmother carrying a little of the same blood and she will be a very good test for the quality of his first litter. If one or two of his first puppies begin to do some useful winning, breeders will begin to take note of him and stud enquiries will start to come your way.

Managing the Stud-Dog

There is a great deal more to putting a dog at stud than is dreamed of by the novice owner. The early training and management of your promising dog puppy is of vital importance. If he is bullied and harried by older puppies he may become too submissive. If you consider the position of a young dog in the wild you arrive at some interesting conclusions. By nature, the dog is a pack animal and subject to very strong family discipline. The pack is often matriarchal in structure and if food is scarce only the dominant female will produce a litter each year. She will select as her mate the strongest and swiftest of the males in order to pass on these characteristics to her offspring. Thus, nature ensures the survival of the fittest. Unless it is an exceptionally good year and food is plentiful, none of the other bitches will be allowed to produce litters. Many of the males will pass the whole of their lives without ever reproducing themselves. Their sexual instincts will be repressed and they will devote all their energies to hunting and caring for the pack.

It is important not to mirror this situation in your own small pack. From an early age, your young dog should be encouraged to be an extrovert. Do not let him be dominated by his elders, particularly older bitches, or he may have psychological difficulties in bringing himself to mate when the time comes. Do not feed him with a dominant bitch or she will bully him into surrendering his rations as soon as your back is turned. His natural instincts will tell him that it is his duty to hunt and provide for her and he will stand back and watch her devour his food in the most gentlemanly manner.

In fact, he is the one who should be getting the increased rations. By the time he is twelve months old, he should be receiving about twice the amount of food required by a non-pregnant bitch. A stud-dog that has a reasonable amount of stud work needs plenty of exercise and a high-protein diet to keep him fit. Supplements are largely a matter of personal taste but many breeders believe that vitamin E, the 'fertility vitamin', is a useful addition to the stud-dog's diet. I have yet to be convinced that a dog on a well-balanced, varied diet needs any supplements to improve his fertility but Vitamin B, in the shape of brewer's yeast tablets, is greatly enjoyed by dogs and encourages appetites. It is claimed that these tablets form a metabolic stimulant for infertile dogs and bitches, and anything that improves general health and appetite is bound to be of benefit.

It is important that your dog should be maintained in robust health, well fed and well exercised if he is to remain at maximum fertility. Ill health will take its toll and disease, particularly Parvovirus, has been proved to cause sterility in the male dog for periods of anything up to one year. Keep your parvo boosters up and keep careful records of their timing. It is so easy for them to get overlooked when you have a number of dogs. If you have been unfortunate enough to contract this scourge in your kennel then it is wise to have a sperm count of your male dog done, at the end of the quarantine period, before putting him back at stud.

It has been proved that the sperm count drops significantly when the temperature is raised. In some countries, where infertility is aggravated by the hot climate, stud-dogs benefit greatly from being kept in air-conditioned surroundings. The temperature in Britain seldom rises sufficiently to make this a problem but it is worth making every effort to keep your dog in cool conditions during the occasional heat wave.

To maintain maximum fertility it is wise not to allow your dogs to drink from streams or puddles during their daily exercise. Both farmers and local authorities fertilise their grasslands with nitrates to encourage growth, particularly in the spring. These nitrates drain into streams and ditches and can produce infertility in both male and female dogs. There is some evidence that they can also account for puppy losses.

If your dog appears to have a low sex drive which cannot be attributed to a psychological hang-up, and if those bitches he is able to mate, fail to conceive, then it is worth asking your vet about the possibility of hormone treatment. This can have dramatically beneficial results but is only to be recommended if your dog is a genuinely superior animal that is likely to make a valuable contribution to the breed. Interfering with nature carries its own hazards and, if continued through several generations, is liable to result in sterility.

The number of times a dog is used when young, appears to affect his fertility at a later stage. Most breeders like to use a young dog while he is still a puppy, at around ten months of age. It is then recommended that he is not used again until he is eighteen months. Statistics seem to support the theory that if a young dog is used extensively at an early age he will become infertile at an earlier stage in his life than would otherwise be the case. It is surely better and far more useful if one is endeavouring to build up a blood line, for a stud-dog to have his active sex life prolonged as long as possible.

Training the Young Dog

It is a great mistake to choose a compliant female for your novice stud-dog and shut them up together in the hope that nature will take its course. It will probably seem delightfully easy to him but he is in for a rude awakening when faced with a cantankerous bitch that values her virginity above all else. Your young dog will not only lose all his self-confidence, he will lose condition at an alarming rate which can be disastrous for his show career. It is vital that he should be trained to mate a bitch with a minimum of fretting. Confidence in himself is the name of the game. It is up to you to make sure that the whole operation is carried through smoothly with the least possible fuss. It is important that the same procedure should be followed on each occasion so that the dog knows exactly what is expected of him. Always use the same place for stud work, such as a covered run or utility room that can be used in all weathers.

For his first bitch it is preferable to use a proved matron, known to be placid and easy to mate as long as it is not one which he knows well and holds in awe. Even if you can persuade him to mount such a bitch, he may well be unable to mate her. Sometimes a young flirtatious bitch, even if she is a maiden, will be easier for him to dominate. Provided she is presented at the right time, she should raise her tail and twist it to one side as an invitation to the dog, and he should have no difficulty.

I find it helpful to introduce the dog on a lead while allowing the bitch to run free. She will not then take fright at his over-enthusiastic advances. Given time, she may decide she likes him and she will then give him every encouragement. Allow them a little love play but not sufficient to tire the dog. Put him away or tie him up somewhere where he can see you while you go through the routine of preparing his bitch for mating.

However amenable she seems, muzzle her with a soft tie wrapped twice round her foreface, crossed underneath and tied securely behind her ears. She will not like it but once a dog knows his bitch is unable to bite him it will give him confidence when he has to mate a difficult bitch. Most Collie bitches have an excessive amount of hair around the vulva. It can be cut away if her owner does not object but it is better to grease it down with copious amounts of Vaseline. If the bitch is ready, the swelling will already be subsiding and the bright red discharge will have turned to a watery almost transparent pink. Grease your little finger and insert it gently upwards into the vulva. (Needless to say, your nail must be kept short if you are not to damage the delicate membrane.) You will feel a ring with the tip of your finger. If this is too tight for your finger to pass through then the bitch is not yet ready, but if your finger slips easily through, then move it up and down gently and you should feel her contracting on to it. If this is the case she is good and ready.

Get the owner, or better still an experienced assistant to hold the bitch's head firmly, and release the dog. Do not allow him to mount the bitch until you are in position. Kneel beside the bitch on whichever side seems easier to you to work from. Always use the same side so that the dog gets used to a routine. Place one hand underneath the bitch between her hind legs, take the vulva between two fingers and encourage him to mount. It is not, in my opinion, a good idea to touch the dog, merely manoeuvre the vulva directly over the dog's penis and let him do the work. Some breeders prefer to manipulate the dog but too much reliance on this method will spoil a good dog. If your dog is a little short on the leg it may be necessary to stand him on a rug or board to raise him a couple of inches. On the other hand, if the bitch is very small, it may be advisable to raise her to his level. If the dog persistently fails to get close enough it is sometimes helpful to back them both into a corner where it will be easier to man-oeuvre the bitch into the required position.

As soon as penetration has been achieved, the dog will start to tread air with his hind feet. Once this is completed it is important not to let the dog dismount but to wait until the bulbous gland on the dog's penis swells up and holds him 'tied' to the bitch. When she is ready, she will release him. This 'tie' may last anything from three minutes to three-quarters of an hour. Some dogs are slow to swell up inside the bitch and if allowed to turn too soon, will slip out. If your dog is prone to do this it is advisable to change the procedure slightly. As soon as the dog has finished treading air, rise from the kneeling position and move behind the two animals. Grasp the bitch firmly by both thighs at the same time pressing the knee gently into the dog's back to make sure he cannot withdraw. Once you are confident that a tie has taken place, the dog can be allowed to dismount in the usual way.

Slide one of his front paws over the back of the bitch so that he can place both front feet on the ground and relieve her of a good deal of his weight. Let him rest like this for a few minutes and when he indicates that he wants to turn completely you can slide his hind foot over and hold them together back to back. You can do this by clasping both arms round their hind legs or by holding their two tails together. Never, on any account, leave them to their own devices during this rather boring period. The bitch can drag the dog about all over the place and make it an experience he will not be anxious to repeat.

Some breeders like to help their dog dismount and turn in one swift movement. It may look very efficient but it is doubtful if there is any advantage in this method. Left to their own devices, the pair would stand for some time with their heads together before the dog slowly shifted his position, gradually inching round till he was facing in the other direction, finally lifting his hind leg over till they were resting in the back to back position. It is as well not to rush things. Provide a small stool for the handler to sit on, as it can get pretty cramped in the crouching or kneeling position if the tie is prolonged.

If the owner of the bitch has elected not to be present at the mating, it is etiquette to call him in to witness the tie. In this way he can be certain that the mating has taken place and to the dog he selected. In other words, he is getting precisely what he is paying for. Most breeders will not accept a stud fee if a tie has not been obtained, pre-ferring to rely on the owner of the bitch to send them the fee, should a litter result. Although it is perfectly possible for a Collie bitch to conceive without a tie, it usually indicates that the bitch was not ready and every effort should be made to obtain a second service, taking the precautions previously outlined.

If the mating is normal then there is, in my opinion, no need for a second mating. There are two exceptions to this rule – if the dog is young and is being used for the first time and if a dog has not been used for some considerable time. In either case, the count of live sperm will be considerably higher on the second service. Many experienced stud-dogs who are frequently used will flatly refuse to give a second service when they consider the first to be successful. They are almost invariably right.

The fluid in which the sperm is floating passes into the female's vagina in three stages. There is a first emission before the tie takes place, then a slow 'drip feed' emission during the tie and finally a colourless watery fluid which completes the tie but which does not appear to be essential to conception. Provided the bitch is presented to the dog at the right time, there is little or no evidence of higher fertility from two or more services.

This was brought home to me on one occasion when a breeder sent two bitches, a mother and daughter who had come in season at the same time, to my stud-dog. She was particularly anxious that the daughter should have a litter so it was decided to give her three services and the mother one. The daughter was mated on day one, day two and day four while the mother was given one service on day three. The daughter produced one puppy and the mother produced ten, which they happily reared between them. Ever since then, I have been extremely sceptical about the benefit of two services. The sperm can remain alive inside the bitch for approximately four days, so there is a good chance that one of the days will coincide with her ovulating period. Thus, even with one service, there is a certain amount of leeway. The number of puppies a bitch produces will depend entirely on her reproductive system. High or low fertility does seem to run in families or even strains.

I have described in some detail the mating of the dog with a willing bitch and it probably all sounds very straightforward. Believe me, this is far from the case. For every willing receptive bitch that comes to your dog, there will be two fractious cantankerous females determined to protect their virtue at all costs. There is a vast difference between the attitude of a kennel bitch who is used to other dogs, and a pet who believes she is part of her human family and wants nothing to do with nasty strange dogs. This is not surprising when you consider that, from the age of eight weeks, she has been bonded to humans and undoubtedly considers that she is herself one. So much so that she becomes hysterical at the approach of the male.

Never, never be persuaded by the owner that, 'Darling Lassie would never bite anyone!' Darling Lassie has never been subjected to the indignity she is about to undergo, so ignore the owner's protests and muzzle her. Otherwise the one most likely to get bitten is your dog. Some owners are totally incapable of holding the head of even a muzzled bitch (some cannot bring themselves even to watch), so experienced help with a difficult bitch is invaluable. Get them to hold her head securely. You will find that you need all your strength to hold Lassie's rear end up when she is determined to sit modestly but firmly on her 'naughty bits'. The dog will be watching this procedure with interest. He knows the routine and provided he has confidence in you, he will not be put off by her performance, however loud her protests. This is possibly because his instincts tell him that some of his most reluctant mates make the best mothers when the time comes for them to rear their families.

Occasionally you get a bitch that appears to be perfectly willing but for some reason the dog refuses to mount her. He may spend his time blowing down her ear or playfully pulling lumps out of her fur. There are several possible reasons for this. She may be a dominant female whom he holds in awe, there may be something wrong with her season or she may simply not be ready. There are also some nymphomaniac bitches that will stand hopefully in front of a dog throughout their entire season but there are only a few days in which they are actually ovulating. You must give your dog the credit for knowing, better than you, when this period is taking place. Some bitches go on showing colour up to their nineteenth or twentieth day and only when the colour changes are they ready to mate. Other bitches are ready as early as seven or eight days from the time they first show colour. There is no hard-and-fast rule.

The time of day can affect a dog. Most matings in nature take place in the early morning or the evening. All the books I have read tell you not to feed a dog before mating and he will then be at his keenest. I think this is a fallacy. If your dog is a reluctant lover, try the soft lights and tasty meal approach for both of them, preferably in the evening. I find this relaxed, 'in the mood' prelude can work wonders. I am not one to study biorhythms but all puppies have a mad half-hour, just after dawn and just before sunset, like fox cubs. They may not rush about in the same way as they get older but the instinct is still there.

Finally, when the mating has been completed, sponge the dog with mild antiseptic to safeguard him from infection. Some breeders like to raise the bitch by her hind legs in the wheelbarrow position, to allow the semen to flow up the vagina. My own feeling is that if this was meant to happen the bitch would stand on her head, but by all means do it if you think it will bring you luck.

8

Ailments and Diseases

Fortunately, the Collie is not prone to disease and is free from many of the hereditary disorders which afflict some breeds. A special section is devoted to the hereditary defects which do affect the Collie and great care should be taken by any newcomer, seeking to start their own kennel, to avoid such defects in their foundation stock, but in this section I will deal only with common ailments. If there is real cause for concern then prompt veterinary help should be sought.

Common Ailments

Arthritis

Arthritis, or inflammation of the joints, may be caused by injury at some previous stage or may be due to a hereditary problem such as hip dysplasia or may simply be due to advancing age. The symptoms are difficulty in getting up and reluctance to go upstairs or to walk. Chronic pain is often present so consult your veterinary surgeon about its alleviation. The administering of cod-liver oil in daily doses is sometimes beneficial over the long term. Short walks at frequent intervals are better than one long daily walk for exercise.

Bloat

Caused by fermenting food releasing gas into the stomach, bloat affects many large breeds. The Collie is not susceptible to bloat although occasional instances have been recorded. The main symptom is a rapid swelling of the stomach which becomes hard and distended causing the dog great pain. Get your patient to your veterinary surgery immediately. Delay may prove fatal.

Brucellosis

Brucellosis affects various animals, particularly cattle. It is an infectious bacterial disease which causes abortion in females and infertility in males. The canine form of brucellosis is rare in Great Britain and is usually only found in imported dogs – particularly bitches in whelp. Abortion or the early delivery of a litter usually takes place around the sixth or seventh week of pregnancy. It can be caused by shock or injury, but brucellosis should always be suspected and veterinary help sought. A slide agglutination test will quickly establish whether or not Canine Brucellosis is present. The disease is passed on in the same way as a venereal disease. It can also be passed from female to female in mucous membrane and is highly infectious. In the USA stud-dog owners require a bitch to pass an agglutination test before accepting them to their dog. So far, this has not proved necessary here, but *Brucella canis* is a scourge that can ruin the breeding plans of a whole kennel and constant vigilance must be maintained against it. At present there is no vaccine available.

Burns or Scalds

House pets can frequently get burned or scalded. Speed is essential here. Clip off the hair to establish the affected area. If at all possible, immerse the part in cold water. This will often prevent the burn or scald penetrating deeper into the tissue. If this is not possible, continually pour water over it to ease the pain. Cover with tissue and if anything more than reddening of the skin occurs, go to the veterinary surgery.

Car Sickness

This is more frequent in puppies and young stock. Just as children often outgrow travel-sickness, so do puppies. My experience leads me to believe that it runs in families with Collies. Some strains are never sick, others are sick after travelling only a short distance. It usually manifests itself by drooling long ropes of saliva, before vomiting starts. This is particularly distressing when the animal is on the way to a show. Not only does he arrive feeling very sorry for himself, but his coat is in a deplorable state unless you have had the foresight to tie a towel round his neck beforehand. Treatment consists of giving the animal travel-sickness pills at least two hours before the journey. Careful management can prevent travel-sickness altogether. If the puppy is taken for very short journeys by car and released in an open space where he can exercise and play, then he will look forward to travelling by car from an early age and the problem will never arise.

Collie Nose

Collie nose is a distressing complaint, infrequently seen in Collies, Shetland Sheepdogs and Border Collies. The skin of the nose becomes crusted, inflamed and frequently raw. The dog constantly licks it which aggravates the condition. Not a great deal seems to be known about this condition but it has been diagnosed as nasal solar dermatitis and is considered to be an allergic reaction to ultra-violet light. Both sunlight and snow can trigger this condition and it is advisable to keep the dog indoors or in the shade as much as possible. Sun barrier creams provide some protection and should be used if the dog is taken out in snow or sunlight.

It is said not to be hereditary but there is some evidence that it runs in families. I have only encountered the condition twice, in different parts of the country. On enquiry, it was discovered that the affected animals were brother and sister but that they had not inherited their condition from either the sire or the dam. It would seem advisable not to breed from affected animals. Recent research has linked Collie nose with other skin lesions round the eyes and mouth, symptomised by loss of hair, crusts, scabs and changes in colour of pigmented areas. These are believed to be caused by a breakdown in the immunity system. Most respond well to steroid treatment but symptoms tend to recur at a later stage.

Convulsions

These were once common in puppies fed on products containing bleached flour. Convulsions are now rare in young stock. A fit is characterised by rapid jerky movements of the head and limbs and frothing at the mouth. Usually it will last only a minute or two, gradually becoming less violent until all movement ceases. The victim rapidly regains consciousness but has difficulty in walking, or finding his way about, often bumping into furniture which he seems unable to see. Try to keep the patient quiet and warm and when fully recovered take him to your veterinary surgeon. Convulsions may be a symptom of epilepsy, particularly if the dog is two or three years old before the first fit occurs. Fits may be brought on by brain damage due to an accident, or caused by a tumour. They were, at one time, a frequent legacy of distemper but this scourge is seldom encountered today. Epilepsy can be controlled by drugs which if carefully administered each day will allow a dog to lead a normal life.

Cough

It is not uncommon for a dog to cough in isolated instances, but persistent coughing should be viewed with concern. The most common cause in young puppies is worms and treatment should be given accordingly. If worms are not suspected make sure the puppy does not have an obstruction in the throat. Puppies will devour anything in sight and something may be stuck in the throat. Occasionally a piece of stick or bone will be lodged across the roof of the mouth and this should always be inspected. If you are unable to remove the object, consult your veterinary surgeon.

A persistent dry cough is often a sign of the dreaded kennel cough. Veterinary help should be sought at once but it is not advisable to take a coughing dog into the surgery as it is highly infectious. Better to leave him in the car. Your vet will usually treat him outside. The patient should be isolated from all other dogs. This is particularly important in respect of brood bitches. As already stated in the section on fading puppies, there appears to be a link between the two and kennel cough may be the unsuspected cause of many fading litters.

Coughing can also be a symptom of heart disease, inhalation of fumes, chemical irritants or bronchitis and should never be ignored. All will require veterinary treatment.

Cuts and Wounds

A small cut or wound that a dog can reach with his tongue can frequently be left for him to clean himself. Excessive licking will damage the tissue, however, and in that case, the wound should be washed with antiseptic. The surrounding hair should be cut off with a pair of curved scissors and the area treated with lint and bandaged. It may be necessary to fit a lampshade or Elizabethan collar to prevent the dog removing the bandage. Dress the wound daily, applying fresh lint and antiseptic until it has healed. Care must be taken if it is caused by a dog bite, for the deep puncture may heal over the surface leaving infection underneath. A course of antibiotics will assist.

Cuts to the pads are particularly difficult to deal with. Stitches are inclined to break open from pressure when the foot is on the ground. Butterfly stitches, which are made out of strips of sticking plaster placed criss-cross over the wound, pulling the edges together, may prove more effective. Bandage the foot and place in an old sock covered in a polythene bag, to keep out the wet, and tape firmly in place.

Scars on the face, caused by dog bites, are a major disfigurement in the show ring. Prevention is better than cure, but here again butterfly stitches can pull the wound together so that the scar is less visible when healed. A real emergency can arise if the dog is spurting bright red blood indicating that an artery has been severed. Make a pad using a clean handkerchief or bandage and place it over the wound applying sufficient pressure to stop the bleeding. Take the patient to a veterinary surgery at once. In the case of a road accident, try to get the dog on to a flat board before lifting. Cover with a warm blanket and keep warm to lessen the shock.

Cystitis

An infection of the urinary system, cystitis often causes pain or intense irritation. Symptoms include the frequent passing of urine tinged with blood. Prompt veterinary treatment is required.

Diarrhoea

Diarrhoea is frequently found in puppies, caused by stress and change of diet on arrival at their new homes. When collecting a new puppy, always ask for a diet sheet from the breeder and if possible a week's supply of the main food the puppy has been reared on. Be prepared to pay for it. Try to obtain a piece of blanket or cloth that will remind the puppy of his mother and siblings and will prove of comfort to him when he is left alone. Avoid stressful situations and the problems should not arise.

In a litter of puppies, just one puppy may be affected. This may be due to gastro-enteritis or canine parvovirus infection. If any blood is found in the stool, veterinary help should be sought immediately. Diarrhoea may be caused by overfeeding, or feeding too much milk or raw eggs or unsuitable food. Treatment is threefold:

1. Starve for twelve hours but keep a supply of fresh water available.

2. Offer Bovril or Oxo to which you have added a little sugar for the next twelve hours. Spoon feed, if necessary, about one tablespoonful every hour.
3. Begin feeding small amounts of cooked rice and fish every four hours.

If diarrhoea persists, consult your veterinary surgeon. In adults, diarrhoea may also be associated with stress particularly in highly strung dogs. Demands for instant obedience may cause stress to a dog and sometimes result in chronic diarrhoea. This is particularly common in German Shepherd Dogs, but Collies can be equally affected. Avoid stressful situations.

Distemper

Until a vaccine was found during the post-war period, whole kennels of dogs were wiped out by this terrible disease. It is still found in unvaccinated dogs. It usually starts with a cough and a runny discharge from the eyes and nose. A high temperature is present. The disease itself does not usually prove fatal but the secondary infection which follows may well do so. Pneumonia is a common secondary infection but with modern medicine and careful nursing this can be overcome. If the nervous system is affected, resulting in fits, then the prognosis is not good. Hard pad symptomised by thickening of the pads and nose often follows distemper. It is not a separate disease. On no account should a dog suspected of suffering from distemper be taken to a veterinary surgery. Consult your vet by telephone to find out where he would like to see the dog. The house and kennels should be thoroughly disinfected with strong bleach and all bedding burnt. Puppies should be vaccinated against distemper as early as possible and it is important to keep up regular booster vaccinations.

Ear Problems

Collies, with their semi-erect ear carriage, do not suffer from ear problems as much as the breeds who have heavy pendulous ears which restrict the flow of air to the ear canal.

Canker of the ear is characterised by an evil-smelling brown waxy discharge. The condition can cause considerable pain to the dog. As always, prevention is better than cure and a weekly inspection of ears should be carried out. The ears can be cleaned out with cotton wool dampened in weak antiseptic. Severe cases need veterinary attention. Ear mites can cause the dog irritation and these should be treated by a veterinary surgeon. They are often transferred from cats so if there are any cats in your household, they too should be treated or reinfection will occur.

During the summer, a constant watch should be kept for awns or sharp grass seeds which can penetrate, deep within the ear, and cause intense pain. An operation may be needed for their removal if they are not noticed in time.

Eclampsia or Milk Fever

This is caused by a drain on calcium from the system of a lactating nursing bitch. All in-whelp bitches should have calcium and vitamin D added to their diet but even this will not prevent the illness taking hold occasionally, usually in the case of a large litter. Its onset is sudden and is characterised by a staggering gait, lack of co-ordination of the limbs, followed by total collapse. Sometimes the bitch will lose consciousness. Death will result if prompt veterinary treatment is not sought. It cannot be over-stressed that this is an emergency. An intravenous calcium injection will effect what seems to be a miracle cure. The bitch appears to suffer no lasting ill effects and, once back to normal, will happily return to nursing her litter. However, she must be carefully watched as very rarely the symptoms recur.

Eczema

Eczema is a skin problem familiar to most dog breeders though not often found in Collies. It is characterised by the sudden appearance of large, wet, hairless patches usually on the back or in a place accessible to the dog's teeth. This was previously considered to be a dietary problem and treated by changing the diet. Modern thinking attributes it to an allergy usually to fleas or other parasites. An injection from your veterinary surgeon, to alleviate the itching, and thorough disinfestation of the dog and his environment will usually solve the problem. New hair will grow through the bald patch surprisingly quickly, although it may be of a darker colour.

Eye Trouble

A runny discharge from the eye can be caused by the dog lying in draughts or putting his head out of the car window. This last is a dangerous practice which should never be allowed. Eye trouble may also be caused by dust or some other irritation in the eye which can be washed out with warm water or eye lotion in an eye bath. If it persists seek veterinary help.

The Collie does not suffer from entropion which is caused by in-turning eyelids which can only be corrected by an operation. Occasionally, however, you find Collies affected by a few extra hairs growing on the eyelids which point inwards and cause the dog to blink frequently. These can be removed with tweezers but it is usually better to ask your veterinary surgeon to do this for you.

Loss of hair around one or both eyes is occasionally seen in the breed. This is not really an eye problem, but is usually a symptom of demodectic mange. There are several serious inherited eye diseases only two of which affect Collies and these are dealt with fully in the section on hereditary diseases.

Halitosis or 'Bad Breath'

This can be caused by gastric problems or distemper, but the majority of cases are due to gum infection caused by tartar on the teeth. Prevention is better than cure and regular cleaning with a tooth brush and anti-tartar toothpaste will do much to prevent the condition occurring. If tartar has already accumulated, then it can be cracked with a dental tool and scraped off. In really bad cases, it is advisable to ask your vet to perform the operation. Often, this can be combined with another small operation while the dog is under anaesthetic.

Heat Stroke

Collies are not as susceptible to heat stroke as are some of the short-haired or short-nosed breeds. Their thick coats act as insulating material and they can withstand most climatic conditions. The most common cause of heat stroke results from leaving dogs in locked cars. The sun shining through the glass causes a rapid rise in air temperature and the dog becomes distressed. Collapse and death will occur if the dog is not rescued in time.

Emergency treatment consists of reducing the body temperature as quickly as possible either by submerging the dog in a cold bath, stream or pond or applying ice packs. Even frozen food packs can be used in an emergency! Afterwards the dog should be checked over by a veterinary surgeon.

Hepatitis

Hepatitis in dogs has no connection with hepatitis in man and is not transferable to him. It is an infectious disease passed from dog to dog and affects the liver. It is characterised by lack of appetite, vomiting, diarrhoea and a high temperature. Sometimes the whites of the eyes acquire a yellow shade. Occasionally, the whole cornea becomes blue (this can also happen after vaccination against hepatitis). Early vaccintion of puppies against this disease is the best preventative. Once it has taken hold in a kennel it is a difficult disease to eliminate as the virus may be passed on in urine or faeces for several months after the patient has recovered. Some dogs remain carriers all their lives and only blood tests will identify them. Close co-operation with your veterinary surgeon will be necessary for many months before your kennel can be given a clean bill of health.

Incontinence

The involuntary passing of urine usually affects young puppies or elderly dogs. Some very excitable puppies have a distressing habit of passing small puddles of urine when they get excited, particularly when greeting their owners on their home-coming. Scolding or disciplinary action should be avoided as this seems to make the problem worse. Try to ensure that the puppy greets you outside or on a hard surface where it will not matter so much, rather than on your best carpet! Greet the puppy casually, do not over fuss and the habit will die out with age. It is sometimes a symptom of an over-submissive dog and steps should be taken to try to instil confidence. Collie puppies are not prone to this habit.

Incontinence in the elderly dog is a more intractable problem. It particularly affects elderly spayed bitches and is one of the reasons I would never advocate spaying except in cases of medical necessity. It is distressing to the elderly dog who inevitably finds herself demoted from the owner's bedroom to the kitchen or outhouse. Not a great deal can be done to relieve the problem, though it sometimes responds to hormone treatment. It is essential to keep the sufferer warm. Plenty of newspaper underneath covered by an easily washed vet-bed or blanket make the best bed. It is advisable to cut away a good deal of the long hair surrounding the vulva to prevent it becoming stained. Frequent washing of the hindquarters may be necessary to eliminate the smell of urine. The patient must be treated with the utmost kindness throughout. If made to feel a nuisance, an elderly Collie can easily become depressed.

Interdigital Cysts

Interdigital cysts are inflamed swellings between the toes and are extremely painful. They are usually recurring. They are often found in overweight dogs and can sometimes be prevented by reducing obesity. They are believed to be due to the infection 'staphylococcus aureus' though there can be other bacteria involved. They are probably due to a breakdown in immunity and for this reason steroids are not recommended as they would make the lack of immunity worse. It is considered better to treat the condition and allow the dog to build up his own resistance. A change of diet should be introduced. Cut out all cereals and feed on fish, meat and mashed green vegetables only until the weight is reduced. As soon as a cyst begins to form, paint with iodine twice daily. This will often reduce the cyst in size and prevent it from bursting. If it does burst, bathe with warm salt water but do not cover. The dog will normally keep the area clean with his tongue.

Interdigital Eczema

Interdigital eczema is the equivalent of 'athletes foot' in humans. It causes intense irritation to the dog who will constantly nibble and bite at the area, often making himself badly lame. It is important to get the air circulating around the inflamed area. Cut out all the hair between the toes and paint twice a day with a proprietary lotion for 'athletes foot'. The first few applications will sting until the area heals, so it is advisable to paint it on just before mealtimes or exercise times to distract the dog's attention.

Lameness

It is not always easy to see which leg is the problem when the dog is moving but usually the dog will take the weight off the affected limb when standing. If he raises his paw off the ground it is likely that this is where the problem lies. If he merely takes the weight off one leg, then the problem is more likely to be found in the limb itself.

Examine the foot first for any foreign body – a thorn or cut in a pad, or a piece of glass or stone embedded. Collies carry a lot of fur on the underside of their foot and a ball of tar can sometimes form between the pads. Often snow will form a hard ball underneath the foot making it impossible for the dog to walk. The lameness may be caused by a sprain or the dog twisting the leg in exercise. In such cases all that may be needed to effect a cure is rest, but if the limp persists seek veterinary help.

Leptospiral Jaundice

Leptospiral jaundice is carried by rats and can affect dogs or puppies which are sited near farms, chicken runs, sewers or streams, which carry a rat population. It is one of the reasons you should never allow your Collie to drink from a stream or puddle while out for a walk. Never leave your dog's water bowl out at night for the same reason. The infection is passed in the urine of rats. Infection may linger in the ground for many months even if the area has been totally cleared of rats.

Puppies will normally be vaccinated against it by the age of twelve weeks and this gives good immunity provided the annual boosters are kept up. Leptospirosis can not only be passed to other dogs, but to humans, also, and very careful precautions should be taken to maintain the highest standards of hygiene when nursing an infected dog. Symptoms include lack of appetite, thirst, diarrhoea and vomiting and are sometimes insidious in onset. If the dog also has a high temperature and rats are known to be present, leptospiral jaundice should be suspected.

A similar disease which used to be called Stuttgart Disease, now usually know as Leptospira canicola, has the same symptoms. It infects the kidneys. Dogs inhale the bacteria from the infected urine of other dogs. Over the years this builds up into chronic nephritis and the symptoms are often not apparent until the dog reaches middle age. Prevention of both these diseases is better than cure. Puppies should be vaccinated as early as possible and regular annual boosters should never be neglected. Infected dogs should be isolated even after they have recovered, for six to nine months, as infection is passed through urine for a long time afterwards.

Mange – Demodectic

This is the most commonly met mange and is caused by demodex mites which are present in most canine follicles, particularly eye lashes. They normally cause no problems at all but for some reason they occasionally multiply causing hair loss, usually around the eyes or lips and also spots on the lower limbs. It seems to be caused by a breakdown in immunity inherited from the mother and often whole litters will be affected even though the symptoms do not appear until long after they have left for their separate homes. A scraping from the affected area will readily reveal the mite to a veterinary surgeon. Treatment of the affected area must be applied carefully, several times a day. This seems to quickly clear up the trouble which seldom recurs in Collies.

Mange – Sarcoptic

This is caused by mites which burrow into the skin which arouse intense irritation in the dog symptomised by constant scratching. It is usually found in the outside edge of the ears and between the elbows and thighs of the dog. Treatment must follow veterinary advice and be repeated at weekly intervals in order to break the breeding cycle of the mites. All bedding should be burnt and the dog isolated, as sarcoptic mange mites are transferred from dog to dog.

Obesity

Some years ago Collies as a breed were considered poor eaters and the utmost ingenuity had to be used to get many of them (particularly males) into show condition. This is a problem which can still occasionally be encountered but which is becoming increasingly rare. Far more common nowadays is the problem of getting an overweight Collie into show trim. One of the causes lies in our new system of feeding puppies ad lib. Faced with competition from litter mates, it is surprising how much a young Collie puppy can put away. Fat, roly-poly puppies may look very attractive but they turn into fat, roly-poly adults. The extra weight on their rib-cage obstructs the free swing of their forearms thus restricting the stride, forcing the elbows outwards and the front feet inwards. This in-toeing is probably the most prevalent of all the gait faults of the modern Collie.

Overweight puppies are more likely to develop hip dysplasia

because of the strain on their hip joints. Greyhounds and Siberian Huskies who carry very little weight on their hindquarters score extremely low marks in the BVA HD scheme. There is no doubt that force rearing (the overfeeding of Collie puppies to get them into the ring at six months of age), is responsible for a lot of the bad movement noticeable in present-day Collies. There is a fixed weight for adult Collies laid down in the Standard and a healthy Collie should not deviate far from this. Many breeders seem to have difficulty in recognising obesity when they see it. If you imagine your Rough Collie is a Smooth and mentally strip off the coat, you will have a better idea of how much weight your Collie should be carrying.

Medical opinion is united in proclaiming the disadvantages of obesity in humans, it can lead to all sorts of problems. Dogs are no different. You may be shortening the life of your beloved Collie if you overfeed him.

To treat obesity you should first weigh your Collie and compare the weight with the Breed Standard which recommends a maximum weight of 65 pounds (27kg) for dogs and 55 pounds (25kg) for bitches. This is easily done by picking up your dog in your arms and weighing yourself on the bathroom scales. Then weigh yourself. The difference will be all dog. Decide whether your Collie is a few pounds overweight which may be safely ignored, or grossly overweight which will need treatment. It is better to achieve a slow reduction of weight over months rather than put the dog on a crash starvation diet. Aim for a weight loss of between one and two pounds (0.5kg) a week. Weigh the dog weekly to make sure you are achieving the desired results. The diet can be adjusted accordingly. The simplest method is merely to reduce the quantity of food. To reduce hunger pangs, feed the dog in two small meals rather than one large one. You can speed up the process by adding bran and chopped lettuce or raw cabbage to replace the biscuit content of the dog's diet. Do not allow other members of your family to succumb to pleading eyes and feed titbits behind your back. Reassure them that the dog is not going to starve to death! It is for his own good that he is being put on a diet.

Exercise can play an important role in the process. To start with, it will help to take the dog's mind off food! As his weight decreases, so will his activity increase. Slowly, muscle will replace fat and you will have a far fitter and healthier dog as a result of the diet.

Parasites

We are fortunate in this country in that we do not have to contend with heart worm and other such parasites as lung worm, hookworm and whip worm which are rarely found in domestic kennels. The most common internal parasite to be found is roundworm or *Toxocara canis* and is present in most puppies. Adult dogs usually carry dormant larvae which in the male dog may never be released but which in the female, become active during pregnancy. Some will migrate to the foetus while others remain in the bitch until her next litter. Often, the quantity of worms found in a bitch's first litter will be far more noticeable than those found in her third litter, as the amount of larvae she carries decreases with each subsequent litter. The larvae within the puppies continue to grow after birth and more will be transferred via the dam's milk so that by the time they are three weeks old they may be heavily infested.

It is advisable to worm a litter of puppies at three weeks of age and again at two weekly intervals until the puppy reaches twelve weeks of age. Thereafter, at six monthly intervals will be adequate. This is particularly important when there are children in the family. The eggs of the roundworm may be swallowed by children and, although they do not develop or breed in man, they can migrate around the body and very rarely may affect the retina of the eye and impair vision. A similar process takes place in kittens which are less likely to be wormed than puppies and similar precautions should be taken where there is a cat or kitten in the family.

Modern vermifuges seldom result in the piles of worms which the old-fashioned remedies expelled, but do not stop worming because you see no worms. The dead worms have been absorbed and will be passed out, unnoticed, in the digestive process. There is a modern worming remedy which is safe to give a pregnant bitch which is claimed to destroy all reactivated larvae and thus ensure that none are passed on to the developing whelps. This remedy is very reliable but can only be obtained from your veterinary surgeon. Be very, very careful that the drug Ivermectin is not administered to either Collies or Shelties in any circumstances. (*See* Poisoning.) Ivermectin is also known as Avermectin.

Tapeworm   Tapeworms are long segmented worms that can be seen in the faeces or clinging to the fur around the anal area. Infection is not common, particularly in puppies, and in adults it usually occurs through ingesting larvae in raw offal. Dogs should be wormed regularly against tapeworm, but not all reported infestations are what they seem. I once sold a puppy, only to be informed that he was infested with tapeworm. I found this difficult to believe but advised the owner to obtain a suitable vermifuge and worm the puppy. An agitated phone call revealed that this had had no effect and the puppy was still passing worm segments. I advised the disgruntled owner to take the puppy and a sample of the tapeworms to their veterinary surgeon and follow his advice. Subsequently, I received an apologetic phone call. The tapeworm segments turned out to be grains of rice! Fleas are part of the life cycle of the tapeworm so it is important to eradicate all fleas.

Fleas   Dog fleas are reddish brown in colour and run rapidly through the coat when you part it. Their presence is often indicated by flea dirt (little black specks which turn red when placed on wet paper). The dog is often a host to cat fleas and hedgehog fleas which are smaller and darker in colour. Dog fleas multiply rapidly unless steps are taken to eradicate them. It is important to treat the bedding, warm spots under radiators and other places where the fleas breed as well as the dog itself. Some dogs will tolerate a large number of fleas without showing any signs of irritation such as scratching or biting. Other dogs will be driven almost mad with the allergy caused by just one flea bite.

There are various sprays and powders that are effective. Bathing with a good insecticidal shampoo is very beneficial. In severe cases, a proprietary form of sheep dip suitable for dogs can be obtained from your veterinary surgeon and this will give immunity for up to three months. Flea collars are effective for about the same period. There have been reports of ill effects on some dogs from the use of flea collars, but Collies seem to tolerate them well. Their main drawback is that they have a limited life.

Lice   Tiny greyish insects that affect small patches of the dog, usually around the edges of the ears and around the neck. They do not jump like fleas but pass from dog to dog with ease. Eggs are laid on the hair and are difficult to remove even with a nit comb. Puppies can easily become infested with lice and become debilitated. Lice breed on the dog so there is not the same need to destroy bedding and treat cracks and crevices. Wash with a good insecticidal shampoo at weekly intervals paying particular attention to the tips and base of the ears.

Ticks Dogs that have access to the countryside frequently pick up sheep ticks which bury their heads into the dog's skin and suck the dog's blood. They are grey in colour and vary in size from a pin-head to the size of a round pea. Do not try to remove them with tweezers as the head will remain buried in the dog's skin. Instead, dab the tick's body with methylated or surgical spirit to make it release its hold and then remove the tick intact.

Harvest Mites These are small red mites which are barely visible to the human eye. As their name suggests, they are a seasonal problem. They usually affect the feet and cause the dog intense irritation. Thoroughly wash the feet with insecticidal shampoo taking particular care to get between the toes, dry thoroughly and dust with flea powder. Repeat at regular intervals throughout the late summer. Harvest mites can also affect the ears. The treatment is the same.

Parvovirus

This comparatively new disease made its appearance in the late 1970s and swept through many kennels. It appeared to make an almost synchronised appearance in many parts of the world bringing disaster. Many promising puppies and well-known winners succumbed to this dreadful disease before a vaccine could be found. Even then, vaccination was not always successful as the extent to which maternal antibodies could block immunisation in the puppies was not realised.

The incubation period is only about five days and the disease is virulently infectious. The infection is carried on clothes, boots and utensils and can remain active for a very long time. The disease manifests itself in two ways. The severe enteritis is often preceded by twenty-four hours' lack of appetite and interest in the surroundings. Usually the puppy will arch his back, indicating stomach pains. This is followed by vomiting, often streaked with blood and severe diarrhoea of a pale grey colour gradually becoming blood stained. In bad cases, pools of blood are passed and this may persist for some days. Dehydration follows and unless steps are taken to counteract it, death usually ensues. It is often impossible for the animal to keep down any liquid and the continuous vomiting merely weakens him. An intravenous drip, administered by a vet, is often the only solution as it may be several days before the patient is able to take liquids.

Thereafter, the treatment can be the same as for severe diarrhoea and a solution of one pint of boiled water made up with one teaspoonful of salt and one tablespoonful of honey can be given in small quantities every hour. There is a secondary form of Parvovirus which affects young puppies that are not protected by their mother's antibodies. The virus attacks the heart muscles of the growing puppy at between four and ten weeks of age and the puppy will collapse and die suddenly, often while playing. Sometimes one puppy in a litter will be found dead in his kennel with the other puppies asleep around him. It is probable that the whole litter will be affected even though they show no symptoms at the time. From time to time, just one puppy seems to slip through the net and is not protected by the mother's antibodies to the same degree as his brothers and sisters.

The best method of protecting a litter is to give the mother a booster vaccination before she comes into season. It is possible to give a booster while she is in whelp but in this case, the vaccination of the puppies must be delayed as the vaccination will not be effective while the maternal antibodies are active. In-whelp vaccination is often, therefore, counter-productive. If in any doubt, a blood test can be given to the mother to decide on the best age at which to vaccinate the puppies. A word of warning should be given here about hand-reared puppies. If they have received no milk from the mother they will have received no antibodies at all and will be particularly vulnerable to parvovirus infection. They should be vaccinated as early as possible.

Any sufferer from parvovirus should be kept in strict quarantine and humans in contact with such a dog should refrain from contact with other dogs. The virus is difficult to eradicate. Various proprietary parvocides are available, but a strong solution of household bleach or chlorine is very effective. Kennel walls, floors and runs should be thoroughly scrubbed at least twice and the kennel should not be used for the rearing of puppies for at least six months.

Poisoning

Symptoms include vomiting, foaming at the mouth and diarrhoea, often followed by total collapse. Take the dog to your veterinary surgeon immediately, together with any suspected substance. Most poisoning is caused by carelessness. Some dogs will eat absolutely anything and care should be taken to keep all medicines, solvents, insecticides etc. well out of their reach. One of the commonest causes of poisoning in the garden is the laying of slug pellets which are extremely attractive to dogs. They are highly poisonous, in spite of the labels which say they are harmless to pets. Weed killers, particu-

larly Paraquat, can be lethal and even inhaling the fumes will seriously damage canine lungs. Dogs should be kept well away from
areas where weed killers have been used whether it is in the garden
or municipal park. Rat poison, of which the most commonly used is
Warfarin, is claimed to be harmless to pets in small doses. It has a
cumulative effect which can result in haemorrhaging and great care
should be taken to remove all Warfarin bait laid down for rats before
dogs have access to the area. Even greater care should be taken when
using phosphorus or arsenic-based rat poison.

There are many poisonous plants and seeds in the garden which
can be harmful, particularly to omnivorous puppies. Notably, some
toadstools, foxgloves, laburnum seeds, yew leaves and thorn apples.
Remove all sources before allowing puppies access.

Ivermectin   Ivermectin is a drug widely used in veterinary surgeries.
It is a type of wormer approved for use in horses and goes under the
tradename of Equalan. Because of its effectiveness in treating worms
and sarcoptic mange, it has been used on dogs with great success but
must *never* be used on Collies and Shelties. I quote from Dr Sharon
Vanderlip's article on the subject in the International Collie Handbook: 'In some dogs and in the Collie and Shetland Sheepdog breeds
in particular there is either a congenital sensitivity to Ivermectin or a
defect in the blood brain barrier. In either case, the Ivermectin can
cross into the brain and spinal cord in Collies or Shelties and affect the
animal.'

Not every Collie injected with Ivermectin will be affected. Those
that are will normally display symptoms within twenty-four hours.
Usually the dog appears to be hallucinating, staggers and loses all co-
ordination of his limbs. He will appear to be hungry but physically
unable to eat. He will lose control of his tongue muscles and will be
unable to lap. It is important to keep up his fluid levels and the best
way to do this is with a human feeding cup with the spout inserted in
the side of the mouth. It is wiser not to put the dog on a drip if this can
be avoided as it is important not to let him pass into a comatose condition.

Antibiotics and antihistamines are helpful but barbiturates should
not be given. Careful nursing is the key to success. The dog should be
raised on his feet every half-hour, physically held up and 'walked',
right round the clock. If the dog survives a week, he will usually
recover, but it will be some time before he is able to eat and drink normally. In spite of the fatalities that the breed has suffered and the

devastating effect this has had on Collie breeders in several parts of the world, veterinary surgeons do not seem generally aware of the danger of this drug. It is up to you, therefore, to make absolutely certain that Ivermectin is never given to your Collies in any shape or form.

Pyometra

It is my experience that the Collie bitch is prone to this infection of the uterus. It is considered to be more prevalent in bitches that have not been bred from, but with Collies the reverse seems to be the case. Symptoms are not always visible other than the bitch appearing to drink large quantities of water. The infection occurs four to six weeks after the bitch has been in season so if a bitch is running a temperature and has a heavy thirst, about this time, then pyometra should be suspected. More commonly an evil-smelling, brownish-black discharge appears from the vulva. Veterinary help should be sought at once as delay will result in collapse and probable loss of the bitch.

Treatment may consist of antibiotic injections, but usually hysterectomy is advised as the symptoms tend to recur as the bitch gets older. It cannot be over-stressed that prompt action is necessary. If the womb has to be removed, then the quicker the infection is dealt with, the easier and quicker will be the recovery of the bitch.

Shock

Shock is often the result of a road accident or other traumatic experience. The dog may be in a collapsed state, the gums and inner eyelids will be pale and he (particularly his paws and limbs), will feel cold to the touch. Follow the normal treatment for shock. Cover with a rug or a blanket and keep warm while he is unconscious. When conscious, administer a few spoonfuls of warm, sweetened milk or tea. Allow the dog to rest for several hours in a quiet warm place and keep a watchful eye on him.

Stings

Most young dogs will chase anything that flies and bumble bees are quite irresistible to Collies. Honey bees and wasps are not far behind and result in many a swollen face during the summer season. Stings are not normally dangerous unless they are in the throat, where the swelling can cause an obstruction. If you have any reason to believe that your dog is allergic to stings, then your veterinary surgeon should be approached for a supply of antihistamine tablets. Otherwise, a soothing paste made of bicarbonate of soda and water can be applied if the dog appears distressed. Most Collies seem to think it's all part of the fun and few learn to leave bees and wasps alone.

Tooth Abscess

The main symptoms of a tooth abscess is a painful swelling of the face, usually just below the eye. This can be treated successfully with antibiotics but when the swelling has subsided, it is advisable to have the offending tooth removed, otherwise the symptoms are likely to recur. Problems with teeth can largely be avoided in Collies by regular cleaning and the feeding of a certain amount of hard biscuits. Marrowbones to chew are very helpful in preventing the formation of tartar, the usual cause of gum trouble and tooth abscesses.

Inherited Defects in the Collie

Achondroplasia

I have heard of only one reported case of this disease in Rough Collies but it would suggest that there may be others which have gone unreported. It was originally thought to be confined to Scottish Terriers and Poodles. The symptoms of the disease are failure of the limb bones to grow.

In the case reported to me, all but one of a litter of five Collie puppies were affected. No symptoms were visible at the age of eight weeks, when the puppies left for their new homes, but all the affected puppies had to be euthanised by the age of fifteen weeks, causing great distress to their new owners and breeder alike. It is vital that all cases should be reported so that an inheritance pattern can be established and any carrier lines eliminated from breeding programmes.

Congenital Eye Disease

The most common of these is Collie Eye Anomaly which affects approximately two-thirds of all Rough, Smooth and Border Collies as well as Shetland Sheepdogs. A less common disease that affects a small percentage of these breeds is more serious in its effect. It results in total blindness by the age of three. This is Progressive Retinal Atrophy. There is also an extension of PRA which does not affect dogs until they are eight or nine years of age. This is known as Central Progressive Retinal Atrophy.

Collie Eye Anomaly or CEA   There is no doubt that this disease has existed for a great many years, but it was only in the 1970s that it was brought to the attention of British breeders by Dr Barnett and Dr Bedford. A glance at the history of the Collie will reveal the large number of Collies exported to the USA in the early days. Since World War II these exports have dropped to a trickle and yet the incidence of CEA in the USA is even greater than it is here. Some 85 per cent of USA Collies are estimated to be suffering from CEA and it must have come from the early English imports. It would seem, therefore, that this disease has been with us for a very long time.

It is the united opinion of the canine eye specialists that the mode of inheritance is a simple autosomal recessive. It is difficult to understand, in this case, how the disease has got such a hold on the breed. It can only be due to excessive line or inbreeding to affected dogs. Most of this would seem to have taken place before World War II, although some has undoubtedly taken place since then. There are five grades of Collie Eye Anomaly that are currently accepted in the UK.

Grade 1   Choroidal hypoplasia is the most common and mildest form of CEA, distinguished by an area, or areas, lacking in pigment on the choroid layer at the back of the eye. It does not affect the vision and is not progressive. It is perfectly acceptable for pet Collie puppies who are not to be bred from. Owners can be satisfied that the sight of their Collie will not deteriorate with the years.

Grade 2   Coloboma or staphyloma. This manifests itself as a hole or very thin area adjacent to the optic nerve. Provided it is not so large as to affect the attachment of the retina, this is again a non-progressive state and will only slightly affect the Collies' field of vision. Very large colobomas may lead to partial detachment of the retina with a resultant blurring of vision.

Grade 3   Partial or complete detachment of the retina. This results in partial or complete blindness according to the severity of the condition.

Grade 4   Intra ocular haemorrhage or bleeding in the eye. This sometimes follows the detached retina stage and can be due to a blow on

242

the head or from bumping into an object. It causes severe pain which can only be relieved by removal of the eye itself.

Go Normals There is one other grade which bedevils the whole of the CEA elimination programme. This is commonly known as the 'Go Normal syndrome', or, as some eye specialists prefer to call it, the 'Look Normal syndrome'. This occurs when a certain lack of pigment in the back of the eye, detectable in a six-week-old puppy, colours in at a later stage becoming indistinguishable from a CEA clear eye. A dog tested at this later age will often be given a Clear Eye Certificate. This dog is not a true clear, however, and for the purposes of breeding is an affected animal.

This can lead to very disappointing results for a breeder who has searched diligently to find a CEA-clear stud-dog of blood lines suited to his bitch, only to find that the resultant litter is badly affected with CEA. Breeding from 'Go Normal' or 'Look Normal' clears is, I believe, responsible for much of the disillusionment that overtakes enthusiastic breeders trying to establish clear-eyed strains.

The only age at which CEA can be accurately and permanently diagnosed is at five to seven weeks of age. A puppy that is clear then, is known to be clear for life and will be highly valued as a breeding proposition. A high proportion of his or her progeny should also be clear.

Eye specialists charge the breeder only a small fee for screening whole litters at this age. Certification, which is more expensive, can be left to a later date when the Kennel Club Registration papers arrive. As in the consultant/doctor relationship, a canine eye specialist can only be approached through your veterinary surgeon who will make the appointment for you. Take along your Registration Certificate for stamping if it has arrived from the Kennel Club. Some breed clubs arrange for collective eye testing at a cheaper rate.

It has been suggested that specially coloured BVA Certificates should be issued for six-week-old clears. This has much to recommend it as these are the only certificates of value when it comes to breeding. The other method would be to issue CEA-free Certificates only to puppies under eight weeks of age, thus eliminating the 'Go Normal' factor once and for all. At present, there is no means of knowing (without close examination of the certificate), the age at which it was secured.

It is only from the ranks of the six-week clears that we can hope to discover a genetically clear Collie. A genetically clear Collie is one that breeds only clear progeny. Whether the mate is affected, 'Go Normal' or a six-week clear is immaterial, all the puppies will be six-week clears. A genetically clear Collie is the corner-stone that we seek. At present no such Collie exists.

If we could find such a Collie and it was a male Collie of merit, the whole picture of CEA could be transformed. By careful line and inbreeding to this one dog, many more genetically clear Collies could be bred who would, in turn, only produce Collies free from CEA. If we assume, as we are led to believe, that CEA is due to a simple recessive gene inheritance, then CEA should be no more difficult to eradicated than the tricolour factor from sable breeding. I have already discussed how difficult it was for post-war breeders to believe that tricolours could be eliminated from sable breeding. Yet now we take it for granted. Just one dog achieved that feat for us – Champion Lochinvar of Ladypark. If we could find another Lochinvar that was genetically clear from CEA, our problem would be solved!

It is important that breeders believe that it can be done. They must have faith in their own efforts. Personally, I think it will be achieved by an enthusiastic newcomer to the breed. It is far easier to start out and continue on the right lines than it is for established breeders to discard their best stock and start their breeding programme all over again. Meanwhile, conscientious eye testing at six weeks and rigid selection will help us to keep the problems at bay until genetically clear Collies can be bred. Until then, every Collie must be regarded as a carrier.

Puppy purchasers should ask to see copies of the BVA Eye Certificates of both parents and if they intend to breed from their puppy, they should insist that it has been screened eye-clear at six weeks. If, on the other hand, the puppy is intended only as a pet, then a screened result of Grade I CEA or mild Grade 2 CEA will be perfectly acceptable. It will mean that the puppy's eye status will not deteriorate and that he will never have problems with his vision.

It is not sufficient to accept the breeder's word that he has never had any eye problems with his line. CEA is virtually impossible to detect without the aid of sophisticated ophthalmic instruments. Even severely affected animals, due to their heightened sense of smell and hearing, can show very little evidence of their defective sight.

I was once given a sharp lesson in how difficult it is for the layman to correctly diagnose CEA. I was interested in purchasing a blue merle dog puppy from a litter of blue merles whose breeding was not familiar to me. When they were seven weeks old I went to inspect them. There were four merle dog puppies amongst the litter. I particularly wanted a merle with dark rather than wall eyes and held up each puppy in turn to examine their eyes carefully in bright sunlight. All had lovely dark eyes that appeared perfectly normal, but I decided to wait for the result of their eye tests before coming to a decision. Two days later they were eye screened under the BVA scheme. All four dog puppies had detached retinas. They were blind in one eye and badly affected in the other. Their breeders, who had been so proud of them, were devastated. They had never had the slightest suspicion that there was anything wrong with the puppies' eyesight and would routinely have sold them for stud and show purposes if they had not been tested. So now when breeders tell me proudly that they have never had any eye problems in their line, I think of that merle litter with CEA and wonder how many puppies they have unsuspectingly sold. It is not only important for breeders to eye test, it is also important that they are honest with themselves and with other breeders. They must publish their results and share all information for the improvement of the breed.

Cataracts

Collies do not suffer from hereditary cataracts which affect some other breeds. For information on nutritional cataracts, *see* page 209.

Progressive Retinal Atrophy or PRA

PRA has been known to exist in Collies for some forty years. Obviously, it has been in existence much longer than that, but the disease was not recognised until research into night blindness in Irish Setters revealed the true cause. It affects several breeds, and is now less common in Collies than it was forty years ago. It affects the retina – the light-sensitive area of the eye. Gradual deterioration takes place until, at about three years of age, the dog becomes totally blind. Originally it was thought that if a Collie was free from PRA at the age of three he would be free for life. This no longer appears to be true. A latent form of PRA known as Central PRA has now been diagnosed. As its name would suggest, it starts in the centre of the eye and spreads outwards. Appearance can be delayed for up to eight or nine years. It is thought to be inherited from close ancestors, i.e. parents and grandparents. It is impossible to delay breeding from a Collie until such an advanced age, which adds to the difficulties of eradicating PRA from the breed. It is vital that Collies used for breeding should have their eyes checked annually for CPRA.

245

PRA has a different inheritance pattern and can appear after a gap of many generations. I have known of cases where it can be traced to a dog seven generations back with no known cases in the interim. Breeders can take some credit for the fact that PRA is not as prevalent as it was in the post-war period. At that time nothing was known about the disease or its mode of inheritance. Blindness was thought to strike dogs at random, just as it seems to do with man. There was never any suggestion that it was hereditary; consequently, blind dogs were advertised and used at stud in the same way as normal dogs. I can think of one very successful post-war sire that was totally blind.

Haemophilia

Haemophilia is a rare disease where the blood fails to clot, which has been reported in Collies. It manifests itself only in males but is carried through the female line. Unfortunately, it is often not until a bitch has a litter containing male sufferers that the disease is recognised. On the very rare occasions that it has been found in Collies, great efforts have been made to neuter any suspected carriers and the disease has not been able to take hold.

Hereditary Epilepsy

See Convulsions. A few years ago there were very real fears that hereditary epilepsy was becoming established in the breed. Efforts were made, at that time, to eradicate the disease and they appear to have been successful. Isolated cases still appear occasionally but there seems to be no set pattern of inheritance. Epilepsy can be controlled by suitable drugs as it can in man. It goes without saying that no Collie suffering from epilepsy should ever be used for breeding.

Hip Dysplasia or HD

This is probably the most common of all the inherited diseases that afflict the canine race. Large and medium-size breeds are more seriously affected than small breeds. A great deal of research has gone into HD in an effort to discover the cause and the mode of inheritance. It is now established that it is polygenically controlled. This means that there is no single, isolated gene that can be held responsible, but that it is controlled by a number of genes within the cell. This makes it difficult to control.

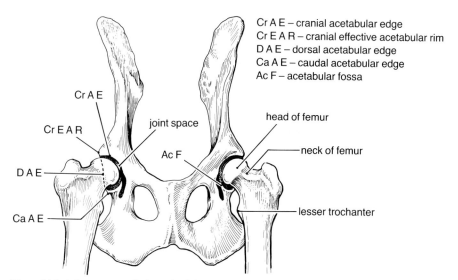

Cr A E – cranial acetabular edge
Cr E A R – cranial effective acetabular rim
D A E – dorsal acetabular edge
Ca A E – caudal acetabular edge
Ac F – acetabular fossa

Normal hip joints – ventral view of pelvis.

Basically, HD is the faulty fitting of the head of the femur into the hip socket or acetabular cup. This is due either to the head of the femur being deformed or to the cup being too shallow. Mild or moderate HD is difficult to diagnose without resorting to X-rays. It results in little or no pain until the dog reaches middle age when arthritis often sets in. When the dog is in pain from early life, there are three possible methods of treatment. Pain can be relieved by some of the modern drugs that are available. It is important to keep the dog's weight down and give exercise in moderation. Several small walks during the day are best and are good for morale. It has been reported that many police dogs that have HD still manage to fulfil a useful working life until they reach retirement. From then onwards they seem to grow more aware of their hip problems, become depressed and often have to be put down.

If the HD sufferer is young, a small operation called pectineal myotomy may be the solution. This entails severing the pectineal muscle that runs tight up under the hip-joint. In cases where the joint is loose and badly fitted, this muscle gets a lot of wear and becomes enlarged, tight and fibrous. Just sectioning this muscle will often dramatically relieve the pain. Sometimes, after a simple twenty-minute operation, the patient will walk home from the surgery, with all signs of discomfort gone. The pressure on the arthritic joint has been relieved but, of course, the diseased joint remains.

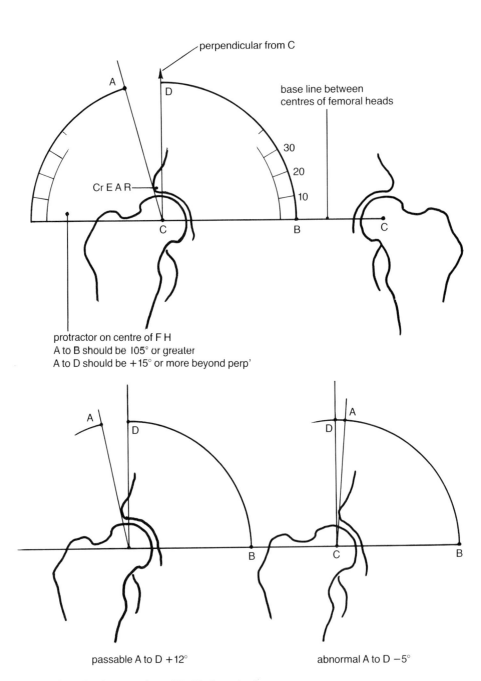

perpendicular from C

base line between
centres of femoral heads

30
20
10

Cr E A R

A

D

C

B

C

protractor on centre of F H
A to B should be 105° or greater
A to D should be +15° or more beyond perp'

A

D

B

passable A to D +12°

A

D

C

B

abnormal A to D −5°

How the HD scheme works: 1. The Norberg Angle.

In severe cases, major surgery may be required. In this case, the head of the femur can be cut off. The dog is left with a bag of fluid which produces a reasonably good fit in the socket. The dog will carry his weight on the front legs using the back legs for propulsion. Again, it is important the dog's weight should be kept down and only moderate exercise given.

A new method of treatment is a hip replacement operation and this is probably where the future lies. At present it is uncommon and expensive, but the operation is producing excellent results. The only alternative in severe cases is euthanasia. Rather than condemn a dog to a life of pain, this may, in some instances, be the only solution. Of course, all these problems could be avoided if HD had been prevented in the first place. There is no doubt that with careful selective breeding and routine hip testing, this disease could virtually be eliminated. Many Collie breeders still refuse to accept the hereditary nature of HD. They accept that width of skull, length of tail, angle of shoulder and so forth are all skeletal parts that are inherited from parents and grandparents; but not the structure of the hip-joint. Unfortunately, they are deceiving themselves.

Environmental conditions also play a part. This is not to say that poor rearing is the cause. Rather, the reverse appears to be the case. It seems to be the overfed, overweight puppies that are more likely to suffer from HD in later life, probably because of the strain put on their joints at an early age. The underweight, badly reared puppies,

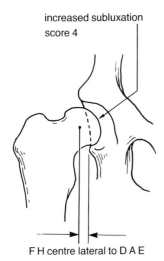

increased subluxation
score 4

F H centre lateral to D A E

2. *Subluxation.*

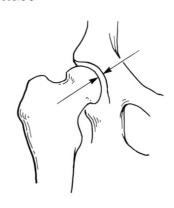

smooth even curve parallel to femur head
score 0

3. *Cranial acetabular edge.*

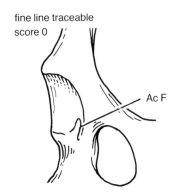

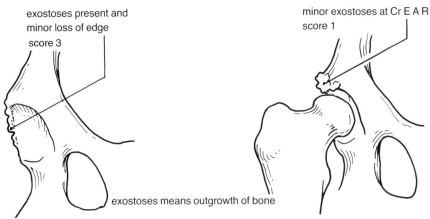

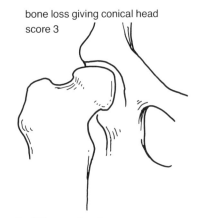

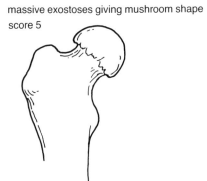

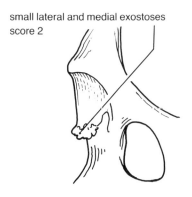

exostoses present and
minor loss of edge
score 3

exostoses means outgrowth of bone

4. Dorsal acetabular edge.

minor exostoses at Cr E A R
score 1

5. Cranial effective AR.

fine line traceable
score 0

Ac F

6. Acetabular fossa.

small lateral and medial exostoses
score 2

7. Caudal acetabular edge.

massive exostoses giving mushroom shape
score 5

8. Femoral head and neck.

bone loss giving conical head
score 3

9. FH re-contouring.

whatever other problems they may have, are less likely to suffer from severe HD. I was interested to learn that it has recently been proved that puppies which have been denied the colostrum in the first few days of life are less likely to suffer from HD than their luckier siblings. It has been my experience that such puppies are very difficult to get into good show condition in later life. It seems impossible to put any weight on them no matter how good their appetite. This would seem to support the theory that carrying too much weight at an early age is detrimental to good hips. It is thought but not proved, that over-exercising young puppies may have a bearing on HD. It is common sense that puppies should not be taken on long walks at too early an age.

It seems indisputable that dogs with good hips bred together are more likely to produce puppies with good hips, than dogs with bad hips bred together. The only way to be certain that a dog has good hips is to have him hip scored under the BVA scheme. This is a comparatively new scheme devised by the geneticist Dr Malcolm Willis and is known generally as the 'Willis Scheme'. It was originally designed for the use of German Shepherd breeders and since its inception there has been a dramatic improvement in the status of GSD hips. So much so, that the BVA decided to extend the scheme to all breeds. Dr Willis continues to give a great deal of his time to analysing the scores and produces an annual average score for each breed. At present the average score for Rough Collies is 11.42 – an improvement of several points on their score at the start of the scheme.

A study of the diagrams will reveal that the hip has been divided into nine areas. Each area has been given a fault score of up to six marks. The more marks scored against an area, the worse the hip. For instance, a dog with perfect hips would have a score of 0/0, i.e. nil for each hip. In the worst conceivable case, a dog would have a score of 54/54.

I leave you with an extract from *Our Friend the Collie*, first published in 1934 – A brief eulogy by Captain Thomas Brown FLS:

> This useful and intelligent animal is one of the most placid, obedient, serene and grateful members of the canine race. He is ever alive to the slightest indication of his master's wishes, prompt and gratified to execute them; and he seems to enjoy the greatest delight when employed in any kind of useful service. Formed by nature with an instinctive propensity to industry, he is never more pleased than in exerting his talents for the benefit of man, and in giving constant proofs of his inviolable attachment.

Locating a Collie Club

A natural development of the Collie's popularity is the growth of numerous clubs in most parts of the United States. The single national organization is the Collie Club of America. The CCA takes a leadership role in developing the breed standard and other matters of vital importance to the breed. In addition to the parent club, regional clubs serve the needs of local Collie fans in a variety of ways. To find the name and address of the current secretary of the CCA or any of the regional clubs listed below, write to the American Kennel Club, 51 Madison Avenue, New York NY 10010.

Alabama
Collie Club of Alabama

Alaska
Collie Club of Alaska

Arizona
Arizona Collie Club
North Arizona Collie Fanciers
Tucson Collie Club

California
California Collie Clan
California Collie Fanciers
Collie Club of Northern California
Los Padres Collie Club
Modesto Collie Club
Sacramento Valley Collie Club
San Diego Collie Club
San Gabriel Valley Collie Club
Southern California Collie Club

Colorado
Collie Club of Colorado
Pikes Peak Collie Club

Connecticut
Collie Club of Connecticut
Hartford-Springfield Collie Club

Florida
Collie Club of Greater Miami
Greater Jacksonville Collie Club
Greater Tampa Bay Collie Club

Georgia
Collie Club of Georgia

Hawaii
Collie Club of Hawaii

Illinois
Central States Collie Club
Chicago Collie Club
Illiana Collie Club
Peoria Area Collie Club

Indiana
Indiana Collie Club

Kansas
Central Kansas Collie Club
Kansas City Collie Club

Kentucky
Collie Club of Kentucky

Louisiana
Collie Club of Louisiana

Maine
Collie Club of Maine

Maryland
Collie Club of Maryland
Mason-Dixon Collie Club

Massachusetts
Collie Club of New England

Michigan
Midwest Collie Club

Minnesota
Collie Club of Minnesota

Missouri
St. Louis Collie Club

Nebraska
Nebraska Collie Club

Nevada
Sierra Nevada Collie Club

New Hampshire
Collie Club of New Hampshire

New Jersey
Central Jersey Collie Club
Collie Club of Northern New Jersey
Hunterdon Hills Collie Club
South Jersey Collie Club

New Mexico
Albuquerque Collie Clan

New York
Collie Club of Central New York
Collie Club of Long Island
Collie Club of Western New York
Hudson Valley Collie Club
Rochester Collie Club
Tri-County Collie Club

North Carolina
Piedmont Collie Club

Ohio
Cleveland Collie Club
Collie Club of Southern Ohio
Columbus Collie Club
Miami Valley Collie Club
Toledo Collie Club

Oklahoma
Central Oklahoma Collie Club
Southwest Collie Club of Tulsa

Oregon
Pacific Northwest Collie Club

Pennsylvania
Central Pennsylvania Collie Club
Collie Club of Western Pennsylvania
Keystone Collie Club
Presque Isle Collie Club

Tennessee
Greater Memphis Collie Club
Nashville Collie Club

Texas
Collie Club of Austin
Collie Club of San Antonio
Fort Worth Collie Club
North Texas Collie Club
South Texas Collie Club

Virginia
Chesapeake Collie Club

Washington
Collie Club of Washington
Inland Empire Collie Club
Overlake Collie Club

West Virginia
Panhandle Collie Club of West Virginia

Wisconsin
Collie Club of Southern Wisconsin

Index

255